Karl B. McMillan Jr.

Triumphs
and
Tragedies

A True Story of Wealth and Addiction

The Life of Karl B. McMillen, Jr.

AS TOLD TO BILL HAYES AND JENNIFER THOMAS

FINAL WORD
PRESS

Published by Final Word Press, P.O. Box 3008, Redondo Beach, CA 90277; www.finalwordpress.com. Contact: info@finalwordpress.com or 310.991.7893.

The following is a true story. However, a few names, locales, and descriptive details have been omitted to protect the privacy of individuals whose lives have intersected with Karl B. McMillen, Jr.

Author: Karl B. McMillen, Jr., as told to Bill Hayes and Jennifer Thomas
Editor: Jennifer Thomas
Jacket and Body Design: Jennifer Thomas
Front Cover Artwork: Robert Waxman

Photographs:
  Karl B. McMillen, Jr., Back Cover: Deidre Davidson
  Bill Hayes and Jennifer Thomas, Back Flap: Joanna Jana Laznicka
  Supplemental Photography: Deidre Davidson
  DC-10 Crash, p. 168: Provided by the Los Angeles Fire Department
  All Other Photographs: From the archives of Karl B. McMillen, Jr.

ISBN: 978-0-9884126-2-0 Hardcover

Library of Congress Control Number: 2013937890

First Edition
Published in the United States of America
Printed in the United States of America

All proceeds benefit the McMillen Family Foundation

For my late wife, Thelma,
my sons, Mark and Chris,
and all those whose lives have been ravaged—
directly or indirectly—
by the scourge of addiction.

—Karl B. McMillen, Jr.

Contents

Preface

by Karl B. McMillen, Jr.

Why was this book written?

Hopefully, it will help future generations (and yes, those who are here now) do the following:

•*Avoid* drug problems.

•*Recognize* drug problems.

•*Handle* drug problems.

•*Avoid being an enabler.*

It provides pretty good insights into succeeding in business, too!

Sure, that's a lot to ask of one book, but it's a lot to ask of one life.

My life.

An intense and exceptionally full life.

A life that has posed many questions and has come up with many answers.

A life lovingly laid bare in these pages; laid bare for the greater good. And within that greater good, I can only hope that the triumphs and tragedies I have experienced will inspire, guide, and even frighten those who have, or may encounter, any connection to drugs, alcoholism, addiction, or enabling.

Even as I have written, read, and reread the words in this book, I find it hard to believe that I survived the tragic deaths and lives of my sons and wife.

I also find it hard to believe what alcoholism nearly did to *me*. But on May 1, 2013, I received my seventeen-year sobriety chip.

What I don't find hard to believe is that I survived for a reason. And that reason is simple: to help others. To help them survive, to help them avoid what my family endured—both individually and collectively—and maybe even to help them accomplish some triumphs like those I've been blessed with.

If, in attempting to extend that kind of help, this book offends anyone, I sincerely apologize. My intents are stated above; and with all my heart, I believe that they are so, so important.

So, please—for my reasons and for any personal reasons affecting you within the agonizing cycle of addiction—*read it*.

Acknowledgments

This book could not exist without the support, guidance, and assistance of so many people. I especially want to thank...

My three grandchildren,
for giving me your blessing to share my life in this book.

Jeff Morrow and Richie Davidson,
for your love of my sons
and your hard-won wisdom about addiction,
both of which you were willing to lay bare
in order that it might help others.

Merle Countryman,
for your support and care throughout my and my sons' lives
and for contributing your in-depth knowledge of
addiction and alcoholism.
I am also grateful for your incredible work
as CEO of the McMillen Family Foundation.

Don McDonald,
for being like a son to me
and supporting me through both my triumphs and tragedies.

Ralph Todd,
for having the guts and foresight to open Todd Pipe
and invite me to be a part of it.

Dr. Ken Trefftzs,
for your years of friendship, help, and business insight.
You are greatly missed.

My sister Ruth,
for always being involved in and caring about my endeavors.

Chuck Monnich and his wife, Liz,
for a lifetime of friendship and support.

Jack Clower,
for being my sponsor and friend.

Marc Walmer and Jim Olsztynski,
for your valuable editorial input and assistance.

Rob Waxman,
for capturing the spirit of my life's journey in your artwork.

All the McMillen Family Foundation board members:
Merle Countryman; my wife, Carol McMillen; Jeff Morrow;
Shannon McMillen; Aaron Olsen; Gary Michel; Dave Bishop;
Dan Fiorito; Dr. Moe Gelbart; Chuck Campbell; Dan Patrick;
my son Chris's second wife; and my third granddaughter—
all of whom unselfishly devote their time and wisdom
to helping so many people in need.

Dan Patrick,
my business partner and friend,
for conceiving of a new Todd Pipe and assembling a great team
that is making it a legend renewed.

All four of my partners at Todd Pipe:
Dan Patrick, Tom Morrow, Jason Kemp, and Aaron Olsen—
your hard work will help keep the McMillen Family Foundation
working for the greater good.

———

A special thanks to Bill Hayes and Jennifer Thomas
for your tireless dedication and hard work
in helping me tell and experience my story
in a way I never have before.

And most of all, thank you to my loving wife, Carol,
for your love and strength throughout
this often painful and difficult process.

Triumphs
and
Tragedies

Introduction

by Bill Hayes

The story of Karl Benton McMillen, Jr., is a twofold trip down a much-too-tight path—a path like those carved into the wild walls diving down from the rim of the Grand Canyon or beyond the shredding edges of New Zealand's Rotorua. Rising up one side are sharp, steep, and unforgiving cliffs that the average person could never scale. On the other side—the down side—is the drop-off. The doom hole that will swallow you up if your step goes even slightly wrong.

Karl has experienced both.

He climbed to heights in business and finance that put him in an elite economic league. He made that assent with his bare hands, with no preferential boosts or safety line of inheritance—just the determination of an overtime work ethic and the kind of drive that every now and then turns some blue-collar rags into serious riches.

But more of those riches found their way into his heart than into his pocket. Karl McMillen's philanthropy has become legendary, his benevolence boundless.

But then there's that sheer on the other side of the path. Sometimes you don't even see it coming. Sometimes the rocks and ground slip out from under you before you can grab hold. You fall, and all the money in the universe can't save you. Gravity is a powerful force.

So is addiction.

It's a force that transcends wealth or reason. It's a force that will eat away at your path until you have nowhere to go but down. It's the force that cut so deeply into the family of Karl McMillen. It's the force that pulled Karl's two surfing-champion sons from positions of popularity, potential, and affluence down into the dead end of prison and pity. It's the force that Karl himself had to face when it affected the business empire he fought so hard to build.

And it's a force that grips the souls of so many.

Triumphs and Tragedies is a mirror. It's a mirror some will look into to see the results, possibilities, and ramifications of their own personal choices—both good *and* bad. It's a mirror that will force some to do a double take when examining the lives and activities of their children. It's a mirror that screams out for awareness of exactly what addiction can do—not just to the crack babies and unfortunates born into the bowels of ghettos and inner-city hell, but to those who wake up each morning to a million-dollar view and a path of life that is seemingly paved with gold.

And to everyone in between.

Prologue

A "white Christmas" is rare in Southern California. Christmas *is* cold, however—at least by some standards; and the cold of the season can cut in many ways.

But it was warm in the new Cadillac. The car was making its way north up the I-5 from the rich Pacific shore of the South Bay to the bottom of Five Mile Grade, the long uphill pull that summits into "the Grapevine"—the volatile rocky straits that link the southern and northern ends of the Golden State.

The Caddy wasn't going *that* far.

The end of the line would be Wayside Honor Rancho in Castaic. That jail was about the only thing out there in those days; the residential swell of Los Angeles hadn't yet spread into that particular pocket of wilderness. The area's population was coyotes, cats, hungry hawks, and dinner-sized rabbits. And the prisoners of Wayside.

On that windy Christmas morning, Karl and Thelma McMillen rode up there in their cozy, well-waxed Cadillac to see two of those prisoners.

Their sons.

WAYSIDE—later to become the Sheriff Peter Pitchess Detention Center—was a clearing house for inmates. A layover on the way to the various "big houses" around the state.

The McMillens parked behind the gates and boarded a prison bus to take them along the rest of the two-mile trail into the facility. The bus was in chilled contrast to the Cadillac—with graffiti, filmy windows, and an overall stickiness on the floor that made walking a noisy and nauseating business. Their traveling companions in the stiff seats around them were not like the company they usually kept. This wasn't exactly their social niche.

But they were getting somewhat used to this shabby parallel world.

In *their* world, they knew the comfort of nice restaurants and the calm of coastal campouts and getaways; on the other side of the dim portal, they were becoming all too familiar with destinations like this one. And Corcoran. And Chino. And Jamestown. And Susanville.

NO CHRISTMAS CAROLS brightened the background of the waiting room. No bright decorations or glowing trees lit the visiting area. Just the weak lighting in the "cages"—the thick, glassed-in cubicles where inmates, soul mates, friends, family, and others on the official visitation list could share some magical, hands-off moments through the scratched opaque-and-wire mesh and the greasy short-wired phone receivers.

Tidings of comfort and joy…

This wasn't the first, or last, holiday that Mark McMillen, twenty-one, and Chris McMillen, nineteen, would spend behind bars.

But on that special morning, the prisoner dispersal shuffle worked out in such a way that it gave an appropriately special gift to the McMillens. After all, it *was* Christmas. It wasn't tied with a red ribbon, certainly, or wrapped in the velvet of a jewelry box, but it was something to be cherished. The California penal system's version of gold, frankincense, and myrrh was the convenience of having the McMillen sons both in Wayside at the same time.

The brothers had been arrested separately on unrelated offenses, so the idea that they were both passing through this transitional facility at the same time, en route to separate long-term lockups, really was a Christmas miracle right up there with George Bailey's angel.

The boys were even placed in side-by-side cages, allowing the McMillens to visit with them both simultaneously.

Merry Christmas.

Although Wayside was isolated in one of the last vestiges of scenic rurality in L.A. County, Mark and Chris's home on The Strand in Hermosa Beach had much better views, saltwater scents, and ocean sounds—ones that didn't involve distorted thick plastic, stale cigarette stench, and the rampant roar of growled arguments and orders.

But Hermosa was fifty miles and a million litigious light-years away.

Karl McMillen, Jr., had built a business—and a family, or so he thought—based upon honesty, integrity, and climbing those steep walls to success completely exposed, out in the open. It was so hard being in a facility that was a monument to the antithesis of all that.

It was so hard seeing his two fortunate sons mired in the antithesis of all that.

Karl knew "the good life," certainly, in the economic sense. But at his core, he had always been a jeans, tennies, and camp-on-the-ground kind of guy—looking at each day, each sunrise, each sunset, and each crash of an ocean wave as a miracle to be savored.

His sons grew to look at each day very differently. Sunrises became continuums of lost nights. Each day—whenever it began—was just another exercise in artful dodging and hustling. Dodging the law, hustling for drugs.

Sometimes Chris and Mark would reach out, wanting so badly to reconnect and to re-savor those bright days and miracle waves.

Sometimes.

But drugs have power. Addiction has power.

And sometimes—for a variety of reasons—the good guys lose.

Those reasons haunt. They lead to sleepless nights of second guesses in the restless dark. Karl would spend plenty of those haunted and restless nights, seeking those reasons again and again. He knew that somehow this whole horrible situation needed to become an example for others. That it could somehow help extend strong hands the next time *someone* reached out. That it could help turn lost nights back into days that could be cherished for the miracles that they are— not the distortions and twists of a parallel world of poisons and pain.

BUT NEW IMAGES would add to a lifetime of haunting.

The flat gray of the Wayside visiting room wasn't quite the blue of the Pacific; the concrete chill of the scuffed floor was definitely not the warm shores of Baja or Australia that the family had enjoyed together.

Still, looking at their beloved sons *did* provide a cocktail of holiday cheer for Karl and Thelma—mulled with the spices of sorrow and shame. Prison tattoos had replaced the tans. Handcuffs had replaced the shortboard leashes.

What child is this…?

The tattoos may have been the worst for Karl—hard-hewn scarlet letters that were sick proof that all of this was actually happening.

How did we get here?

VISITING HOURS OVER, the phone receivers hung up, Chris and Mark were ushered back to their cells, and the Caddy headed south—returning to the beach. To a home no longer defined as it had once been.

No parties filled the beachfront patio; the shelves and walls had been stripped of their surfing-contest awards. The high hopes for this family and its sons had changed—from sky's-the-limit potential to a mere day-to-day hope of survival.

And then to mourning and head-shaking sorrow.

What never did change was Karl McMillen's appreciation of those daily miracles. Many more Christmas mornings like that one at Wayside would lead to Karl's showing his appreciation in more intense and tangible ways. His sons' tragic choices would become an example and a caring catalyst for helping others.

CHAPTER I

A Bicycle
& a Backyard Workshop

"We're not going through this Depression
in a mill town!"

MIAMI, ARIZONA, LIES AT THE SOUTHWEST CORNER of Gila County
in the high heat of the central state. It was—and remains—a copper
town. While the big blast has gone out of this once-booming mining
town, the ore still supplies the bulk of the employment—hard, dirty
work that goes on amidst the decaying shacks, booted ghosts, and
other reminders that this one-square-mile community has been
around since Teddy Roosevelt was president.

Karl Benton McMillen, Jr., was born in Miami on September
19, 1928.

Karl was one of those turn-of-the-century "tweeners"—born
between the callous-handed wooden-wheeled pioneers and the war-
affected baby boomers, in an era that offered plenty of the rewards of
the industrial revolution, while remaining raw and wide open enough
to offer even more rewards for hard work, innovation, and enterprise.

A man with Karl's persona and drive was perfect for that kinetic mix.

Karl's childhood years were a combination of America's blue-collar history, the growth of the West, the crazy abandon of a time and place long past, and a textbook on the foundation and footholds of pure entrepreneurism.

THE McMILLEN FAMILY had come to Miami from Butte, Montana, with roots in Missouri and Tennessee.

Karl's mother, Frances, had German parents and a built-in penchant for fierce frugality. If she got a bad piece of meat from her butcher, she'd be right back there telling him about it. No money would be wasted and no bad meat would be served with *her* sauerkraut!

And Frances had as powerful a work ethic as any of the men in the family.

After she married Karl's father, Karl Benton McMillen, Sr.—everyone called him "Mac"—she went to work for an attorney. She began as the lawyer's secretary but eventually ran the entire office.

A true of-the-day letter of appreciation and recommendation followed her leaving of the firm:

Dec. 21st, 1921

To whom it may concern: Frances J. McMillen came into my offices as a stenographer during the latter part of the year 1914 and remained for about four years. In the handling of the general law practice she became an expert amanuensis, took readily to the technique of the business and became almost invaluable to me and my offices. During the latter portion of her stay she had immediate charge of all confidential correspondence in matters concerning my practice. In the course of all of her service, I must say that she proved most capable, energetic and dependable. I know of no stronger language I could use in recommending her to any professional office or lay concern requiring the services of a woman of common sense, ability, honesty, energy, and general efficiency. It will be a pleasure to more fully confirm the above upon written or other request.

Dated at Butte, Montana, this 21st day of December 1921 by William N. Waugh, Attorney and Counselor at Law, the Phoenix Building, Butte, Montana

That was Francis to a T—*a woman of common sense and efficiency…*

J DORHOFER, FATHER OF FRANCES J DORHOFER McMILLE
GRANDFATHER OF KARL B McMILLEN JR

F. J. DORHOFER CO.
PLUMBING, HEATING
AND TIN SHOP
No. 1 W. Silver St.
BUTTE, - MONTANA

FIRST PLUMBING and TIN SHOP IN BUTTE, MONTANA 19

Plumbing pioneering flowed through both sides of Karl's family. His maternal grandfather, Frank Dorhofer, plunged into the profession by 1916!

Mac had a bookkeeping background and was deputy superintendent of a high school.

And he, too, was an entrepreneur.

With that work ethic.

At one point, Mac got involved in an auto repair/ sheet metal shop in Miami. He figured out how to bypass the electric meter, in a basic yet creative "cost-cutting" move.

And then he discovered he was about to get caught.

Karl "Mac" McMillen, Sr.

He needed to spin that meter ahead to make things look normal—*quick!* Use some juice! Cover some tracks. So he borrowed every electric heater in town, plugged them in, and sent the meter dial to the moon.

Resourcefulness like this was apparently in the ingenious genes of the McMillen men. The knack for problem-solving came easy for this family, as proved by their business successes.

But problem-solving in business doesn't always translate into problem-solving on the most intimate of personal levels.

That, too, would be proven.

Mac's father, Robert Thomas McMillen, had been a night watchman at the copper mine. He eventually bought a 120-acre recreational site, halfway between Miami and the nearby town of Superior. It was cooler up on his property, so he built summer rental cabins.

The property wasn't far from a prison, forty miles to the southwest in Florence, Arizona. It was always thought that if someone escaped from the prison, they'd naturally head straight for the cabins and the camp. So Karl's grandfather and his grandmother, Della, always worked as a team when someone came to their front door late at night—one would do the opening while the other readied themselves behind another door with the double-barreled. If there was a problem, they'd handle it.

Isolation breeds on-the-spot laws and judgment.

KARL'S GRANDFATHER never learned to drive; his grandmother did all the driving—in a Model A that began life as a four-door sedan but morphed into a pickup after Della rolled the thing.

Maybe Granddad Robert began to rethink his non-behind-the-wheel decision as the torches went to work on what was left of the Ford—and when Della rode shotgun as she taught Karl's sister Ruth to drive when Ruth was just fourteen.

Frances Dorhofer McMillen

It was a different time. That "growth of the West" was mobilizing America—now on four tires instead of four hooves. Swarming safety regulations, license restrictions and endorsements, and even most DMVs had not been installed, written, or built yet!

But by the time Karl's mother needed to drive, Arizona did have driving schools.

And that's where *she* learned.

Despite (or maybe because of) his mother's intrepid driving habits, Mac didn't believe that any woman should drive—even an "expert amanuensis." So Frances climbed behind the wheel with someone a bit more open-minded.

But even with her double-clutched education, Frances managed to get a traffic ticket early on. (At least she didn't flip the car like her mother-in-law had!)

Traffic courts were maturing as well.

"You are a beautiful young lady," the judge told Frances. "I don't think you should have a ticket!"

And he tore it up.

Times have indeed changed.

And they were changing in more ways than just the country's driving habits.

Karl's parents blazed their own trails in the early 1900s.

1929

When Karl Jr. was barely a year old, the whole family moved to California. The Great Depression was depleting pockets nationwide, and towns that revolved around a single industry—like Miami—were balancing on a very tight economic edge.

"We're not going through this Depression in a mill town!" Mac proclaimed, exhibiting some serious insight and prophesy.

Four hundred fifty-two miles later, the family was in Montebello, California, paying five grand for a house there. Five years later, low on funds and upside down on his mortgage, Mac "mailed in his keys" to the house and the family moved to Pasadena overnight. They would never again own another house; Mac didn't believe in property after that. Renting, he decided, was more economically sound.

And probably less domestically stressful to a man who always possessed a restless, entrepreneurial spirit.

For twenty years, the family lived at 45 South Wilson, a half-block off the Rose Parade route. Every New Year's Day began on a good economic note as fifty cars could be parked on their property—for a fee, of course, of one dollar per car. And even at this early age, Karl Jr. displayed a knack for expanding the family business. Noticing a long line to the ladies restroom at the gas station next door, he announced that for ten cents apiece, the women could use the house toilet. To no one's surprise, the dimes rolled in.

Mac became assistant manager of a foundry that made cast-iron fittings. This foundry was a half-mile long; it required a company truck to haul material back and forth from one end to the other.

Working weekends at the place was nothing unusual for Mac, and he often brought his son along with him.

And he kept him occupied.

It may have been busywork, but having his son clean out buckets and buckets of brass plugs and screw them into fittings had its effect. It was exercise—physical, plumber-dexterous exercise—and it was a mental workout that ingrained an instinct to always be productive in some way.

And it came with a reward.

For now, no paycheck awaited the kid, down at the bottom of those buckets, but what did await was the narrow-railed perk of driving one of the company trucks backward and forward, backward and forward, along that twenty-six-hundred-foot corridor. The rutted track may have been a straight line for that truck, but in Karl's imagination it was a superhighway of adventure.

That imagination and that drive would take Karl far further than that old truck could ever handle.

Then Mac and the next-door neighbor bought a gas station together; entrepreneurism was spreading. Karl had two paper routes and he also sold wreaths during the holiday season—riding his bicycle to Fair Oaks and Colorado Boulevard to buy the piney prizes, and then riding five or six miles to San Marino to sell them door-to-door. Honing his speech with each ring of the doorbell, Karl became an expert salesman. Many neighborhood doors celebrated the holidays with Karl's wreaths—and each of those doors celebrated Karl's soaring business sense.

By 1938 the McMillens had a new ton-and-a-half Chevy cab-over truck and a new Oldsmobile. They were doing well. A feel for business, some gut-level acumen, and hard work was transcending the Depression.

But every so often, they were reminded of the tough times they had endured. One day a sheriff showed up at their front door with a deficiency judgment from Montebello. The "mailing in of the keys" had caught up with them, and their two vehicles were seized until the judgment was paid.

Besides working in the foundry and owning the gas station, Mac began selling concrete trash incinerators in their backyard. The backyard also became the "workshop" for rebuilding hot water heaters. Mac would take them apart, weld up the holes, and put them back together; they'd be good for another generation of baths, showers, and dishwashing.

Twenty years later, people continued to come by the house asking if they were "still rebuilding hot water heaters here? I bought one from you years ago and it finally went out and I need another one."

Eventually, Mac joined a plumbing shop in Altadena, living in a company-owned building for twenty-five dollars a month. The shop employed thirty-five plumbers. They all had workhorse Model A pickups and would go into the tracts that were now erupting all over Southern California—in developing communities like Lakewood— and divide up into assembly-line crews of four or five, plumbing the entirety of the up-quick homes.

Even with the Depression having hammered at America's prosperity, the McMillens were doing okay. People *had* to get rid of their garbage, and those incinerators came in handy. And water, whether hot or cold, was pretty important as well.

BRASS WAS HARD TO OBTAIN as World War II exploded, so Mac would buy the available cast-iron faucets and chrome them, reaching out into the "custom jobs" market.

Karl would be brought into the plumbing shop to do odd jobs on weekends. When the crews finished a tract, they'd have boxes of pipe fittings left, all mixed up with oakum. (Oakum is what you put in the joints for the caulking; all of this is mixed in oil.) Karl would clean everything up and sort the fittings back into the bins, readying them for use on the next job.

Now Karl's work was rewarded with something more commercially fulfilling than driving an old truck back and forth; now, Karl earned some serious pay from his father.

A buck!

And that was fine—for now.

Even more education and "gut-level acumen" would come.

Karl would go with his father to jobsites and supply houses. He'd watch Mac negotiate and deal. He'd absorb his father's price-wrangling and business strategies.

And along with all of that, the legacy-feed of Mac's backyard hot water heater business kept pumping through the McMillen veins. As a side benefit of helping at the plumbing shop, young Karl got access to all the old, irreparable water heaters and side boilers that the plumbers brought back. They were cast iron on the outside with copper coils inside.

Copper at that time sold for about six cents a pound; cast iron, around a penny. So Karl would set to work disassembling the tanks and extracting the copper and iron from the old heaters and boilers. Mac knew where he could take his son to get the best price.

Education.

Acumen.

And Karl still had papers to deliver amongst the hardware sorting.

One of Karl's two paper routes took him into Cal Tech—the top-shelf university of Nobel laureates and big-wheel scientists along Pasadena's California Boulevard—where Karl would slip into lecture halls during Friday night seminars. He didn't exactly get what was being said, but his note-taking was extensive.

So was his vision.

ENTREPRENEURISM, INNOVATION, LOOKING AHEAD at a horizon of success—so much fueled Karl McMillen, Jr., as he grew up. But throughout all of the productive, objective, and businesslike data input, Karl's mind was charged by a couple more slightly eclectic elements that were close to the double-time heart of his father.

Mining was the gilded leafing on the family tree. Karl Jr.'s grandfather had been involved in lead mining in Greenfield, Missouri, in the late 1800s. The family's move to Butte, Montana, where gold and copper mines ran deep, occurred around the turn of the century, shortly after Mac was born. So mining was infused into Mac at a very early age. Even when he worked for the school system in Miami and when he later managed a plumbing shop, the gambling nature of a miner was always pulling at him.

He had money in his blood—that's a gambler. They are always prospecting—new areas, new mines.

This could be it!

On the weekends, Mac would be out looking for the next deal. He was passionate in his ceaseless sift for gold, and he was umbilically tied to the dust and the desert and the badlands that made up the last of the Wild West. He wrangled gold from the hills, snakes in the kitchen, and toilets in the brush—and his son was with him every hot and booted step of the way.

CHAPTER 2

Mining for Experience up on the Hill

MAC'S PERSONAL GOLD RUSH began when his son was about six years old. This quest gave Karl Jr.—"Karlie," to his family—a bonus in the hands-on education that he'd been receiving. In between paper routes, plumbing practice, and negotiation tactics, Karl would get a journey into Americana that would make Mark Twain proud—and jealous. Karl would see and live the grit-over-glamour history of California and the early-twentieth-century West that was worlds removed from Serra's missions, the *Pueblo de los Ángeles*, and the surge of sea trade steaming into the ports of Long Beach and San Francisco.

What he saw were the back roads from 'Berdoo to Baker, from Death Valley to Randsburg. He would get to roam over the Arizona, Utah, and Nevada borders to towns like Ely, forty miles south of the Pony Express Trail. If L.A. and the Bay were the heart and brains of this new California, then Mojave and beyond were the brawn, the backbone, and the expanding net of nerves—feeling the heat, holding onto the Wild West, preserving the toughness of the pioneers, and keeping fantasies charged.

Mac (right) took Karl (far left) and his best friend, Chuck (center), on grit-over-glamour adventures through Americana and the still-Wild West.

THE DEPRESSION WAS STILL CHOKING our nation's prosperity when Mac and a few other men decided to get some mining property in Northeast Nevada, east of Ely, in the now–ghost town of Osceola. A town where in May of 1877, the largest gold nugget ever found in Nevada had been discovered, valued at $6,000—*then*.

That rare rock may have been the ingot of inspiration for Karl's mother, Frances, to compose a song about the adjacent town and gulch of Hogum, with lucky lyrics to the tune of "Is It True What They Say About Dixie?":

Is it true what they say about Hogum,
That it doesn't rain but once in six months,
That the miners work their dry washers throughout the day,
Or hasn't the story been told the right way?

Is it true what they say about Hogum,
That there's gold in the ground all around,
Do they dig, do they sweat, do they pan all they can get?—
If they do, that's where I belong!

Just over the mountain ranges to the east was the tiny town of Baker, Nevada (current population: 68), and the Utah line. The Snake Range was on one side and the Schell Range on the other. Mac and his pals had access to the Lehman Caves and Osceola's mining center with its placer mining—a system that essentially washes precious metals out of soil and sediment.

Mac would head out on their trips clean-shaven and return with a long beard. And all the while, Karlie's knowledge and imagination were growing right along with those whiskers.

Karl saw the intricacies of placer mining firsthand. He saw the Osceola West Ditch and the Osceola East Ditch, built with plows and horses to bring in water from the mountains to use for the mining.

Karl was there when a grizzled veteran prospector told Mac that he and his partners were "out of the loop" but didn't know it. That they were too far down the hill to get anything worthwhile.

But what Karl never saw were signs of discouragement.

Karl's familiarity with the hill got its dusty start with the firing of a camp cook—who actually didn't know *how to* cook. So Karl's mother headed for Ely with some needed nutrition and six-year-old Karlie in tow. *And* a few demands for convenience.

The workers used a traditional outhouse, but it was feared young Karlie might fall in. So a Hercules Powder dynamite box became a semi-sophisticated "comfort station" for him after Mac cut out the top and put a toilet seat on it.

A sewer-safe advantage of being a plumber's son.

It was a sturdy little livin'-off-the-land latrine with a lot of longevity. If it was built tough enough to secure TNT, it would surely stand up to Nevada's heat, wind, and weather.

But sixty years' worth?!

KARLS TOILET 1935

The explosion of Western civilization may have all started with Karlie's dynamite-box toilet!

The "K-Model" commode was still sitting in the *still*-rugged area well into the 1990s, when Karl found it standing ready for action on a nostalgic trip back there with his good friend Omar Tweten. It was the plumber's version of the Lost Ark!

ARIZONA—WITH THOSE MIAMI ROOTS—was also a part of that umbilical wild. And one particular trip back there proved to be *particularly* muddy. Mac and one of his friends, along with Karlie and his lifelong friend Chuck Monnich, did a lot of pushing of the family's 1935 Chevy pickup; four-wheel-drive vehicles weren't suburbia-standard back then.

As the ordeal of sludge progressed, so did the wine-drinking of Mac and his buddy.

The kids wound up neatly tucking the two inebriated men into the bed of the truck and lashing them in so they wouldn't fall out; then they pointed the thing west and headed for California.

Neither kid, of course, had a driver's license.

But *that* wasn't the real problem; the steep grade coming down into Indio was.

And the failed brakes presented the *biggest* problem.

Flying down from the seventeen-hundred-foot Chiriaco Summit, there aren't a lot of flat spots to slow something up—so the boys had to ride it out.

Throughout the entire descending drama, the polluted pair in the back shook but never stirred. Not until after they had safely coasted into Indio to get the brakes fixed did the disoriented dads learn of the wild ride.

THAT WASN'T THE ONLY ORDEAL involving the '35. Actually, the remote outback travel in the days before interstates—the days before a "motel row" at every exit, fast-food and gas station oases every twenty miles, cell phones, phones of *any* kind, car air-conditioning, air-conditioning of *any* kind, and the hint of a threat that a fully-radared Highway Patrol cruiser might pop up at any time—made for an American history lesson in itself.

This specific hairy leg of the trip was Barstow to Needles, a hundred fifty miles or so of some of the most desolate stretches of the revered Route 66.

At night.

Karl was free and easy in the back of the pickup under the canopy that his father had built out of a framework of pipe. Laws governing straps, seat belts, and tight restraints on just who can sit where were still many miles down the road.

The '35 was eastbound; a '36 Ford was heading west. Someone drifted. The two big-fendered monsters hit, and both beasts rolled.

Somehow Karl hung on for the flip. He ended up fine. But in the cab of the truck with Karl's dad was a big guy—a Black mine worker whom Mac was bringing out to one of the mines. He wound up with a broken shoulder and three or four snapped ribs. Both the mine worker and Mac spent a few days in the hospital at Needles.

Back in L.A., Mac's insurance paid the tab—with enough left over to buy a brand new aluminum-framed King bicycle for Karl.

The rough "ride"—at least for Karl—had been more than worth it.

When beasts collide...

As years passed, Karl's father would reveal that he and the mine worker had been listening to a baseball game on the pickup's radio. Auto sound systems and electronics in the age of tubes and low-spark, six-volt loops were not quite what they are now. The radio had evidently run down the battery in the bottom of the ninth, and that was the third out for the Chevy's lights. That just may have been a factor in the drift.

WHILE A LITTLE ROUGH in the cosmetic department, the '35 never let the McMillen men down, transporting them back up to their golden quests in Ely and into other crusades. And that old truck and the road beneath it added mile upon mile to Karl's Americana adventure—shuffling the pages of *Huckleberry Finn* with *Travels with Charley* and composing chapter upon chapter of its own.

One of those chapters could have begun with words from a common sign throughout the mining camps: NO TRESPASSING! But it was a sign often ignored in favor of the camaraderie of the hill. Mac would drive into the forbidden areas, talk to folks with the same pans in their hands and hope in their hearts as his, and be best friends in half an hour.

And that kinetic kinship comes in handy in areas where laws are enforced not by folks with badges or from the outside. It was important that Mac "speak the language" when Karlie and Chuck wandered past those signs during the hare-brained heat of their many rabbit hunts.

When the bunch headed back to the city, they would often stop at the Fontana grapefruit stands where Mac had even more friends. He knew a lot of people.

He taught his son how to deal with those people.

He taught his son how to work hard.

He introduced his son to Tobe Barnes and the entire cast of characters he'd met up on the hill.

THERE'S A CHANCE not even Twain or Steinbeck could have captured all the "adventures," "travels," and mineshaft-mindsets of Tobe Barnes and his gold-panning peers.

Of the loose-lodgers of the hill, Tobe was the most honest and was considered a good teacher. He could talk about religion or any subject you wanted.

Tobe was a legend and a gifted grifter. He had that natural ability to attract friends and associates—and creatures—that made life on the hill a diverse daily delight.

Some of the first people *attracted* were a woman and her hubby who tended to initiate a few too many sermonizing conversations about religion with the miners; the pair was exiled from the digs.

Then "Jim Henry" arrived.

You had the Mullet boys on one part of the hill, the State family on another; you had Tobe working his piece of land, and then here comes Jim to stake a claim.

And it didn't take long for *his* reputation to develop.

If an engineer came up on the hill, and *if* that engineer had the misfortune to engage Jim in a discussion about the worth of his ore or a topic equally economically compelling, and *if* his opinions and Jim's didn't line up in perfect order…well, that engineer would find himself quickly hole-blasted back to the flatlands.

If you went to Jim Henry's house for dinner, you could count on having lamb. It may have been a culinary coincidence, but in the springtime, herds of sheep would be shepherded through the nearby valley to feed.

As tales and tongues further have it, Jim Henry once stole some concentrates of scheelite—a multicolored ore of tungsten—from someone's mine. He *allegedly* took the $CaWO_4$ (as its chemical designation IDs it) to a smelter in Salt Lake City and returned to Ely with about four hundred bucks! *During the Depression!*

This bonus helped ol' Jim become known for shamelessly keeping the town's hookers in high heels and generously tossing quarters to the newsboys. And the hill didn't have a bar he wasn't thrown out of for one reason or another.

One day, Jim found himself in the local movie theater, and he wasn't real sure how he got there. He was nearing the end of his latest binge and right there in the theater, ol' Jim needed to "recycle some booze"—or worse. In his soused state, he decided the lobby restroom was too far of a trek, that the aisle would do just fine. That's where the constables and deputy sheriffs got him. It took a bunch of them— with clubs—to get him to finally "pay attention."

Jim himself would make plenty of others *pay attention* up on the hill.

And the hill itself posed some logistical problems, in terms of "equipment."

Jim Henry definitely had the most raucous reputation on the hill.

When Jim's old truck lost its brakes, the mere inability to stop wouldn't—couldn't—keep him from using it. Boats use anchors; why not a car? Jim hauled a big anvil into the truck and hitched up a heavy chain to it. The truck would get him *down* the hill; the anvil would *stop* the truck before it hit bottom.

Simple gravitational physics.

Simple life on the hill…

At one point, Mac, along with Karl and his buddy Chuck, spent an "Injun Joe's cave" kind of night in Jim Henry's cabin.

The good part was the usual blue-plate-special dinner of *Lamb à la Henry.*

The downside, however, was when Mac began shooting his .410 shotgun-pistol through Jim's roof.

No one was exactly sure why—in particular, Karlie and Chuck, who were tucked into their bedrolls in the next room—but a night of drinking may have had a little something to do with the blasts.

Life on the hill…

Ultimately, through all of the introductions, interactions, and aggravations, Tobe was the gold-dust devil of the underground whom Mac and his son became closest to.

When the McMillens met Tobe, his home was an abandoned mine tunnel, which he said was better than "living out in the open."

Mac brought in lumber so Tobe could have a place of his own.

The men all hauled the lumber up the hill and helped construct a sixteen-by-twenty-foot cabin for the old prospector. A bona fide piece of railroad track served as its main roof support, but the structure had a few details yet to be worked out.

Frank Lloyd Wright didn't exactly help with the design.

The cabin had one-by-twelve-foot siding with maybe a strip or two here or there for weathering. But that was it. It had no inside wall. No finish on the inside. It did have a pitched roof, of course, for weather.

And that hefty length of rail down the middle.

The miners took some two-by-six hardwood that Mac had obtained for free. It simply couldn't be nailed, so they drilled a hole in each end and looped a piece of wire through it. One end of each two-by-six was laid onto the lower flat flange of the rail, with the other end wired to the wall. This created Tobe's *attic*, which he used to store traps.

Tobe's traps were part of how he was able to subsist out there. He knew all the tricks: how to track the animals and how to get rid of his own scent and tracks with sagebrush.

Life on the hill was seldom without its challenges.

Tobe's cabin was on a ridge. When the wind came up, it *really* came up in that eight-mile-long valley vortex! The cabin would sway and creak, squeaking like a scalded mouse.

But it was all good until the attic boards swayed a little too much and came crashing down, along with all of Tobe's traps.

After the attic collapse, Tobe found some serious cable to replace the now-ripped-apart wire; so the next time Mac, Karlie, and Chuck visited, the place looked like the web of a mutant metal tarantula. But it worked.

Even with the cables and the dirt floor, it was home.

On the hill "you got to do what you got to do."

Tobe's cabin-in-motion perched on that high ridge was eventually painted a brilliant white. When the sun was right, it could be seen for miles from the other side of the valley, like a beacon to the always-hoped-for big nuggets below. Nothing else around it, it was like a castle in the moors—a fitting mansion for the honorary mayor of Hogum Gulch.

Tobe Barnes:
"The Mayor of Hogum Gulch"

TOBE KEPT HIS WELL and a big water tank down in the valley, and he'd haul the water up the hill.

Until someone stole the tank.

Someone Tobe eventually ran into in town. *While* Tobe was wearing his gun.

The legend doesn't exactly have Tobe shooting the guy, but he did make the day uncomfortable for him.

There was also an uncomfortable day for the bull snake that hung out in Tobe's cabin. Bull snakes were fine to have around because they caught the rats—convenient natural selection at work. But Tobe did have limits to the extent of hospitality granted to nature's little exterminators. Hanging over the stove, due to drop into the cabbage and salt pork and beans, the snake wore out its welcome. Tobe ended the reptile's stay with a shotgun blast that also added some modifications to the cabin's interior decor.

Other members of the wild kingdom left their mark as well. Including a small mammal poised to permeate the shack's inner beauty forever.

It was evening. Tobe was in bed, with Karl and Chuck in their bedrolls on the floor. The door was open as usual—fresh air was needed. Intruders would be taking their lives in their hands.

Unless, of course, they didn't know better.

The skunk that wandered in was of that rare ignorant mindset.

Chuck awakes and sees the black and white fur in the moonlight (the only shine-source in the electricity-deprived shack). He rouses Karl and lights a lantern.

What'll we do?!

Rattle some newspaper!

The skunk stands his ground. Then he jumps up on the kitchen table. *Crash!* goes the butter dish. He jumps to a nearby bench and lands in a full water bucket.

He's not happy.

He leaps out—shaking but thankfully not spraying!

How this furry show being staged in the moonlight and low lantern glow ended is still anybody's guess.

Tobe woke up and his on-the-hill life-learnings intervened: "Let's all just go back to sleep and hope like hell he leaves! If he doesn't, we'll sure know. Good night…"

Tobe's patience and sagely restraint paid off. By morning, the skunk and his potential for pungent pandemonium was long gone.

TOBE'S EXTERIOR DECORATING included a dry washer for extracting gold—a wooden apparatus that looked like a couple of upside-down folding chairs. It would air-dry the "good dirt" that was pulled up from twenty feet down. Karl and Chuck were taught how to operate the old machine.

Gold mining has always been labor-intensive—then *and* today. And the two main methods of separating the ore from the dirt are both primitive but effective. There's the wet method, using gallons and gallons of water; and then there's the dry method. With an annual micro-rainfall of 9.65 inches (Death Valley gets 5), *dry* becomes a key word for just about everything around Ely.

A dry washer: One of the most important tools on the dusty hill.

In this dry method, once the soil was out of the ground, it was dumped into a wheelbarrow and hauled to a flat area where it was laid out on a tarp and raked to dry. The dirt in this region is particularly sticky and needed to be dried thoroughly before the gold could be separated. The grit was then shoveled into the dry washer, which the miners would hand-crank, sending the whole works trickling through a series of trays to allow the heavy gold-bearing dirt to separate from the worthless dregs. Once completed, the miners were ready to pan. The two boys learned how to work with the screen and the rocks and the water and the pans.

Gold was going for thirty-five dollars per ounce but was sold to the grocery store in Ely for about twenty-nine dollars per ounce due to impurities. In one six-week period, Karlie and Chuck processed forty dollars and eighty cents worth of gold.

CHUCK MONNICH & KARL

A lifelong friendship was forged on the hill.

While fortunate with the gold, the boys needed another spin of good fortune on a certain safari for hare meat. During the hunt, Karl and Chuck found an old mining shaft that had been timbered up. But it still had ladder access.

The pair climbed down, of course—all the way to the bottom. Chuck had brought a camera and wanted a photo of the mine floor.

They got their photo, but they also got a long lecture from Tobe when they told him what they had done.

"What?!" The old prospector laid into the boys. "What if it had caved in? We'd never have known where to look for you or find you. And you couldn't be tracked because you were going on rocks and gravel and sage brush!"

Tobe was a camp counselor, an outdoor educator, and a pioneer philosopher. He believed in reincarnation and often talked about people coming back into this world as other creatures—or sometimes other people. (He never did say who he thought the bull snake might have been, however!)

Tobe would closely examine anyone he thought he had met before. He would discuss the Lost Islands of Mu and Atlantis. He had been a bootlegger and a sheepherder. He had done many things but would never boast.

And then he found the mummy.

On one exploratory jaunt around the area, Tobe was coming down the Colorado River on a float, when he arrived at the Green River–Colorado River junction. While searching through some caves, he discovered a mummy with a duck or some creature tied to its back.

This must have been a queen or someone special, thought Tobe.

He packed up the mummy along with some slippers and a pot that accompanied it. He gave the pot to Karlie and the slippers to Chuck. The queen was bunked in the cabin with Tobe in a glass case at the foot of his bed.

Tobe figured the gal to be about two thousand years old, and because of her size and her teeth and her short red hair, he pegged her as a pygmy.

After a while, no one in the cabin paid much attention to "Ma." She was just a part of life at Tobe's and on the hill.

APRIL 13, 1940

A census taker named Mary O'Connell, working on America's once-a-decade Big List, managed to find her way up the rough dirt road to Tobe's cabin.

Tobe was outside chopping wood.

"Anyone else in there?" Mary asked.

Tobe kept chopping. "Just Ma," he answered. "She's in the cabin; go on in."

O'Connell nodded.

"There's no one in there," she said, coming back outside through the creaky wooden door.

"Well," Tobe told her, "I got a shelf at the foot of my bed there, covering up a box. Sometimes she'll take a nap in there. So just move those newspapers and stuff off. *You'll see her…*"

So the census taker did.

And she *did*.

"Ma" was noted—if not exactly added—to the population of Ely.

A reporter "dug up" the story and wrote about it in the local paper. Her wrap-up of events made for a great human interest piece.

> ## Census Taker Refuses to Count Mummy
>
> ELY, Nev., April 13. (Special) Tobe Barnes' mummy didn't quite make the census, but an inquisitive census enumerator really did not care.
>
> Mrs. Mary O. O'Connell was taking the census in the Osceola gold mining camp and questioned Barnes at length, finally asking if he was the only occupant of the house. "Oh no," said Barnes, "my mummy is inside." "Well, I must get the old lady, too," said Mrs. O'Connell.
>
> "Walk right in," said Barnes, and in she walked, and then out again rather hurriedly. His mummy was a quiet old lady, much too quiet, in fact. It was a mummified body Barnes had found and brought into the district from Colorado. Standing three and one-half feet tall, the mummy was a redheaded woman of perhaps thirty-five, which was uncovered in Colorado in a cliff dwelling, found buried with a duck tied about her back, an old cave-dweller custom.
>
> Scientists claim, Barnes explained, that the old lady is perhaps two thousand years old and probably of the first tribe of basket weavers. Found with her was an arrowhead, which probably caused her death, and a moccasin made of the skin of a mountain sheep. He further stated he has refused all offers to part with his mummy.
>
> At any rate, so far as she was concerned, Barnes should have his mummy, and she was too old for the census, anyway, Mrs. O'Connell stated.

THE BOYS' RABBIT HUNTING eventually progressed to bigger game. It was for survival out there—especially for Tobe, who didn't have the luxury of heading back to the urban conveniences of Los Angeles. For him, eating was never "in" or "out" of season.

But deer were hard to get in the summertime—one step on a dry twig and they'd be gone.

On one hunt, Karl headed out through the Schell Range, across the valley. Tobe stayed behind to fish.

"Whatever you do," Tobe told him, "if you run across a warden, don't give him the gun!"

It was Tobe's gun, of course, and he didn't want to lose it to the law. But what was Karlie supposed to do—*shoot the warden?*

Authority out there wasn't given; it was taken. But it took a lot of living to grasp that. To *feel* the truth in that.

Luckily, Karl didn't embrace Tobe's feral logic, but he did at least begin to feel it. Authority was one thing; starvation was another.

Since the hill had no electricity or refrigeration anywhere, after meat was shot and dressed, it was wrapped in tarps and stored in an old mine tunnel during the day to keep it cool against the fierce force of the desert summer. After sundown, it was hung outside in the cool night air.

The miners would cut off what they needed to eat and then wrap the meat back up. This went on until, eventually, maggots would start to "get ahead" of them. But the meat would be shaved of the leeching larvae and the feeding would continue. Apparently, below the wormed-out level, everything was just *fine*.

As ONE OF THE TRIPS drew to a close and the old pickup was once again California-bound, the bed was filled with Karl, Chuck, and a quarter of an out-of-season deer. Up front were Karl's parents. The hunting theme maintained high volume as Karl and Chuck shot at ducks from the bed of the Chevy as the bunch rumbled through the Alamo, Nevada, region, ninety miles north of Las Vegas.

That's where they saw the red lights and heard the siren. A federal marshal pulled them over.

"What are you going to do with the meat?" Karl's mom asked as the cop confiscated the venison-in-violation, loading it into his own vehicle.

"We'll give it to the local hospital," he told her.

I'll bet, she thought cynically.

Summer 1942

At around fourteen years of age, Karl became rooted even deeper into the fertile guts of old California. Mac was adding another life lesson onto his son's lengthening résumé, sending Karl out to farms in the Indio/Mecca area to pick sweet potatoes. The farms were owned by one of Mac's friends, Elmer Crunk (yes, Elmer Crunk!), and that friend was told to teach Karl "how to work."

And he did. Adding even more fire to Karl's already burned-in ethics.

Karl got a dirty hands-on education in agriculture, and he got it quick.

"The vines are growing in the furrows, kid. The plow goes through and it throws the vines up, and you pick up the sweet potatoes and you put them in the lug boxes. Then the farm truck comes down the furrow, where you've got these lug boxes spread out all over the place—after you've filled them up.

"Now the truck is moving. You take the lug boxes and put them up in the truck, and a guy sitting up in there stacks them. This is a field truck, so you got to keep up with it—you've got to move!

"'Course, you gotta be able to handle all the heat and the sweat and the dirt. The furrows are made up of fine silt, and the truck will kick up more than a little dust. You're sweating in 110 or 115 degrees, of course. Really sweating! Pretty soon you're all caked in that hard mud-like silt.

"But nobody passes out, though. These people know how to work in this killer dust-oven.

"So next you go to this shed and toss the potatoes into the washing vat to get the mud off them…they drip dry on a conveyer belt, where they get a shot of wax and they're rolled over a little. Then they come out…dried and waxed…and the ladies pack them in flashy green or purple paper liners in lug boxes so that they go to market looking great! Your clean and shiny potatoes bring a better price than somebody's dirty sweet potatoes—that's the idea.

"So when the potatoes come out the other end in the boxes, you have another machine that presses the lid down…and you soak the lids…that way you can get the max potatoes in the box as the lids bend…then you go bang-bang-bang and tack it into place…and you take more nails and you seal the lid on tight.

"Then everything is loaded onto the freight truck and it's off to market.

"The crops rotate. The early crop comes in at Mecca because it's warmer, and then eventually we go into Indio. You want your potatoes to be the first ones on the market—that's where the price is.

"Toward the end of the summer, we'll be in Fontana."

In Fontana, Karl would get to ride the truck into the L.A. Central Market with the swampers, sleeping all the way there and back. But he'd put down his time on his timecard—*all of it*. Sleeping or not, seventeen hours is a long day.

Especially for a fourteen-year-old.

It was during one of the dumping-waxing bouts in the packing shed that Karl sliced a huge gash in his hand, catching it on a metal clamp that was holding some of the box's wood together.

The "field incision" required many stitches. A future fortune teller would be highly confused by *that* line in his palm.

Of course, if she could have *really* read what was in store for Karl, her crystal ball would have surely shattered!

NEXT, IT WAS ON TO MILFORD, UTAH, for a summer of even more life lessons, building basements for fifteen new homes. Karl would tote the standard ninety-four-pound bags of cement from box cars, and then he'd hand-mix the clay and grit; continuous pour wasn't even heard of yet. Small section by small section was laid until a basement was formed.

The guy in charge of bulldozing out the dirt for the basements was doing a major project at his own farm in Delta, grading 160 acres worth of land. He saw that Karl was a good worker and invited him to come live with him, promising to teach him to run that magic machine.

Karl thought that sounded wonderful! What kid wouldn't want to drive a bulldozer?!

But Karl's mother wasn't quite as keen on the idea. "No!" she told Karl. "You're going to finish high school!"

The McMillen mining trips eventually petered out like a tapped-out ore vein, and even Tobe left the hill in 1948, moving to the warmth of Searchlight, an easier climate for his worsening arthritis.

When Tobe first moved downslope, he just camped out along the river until the authorities forced him to find "more appropriate" digs between Searchlight and the Colorado's shore.

He wound up on some land with an exceptional view of the water. That's where his dog died, and that's where Tobe buried him and set up a monument. And so began Tobe's Cemetery.

At least thirty people are buried in that cemetery, along with Tobe's dog—and Tobe.

He died in 1955 at an unknown age.

The authorities "took care" of his few belongings, and somewhere "Ma" was lost. It's hoped she might be buried in Tobe's Cemetery along with Tobe, but no one knows for sure.

But wherever she is, she doesn't have her slippers or her pot.

Having not a clue as to their significance, Chuck's mother threw out Ma's somewhat weathered slippers. Karl, however, *still* has the pot—and generous and determined as ever, he is *still* looking to donate it to an appropriate museum.

Karl is cooking up a donation plan for "Ma's" old pot.

The last that Karl or his father ever heard from Tobe was toward the end of his years when Tobe found himself in the local Social Security office. A Native American woman in line ahead of him had just been turned down for some benefits—and they were now giving Tobe a raise in his.

"Give it all to her," he told them, looking at the poor Indian woman. He had all he needed.

This would be Karl's final bit of wisdom from Tobe Barnes and the rest of the cast along the rutted-road backbone of the Nevada desert.

And he would never forget any of it—the resourcefulness, the generosity, and most of all the survival-from-the-ground-up toughness.

They were traits he would need and use to their fullest.

CHAPTER 3

You Just Can't Put Numbers
to Philosophy and Romance

Which of these U.S. Presidents
appeared on the television series Laugh-In?
A: Lyndon Johnson B: Richard Nixon
C: Jimmy Carter D: Gerald Ford

THAT WAS JOHN CARPENTER's fifteenth-level question—the big
one—on *Who Wants to Be a Millionaire?* Carpenter was the show's
first go-all-the-way winner back in 1999; he answered correctly and
opened up a pretty healthy bank account.

Karl McMillen, Jr., never had to rely on modern pop-culture
trivia to make a buck. He never cashed in a quick-fix lottery ticket
either. The questions Karl had to answer on the way to *his* big level
were all about business and about people. They weren't multiple-
choice either—but he could always fill in the blanks just perfectly.

Later along his business-success journey, Karl would be looked
upon as having a Midas touch in business. But it wasn't magical.

Karl's "Golden Touch" was the savvy gained from his father:
from those days in the desert heat, savoring fortitude and hard work;

from studying the Tobes of the world and analyzing characters and character.

His "lifeline" was just that: a connection to life, with eyes open and an awareness of people's needs. Karl understood what people require in the way of marketed consumables and what they need to be productive as employees and partners. And he was always ready to learn more.

Sadly, a time would come when Karl's eyes-open connection would dim in an area where he wanted it to shine brightest. But it would later reignite, illuminating a charitable path that few people have the ability—or heart—to ever travel.

JUNE 1946

Karl graduated from Pasadena Junior College, which at the time also served as a high school, offering eleventh and twelfth grades. Karl's formal schooling blended nicely with his developing street smarts. And neither would ever be neglected.

Just seventeen, Karl considered his options for furthering that formal part. He took a post–high school speech class in summer school. One of his assignments transcended being an oratory topic; it became the first section in his outline of life.

Karl's speech looked into the G.I. Bill in the post-WWII years—years of declared peace, but which were still smoldering with the military heat of war. Karl proposed that strong benefits were available to those who helped replenish the fighting forces. Benefits like a fully financed college education. Karl further analyzed that the maximum bang for the buck could be gained from entering the Marines or the Coast Guard; the "perks" could be taken advantage of after only two years in either of these service branches. It was a four-year commitment in the others.

Two years' commitment…a four-year college degree…and they pay you as well…

Within weeks following his *persuasive* presentation, Karl was adjusting to a four a.m. wake-up call in San Diego and marching in the uniform of the United States Marines.

AUGUST 1946

Karl McMillen's more-than-military march from age seventeen to twenty-five defined the phrase *formative years.*

Certainly, every moment of a person's existence in some way affects its overarching entirety. But when you examine the history of a true success, you generally encounter a window of time when that switch was thrown—when the means to a satisfying later end became electric. When that juice started to flow and somebody screamed "It's alive!"

But it works the other way around, too.

When things, lives, and people fall, a window can usu- ally be found there as well. But that window winds up broken—

Karl's Marine enlistment was the first step in his formative march.

shattered by that first drink, that first drug, that first needle, that first point-of-no-return mistake that, for some, is stronger than any force of healing or forgiveness.

Karl McMillen's life from 1946 to 1954 offers a spotless look at a picture-perfect path to honest success. The pioneer paving to his Golden Touch.

Karl's childhood wanderings around pre-*anything* Southern California and his headfirst exploits into business are both historical gold.

EARLY IN HIS MARINE TRAINING, Karl developed a severe leg infection and missed some integral basics in boot camp. The absences also led to some missteps in paper shuffling, and he was assigned to two different platoons, both of which were being dispatched out.

Karl had a choice.

One was going to Inyokern—described by the platoon's sergeant as a lovely locale "up by San Francisco; a great place!" Evidently, in all his back-road roaming with his dad, Karl never quite made it into *that* city-in-the-sun. He bought into the sergeant's glowing review and jumped in line with that platoon. He was soon headed for the Eden of Inyokern—*in the heart of the Mojave Desert, 397 hot miles inland from the Golden Gate!*

Karl sweated enough to make it to Private First Class as a leatherneck, but not beyond. The theory in his little crew was that once you achieved a higher rank, you became an A-hole. His platoon had a farm-boy-made-buck-sergeant who proved the theory. At the sarge's discharge, some of the boys added a pie-baking dose of sugar to the gas tank of his car. They heard later that the booby-trapped buggy made it as far as Needles before the engine overcooked itself in a blaze of glory.

(A few years down the road, Needles, on the California-Arizona line, would rise up out of the heat and provide Karl with a couple more of those life-is-never-dull exploits.)

Karl's own military discharge came just twenty months after his enlistment, in March of 1948. The military decided that the twenty-four-month stints weren't much more than a Halls-of-Montezuma honeymoon, so they cut the short-timers loose.

Karl had wanted to "see the world," but that wasn't going to happen; Uncle Sam's investment just wouldn't be worth it.

But *Karl's* investment did pay off in Semper Fi spades—his twenty months still entitled him to those four years of college.

By April, within a month of leaving the Marines, Karl was working for Spencer Plumbing. His father had deep ties with the union, which *helped* Karl's military time translate into credit for three years of apprenticeship; he needed just two more to reach the heavy-hammer journeyman status.

Spencer had Karl working mass jobs on apartment units. At first, his assignments were less than high-tech; but whatever the tasks, Karl did them faster than anyone.

Karl's quest now was to outwork and to outlearn everyone; to go as fast as possible without making mistakes. He was developing more of that Touch.

But that matter of college needed to be addressed—formal education to fill in the framework of real-time experience he was building so well.

That formality would come next in Albuquerque, New Mexico.

Karl's best buddy, Chuck—Chuck from the Tobe, gold-mine, and runaway-truck days—had reeled in a good catch of money while running an albacore commercial fishing boat off the Southern California coast. With albacore coming in at about six hundred dollars a ton, he easily bought himself a brand-new 1949 Mercury— the immortal *Rebel Without a Cause* model that James Dean would canonize just six years later.

Chuck and the hot rod would be attending the University of New Mexico. It seemed like a good, progressive idea, so Karl joined Chuck in his sedan and headed east. From January to June of '49, Karl got in a full semester at UNM; then it was back to L.A. to work at Spencer for the summer.

FALL 1949

It was time to return to Albuquerque—but not in that cool new Merc. Chuck had decided to forego school for a while—he had *un problemo*. The Spanish class he took at UNM had assigned all the homework *en Español*.

¿Qué?

That didn't work at all for Chuck.

And besides, the siren call of high-dollar fish was too enticing for Chuck to bail out on; so Karl headed back to the Land of Enchantment alone.

In his Model A.

Karl's Model A wasn't just *any* Model A. It looked like a T-V8: a V8 in a roadster body with a pickup bed. However, Karl didn't quite have the bucks to drop a V8 under the hood. So the trip to Albuquerque took a little longer than it had in Chuck's coupe. The A's maximum speed was a Route 66–scorching forty-five miles per hour! Any faster and the old Ford threatened to blow a bearing, a serious setback out in the remote badlands of Essex or Seligman.

So Karl nursed the Model A eastbound along the nearly thousand-mile stretch. When he reached Needles, he knew that he had to go through Oatman and then make the steep climb up the Summit of Gold Roads grade into Kingman. He also knew that the Model A was going to need water. *And* he knew that because the Ford had no hand brake, he was going to need to somehow keep the engine running while he filled the radiator on that big up-and-over pull.

Well, Karl may not have had a hand brake, but he did spot a hitchhiker up the road.

Karl picked up the thumber and had him work the hose while Karl kept his foot on the brake. He'd give the guy a ride and a break from the late-summer desert heat in return.

It was all good.

Everything was going well until Karl saw a buzzard perched on a fence post. Things don't go by all that fast at forty-five miles per hour, so on a born-from-boredom whim, Karl decided to try to shoot the bird.

From the moving car.

Leaning across the hitchhiker.

Karl whipped out his pistol from under his folded leather jacket and BOOM!

For some reason, when they got to Kingman, the hitchhiker decided to leave Karl's company and find another ride.

Karl was back on his own.

And this was 1949.

On Route 66.

In September.

It was hot, and the road was lined with the diners that helped make Main Street, U.S.A., an asphalt legend.

Karl stopped at one and sat down at the counter. The fan was turning, but the fans of '49 weren't exactly of the cooling caliber of twenty-first-century A/C. But they *were* part of the raw pioneer charm; this was still the Wild West.

Karl ordered up a salad. He *didn't* order the beetle in the middle of it, however. But Karl's eye for opportunity salted any distaste or disgust. He managed to fork all the way around the big bug, leaving only the entomologic eats for the manager to view—and to comp him, with humble apologies, for the meal he'd eaten most of!

KARL AND THE MODEL A made it to Albuquerque, and his second semester of college began—a semester that saw his induction into Delta Sigma Pi fraternity.

That semester ended in January and a lot of students planned on heading back to California for the break.

Not Karl. He simply couldn't afford it. The G.I. Bill was paying him seventy-five dollars a month, and his job setting pins in a bowling alley provided only *spare* change.

It was a tough up-and-down blancing act, but like plumbing those massive units, Karl was the fastest. "No one has EVER set that many pins in a day!" he was told.

Karl could barely walk after the contortions and jumps involved in the endless strikes and splits, and he still didn't have enough money to get home.

There was this card game, however…

By the next morning, Karl had enough capital to get back to California. He also found another student who needed a ride and would split the costs.

Once those cards turned lucky and he had a few bucks in his pocket, Karl decided that this road trip west would be a one-way run. He wouldn't be back for the spring semester.

Karl was tired of being broke. That didn't work for him at all.

He and his friend also decided that the Model A—heatless and windowless—would take them home via the southern route. They wouldn't be rolling through Flagstaff in the snow.

They left Albuquerque and drove all night. At three o'clock in the morning, they stopped in Benson, Arizona, in the rolling hills east of Tucson.

In the *cold-bite* rolling hills east of Tucson.

They needed gas *and* some time huddled around the station's pot-bellied stove. Then it was west to Mexicali and across the Mexican border where lodging, such as it was, was cheaper—a buck a room, or you could sleep in the hall for fifty cents.

Karl finally made it back to Pasadena where rents were a few degrees steeper. His grandfather had a trailer out in rural Fontana that he offered to let Karl bring into the City of Roses. Its social flavor may have tasted of *The Grapes of Wrath,* but it would become home.

Karl hauled the old Airstream into town and parked it behind a boarding house near the Pasadena City Playhouse. The house had ten or fifteen people lodged in the low-budget roosts, mainly struggling actors working at the Playhouse and trying to make the big time in Hollywood. Neither route seemed to be paying off for most of them.

Karl paid twenty to fifty bucks a month to moor the trailer and eat with the crowd. And while the actors tried to act…

"Misery acquaints a man with strange bedfellows.
I will here shroud till the dregs of the storm be past."

…Karl went back to Spencer and back to plumbing.

KARL MAY HAVE BEEN LIVING in a trailer behind a boarding house, eating meals with frustrated and weary would-be stars, and working as a plumber, but he was still himself. He was still the guy who had that eyes–open connection to life.

One of those connections was about to get stronger.

Karl had been in Pasadena for about six months. In June, he decided to shuffle on down to the Pasadena City Auditorium with some of his buddies for a summer dance being held there.

That's where he met Thelma Beatrice Mastraight.

Karl had had a girlfriend back in New Mexico but had never been in a serious relationship. This was different.

For starters, Thelma's parents were from Holland and they had a reputation for being thrifty. Karl highly appreciated that.

He actually liked everything about Thelma. Their three-month, summer breeze–in courtship was like a 1940s movie: in black and white, of course, and heavy on character study. Maybe Jimmy Stewart or Fred McMurray as Karl; Donna Reed or Dorothy Lamour as Thelma.

The "proposal" was more of a calculated shopping errand. Karl had found a place to buy a good diamond ring "at the right price," and he took Thelma along because he didn't want to waste any money buying the wrong ring.

He also took her along to meet his mother.

"I think you should wait," she advised her son.

"No."

SEPTEMBER 30, 1950

The "quicklyweds" took a long weekend and were married in a small chapel on Pico Boulevard in Los Angeles, halfway between Lomita and Pasadena, where each one's folks lived.

The intimate number of guests were treated to wedding cake, but it wasn't a ceremony burdened with frills. Nor an exotic honeymoon: one night in a hotel in Santa Monica, two nights at a hotel south of Santa Barbara, and it was back to work on Tuesday.

This was an obvious part of those formative years that began to weave the business brain and economic brawn of Karl McMillen into the close-knit fabric of a family.

But as always, numbers ruled Karl's data-dominated mind. He took inventory of this new stage in his life.

Thelma had a thousand dollars cash and a 1940 Ford—*paid for.*

That was good.

Karl had the Model A and his job at Spencer.

Not bad.

Thelma also had a job as a secretary at ALCOA Aluminum, and later at North American Van Lines.

That was *very* good.

This would work. There was a lot of potential here!

Karl calculated the potent potential of his union with Thelma.

A woman who worked with Thelma at North American was the sister-in-law of a man named Dal Means. Dal was a junior part-owner in a company that installed water softeners. The majority owner of the company was a guy who was affectionately nicknamed "Curveball."

The new water softener craze was dampened by splashes of a plumbing-Ponzi scheme. Installers made the real money by signing up new "sales partners" into the business.

But the employment/sales gimmick wasn't what excited Karl; he was interested in doing more and more actual plumbing work. And he thought he could make more money installing those water softeners than by apprenticing at Spencer.

Karl arranged to meet Means and Curveball and soon joined their staff of twenty installers at General Installation. It was piecework; the installer supplied the truck, and the company supplied the material and licensing. Karl was paid eighteen dollars for each unit he installed, five bucks extra for San Bernardino and Ventura Counties.

The installers tried to pick the simple houses, the ones in places like El Monte with one bathroom. No one wanted Beverly Hills—not with a basement, boilers, and four toilets to bypass. You could be on a job like that for days!

Karl averaged about 148 bucks a week—not bad for the early fifties.

The "tired of being poor" feeling that had grabbed Karl during his last semester at UNM was easing up. His degree would be on hold for a while. Not ignored, just postponed.

Karl and Thelma's bank accounts weren't exactly fat yet, but that business electricity was boosting the juice of a new marriage.

The Fontana-born trailer near the boarding house had long since been hauled away. Karl and Thelma now rented a place on Orange Grove Avenue in Pasadena. They were surrounded by high-end houses and chauffeured residents—living behind a large mansion in an apartment over a garage, which had at one time been the chauffeur's quarters.

The place cost sixty-five dollars a month. The young couple was there about forty-five days before they decided the rent was too much. Thelma found an apartment over a theater and a dry cleaner for thirty-seven fifty.

Great!

Karl told the landlord he knew he was supposed to give thirty days notice, but explained the situation and said they could only give two weeks' notice.

That didn't settle well with the landlord; he kept insisting on the full month's notice.

Here's where the street smarts kicked in. Karl had offered the landlord two weeks, but since he'd balked at that and the next day happened to be the first of the month, the landlord would get neither the month *nor* the two weeks.

When Thelma got home from work, Karl told her that they were moving that afternoon.

And they did.

The apartment over the theater and dry cleaner may have been half the rent of the chauffer's quarters, but it was easily twice as exciting.

The dry cleaner was directly downstairs from the apartment's main window. The hot steam from pressing the clothes created an air chamber that came straight into the apartment in a constant column of sweltering stale air.

Then there was the landlady. She knew that Karl installed water softeners for a living—that he worked hard and *got dirty.*

"Did you empty the dirt out of your pants cuffs?!" she would ask Karl as he headed up the stairs after a day on the job.

"Yes, ma'am, I did…"

She nearly had a heart attack the time Karl returned from deer hunting with Chuck. His cuffs may have been clean, but the hind quarters he was carrying up her stairs had to be a violation of *some* part of the rental agreement!

EARLY 1951

The year was rolling right along. Business was being taken care of. Thelma's car was about ready to dump its transmission, so they unloaded it and managed to get Karl a new work truck.

In the course of his employment with General Installation, many jobs required local proof that specific tasks were being worked by journeymen who had passed tests. Karl became a water-softening wizard at sitting for those exams—in Santa Monica, in Long Beach, throughout the region.

As Southern California was building, so was Karl's expertise.

Dal Means had a license almost from the beginning. He had lived in the extra-rural mountain community of Big Bear Lake after the war, where a lot of tradespeople moonlighted without licenses or permits. It was one of the last free-construction vestiges of the Wild West, when a hammer, a nail, some wood, and some know-how could build you a home. Dal got his license in a sort of "class action" test, when the state offered legitimacy to the building outlaws if they could pass an exam.

But even with the business end of things improving, Karl regained that formal-education urge. Crawling under houses all day was taking its knee-bending toll, and more and more dirt was collecting in those cuffs.

SEPTEMBER 1951

After Karl and Thelma had been married a year, they loaded up that new truck and headed back to UNM for another shot at scholastic success in the desert.

Karl enrolled at the college and Thelma got a job at the new gas company; natural gas had just arrived in Albuquerque. A meter card had to be typed up for each house in the area, so the company hired a huge typing team at a buck an hour.

Gas may have arrived in Albuquerque, but water softeners hadn't. Instead of softeners, Karl was installing groceries into bags and onto shelves at the local Safeway for a quarter *less* an hour than Thelma was making. With his usual push, Karl was working and sweeping faster than any of the other box boys.

After a few weeks, it was time to ask for a raise.

"No" was the answer.

"I quit" soon followed.

Karl couldn't waste his time in an occupation where hard work didn't get you ahead.

Back in school and back in Delta Sigma Pi, Karl came into contact with a fraternity brother who installed lawn sprinklers. The two quickly formed a partnership and Karl was again able to make use of his long-range perception of what people need.

Galvanized pipe was difficult to get in Albuquerque, so Karl arranged with his father back in California to have the material shipped in. That in itself put his little company way ahead of the plumbing pack.

The two kept busy, but somehow they were not making any money. Karl began to delve inside the financial end of the business. He began to see what cheap labor costs can mean to an overall operational picture. "If you don't come to Albuquerque with money, you can't get ahead because there's so much cheap labor" became a local business axiom.

Things needed to change. And they would.

MID-1952

Albuquerque was home to the McMillens for a year.

Two years of college were finally behind Karl.

In the summer of '52 he enrolled in a summer school class, The Philosophy of Religion. It wasn't exactly his academic forte. Actually, it didn't pan out at all. For Karl, philosophy just didn't compute. Buddhism, Hinduism, Sikhism, Cheondoism, Pantheism—you couldn't put *numbers* to all that!

This wasn't working. It was time to go back to California for some recalculation. But when you drop out of school, it has to be for a reason— at least according to the people who write those G.I. Bill checks.

Karl grabbed another of those savvy lifelines and wrote a long, heartfelt (albeit *marginally* truth-stretching) letter to the Veteran's Administration, explaining the problem:

7 July 1952

Veteran's Administration
1021 W. Tijeras Avenue
Albuquerque, New Mexico

Gentlemen, in attempting to drop out of summer school,
I found out there are complications and so in order to keep
my G.I. Bill and my G.I. training valid, I have approximately
thirteen months left of eligibility which is sufficient
to complete my fifty-three needed hours for a degree in
Business Administration.

This is so important to me.

The reason I wish to drop out of summer school, however,
is an impending divorce. The last few months I have not been
able to study or anything. I cannot concentrate. At the time
I entered school I thought the best thing to do was to keep
busy. This has not proved satisfactory. At times like this I
find myself completely without ambition or fortitude.

I recently sold my half-interest in a lawn sprinkler
installation company in order to give my wife her share.
This was a small business from which I received only a
small profit. However it did have a promising future. It is
hard for one to realize how one feels at a time like this
unless you've experienced the same. As I still love my wife,
and coming from a family tree where everyone has been
married for life, it is doubly hard for me to realize I am
getting a divorce.

I plan to move to Southern California for the fall
semester at USC. I believe the change in locality and school
is the best thing I can do at this time. Please consider this

case thoroughly. I value the G.I. Bill highly and wish to complete college in order to better myself.

Sincerely,

Karl McMillen, Jr.

The "impending divorce" may have been a little white lie—all right, maybe a big one!—but the selling of the lawn sprinkler business was on the level. Karl and his partner split the assets, and part of that deal involved Karl's partner getting the new truck. The McMillens bailed out of Albuquerque, and in yet another scene reenactment from Steinbeck's rough look at Americana, they headed west in a '46 Ford station wagon with the top falling off, towing a trailer with a wooden tongue and wooden wheels.

With the entire train displaying out-of-state plates.

It was an appropriate vehicular wardrobe as they limped home to government housing near the Los Angeles harbor. In that federally controlled heaven, rent was means-tested. Tenants paid one-fifth of their income. With the G.I. Bill as their sole means of support, the McMillens' rent was twenty-one dollars a month.

"I know this…a man got to do what he got to do."
—Preacher Jim Casy, *The Grapes of Wrath*

Now, well into the twenty-first century, it might be somewhat hard to imagine anyone attending USC without the requisite personalized-plated Beamer ("SC4ME"!)—let alone living in government housing as opposed to someplace nicer like Seaver Residence Hall. But Karl has done a lot of things that most people can't imagine.

Karl's sister Ruth had already graduated from USC, and Karl would have been a Trojan in the first place, too, if it hadn't been for that pesky language requirement they imposed on all freshmen.

But he wasn't a freshman anymore. And UNM had taught him how to set a steady curricular pace—USC would be the finish line.

The pace UNM set in Business Law had been strong and fast. But Karl got it, even though the professor had been exceedingly tough. The guy had flunked *his own wife*—before they were married, of course. No one ever got an A in that class; a B on a test would make you the winner of that week's *Survivor* challenge.

But Karl was more than just a survivor; he helped out his fraternity brothers with the class as well. He had a knack.

That knack would serve him well as he entered the campus of the Cardinal and Gold.

In September of 1952, Karl McMillen enrolled in his junior year at USC. It was then that he met Dr. Ken Trefftzs—professor and head of the Finance Department.

The professor trained students to become bankers and to head up savings and loans. He was good at what he did and was well recognized for it.

The professor's father was a blacksmith—a hard job with a hard history that spoke to Karl's in-the-trenches work ethics. Dr. Trefftzs and Karl quickly bonded. Most students at USC had money; Karl had his roofless station wagon. Dr. Trefftzs appreciated who Karl was.

Karl and Dr. Trefftzs began a lifelong friendship. The professor would become Karl's trusted advisor in business decisions. A new lifeline in the arsenal.

His help would prove quite beneficial.

Many lengths of pipe later, a "plumber" would be the one to provide the endowment for Dr. Trefftzs' faculty chair.

KARL AND THELMA WERE IN THIS TOGETHER. She was still working full-time at North American and he got a part-time job at Kennedy Pipe, putting in two or three days a week, so he could attend school and study the rest of the time. For the easier classes, Thelma would read the books, decide on the important material, and underline the parts Karl needed to study.

It was just the start of Karl's propensity to surround himself with key people and utilize their strengths!

JUNE 1953

The day after classes ended for the summer, Karl climbed aboard a cheap multi-stop commuter flight to Anchorage, Alaska. He had taken leave from his part-time piping and was headed north to be part of a massive team of contractors building a four-hundred-home tract in the Last Frontier.

Karl had been brought into the job by a plumber he had long known, "Shorty" Henderson. The elder McMillens met Shorty and his family back in Miami, Arizona.

Shorty was another of those characters right out of the Tobe/ Jim Henry, stand-back-and-stop-look-and-listen mold. He had been a wrestler, then a bus driver.

He had also moved to California, where he and Mac had picked up their friendship. They would gamble together, drink together, and occasionally come close to getting annoyed with one another—depending on who was winning. And how much.

Mac was good at poker. He could bluff, really bluff. He could also play the horses, coming home from the track regularly with money in his pleated-pants pockets.

You don't have a gambling problem as long as you're winning…

He once broke a bookie in Culver City.

Mac got Shorty a job in the plumbing business, but eventually Shorty moved back to the Grand Canyon State, started his own plumbing company, and became the mayor of Wickenburg (you can just picture Twain's take on that!).

At that time, Wickenburg had a "creative" tax policy. Property taxes were paid by the utility bills. So naturally the power company would overcharge; and rental tenants wound up paying the bulk of the property tax so the landowners had a low tax base.

Shorty comes in and wants to fix that.

Nope.

The big boys vote him out.

When Karl finally deciphered his "travels with Shorty," he added a new rule to the playbook: If you're in business in a small town, don't get involved in *those* kinds of politics!

But in Alaska, a guy named Steve Hanson was heading up the project. He and Shorty were distantly related, so Shorty was brought up there.

Since Shorty was close to the McMillens, Karl was a natural to head up there too and be a part of that Last Frontier team.

It would be hard work but good money.

It would also be a chance for Karl's sustained study of the world.

Steve Hansen was a tundra-tough veteran contractor. The job was being worked in the trenches by union labor, and the unions in Alaska are strong.

There would be conflicts.

Hansen was hardened. He had been in Nebraska during the Depression. That wasn't easy. He'd also had some trouble with the law—something to do with needing money and the fact that it was all "inside the banks."

Then he got into ladies shoes—figuratively, that is: he sold a ton of them to American G.I.'s heading overseas during WWII. According to him, "Ladies shoes are the best trading material you can have!"

After the war, Hansen had jumped into Alaska's burgeoning construction. That's where the money was. He'd picked up a partner in Idaho, a good plumber. Their partnership worked—the guy from Idaho knew the technical end of things; Hansen knew the B.S.-ing, job-getting end of things.

The year before the four-hundred-house job came up, the pair had worked a thirty-five-house tract, during which they encountered some stripped threads in their relationship. The partnership had gone south, as had the plumber—back to Idaho.

Hansen wanted this new project, but he needed money to finance it. So he went to work, doing what he did best. He arranged some creative financing.

Karl remembers the numbers explicitly.

Hansen went to the general contractor. "Look," he said, "you're borrowing money at FHA's three-point-five percent, and you could have my cash discount of two percent for ten days on the monthly bills. Why don't you pay the material bills and take the two percent as a bonus for doing that, rather than waiting thirty days to get another draw on all this? That way you'll be sure that the bill is paid but you'll make money because of that two-percent cash discount."

Obviously.

And even more numbers figured in.

The four-hundred-house project featured log cesspools fed by steel septic tanks that were made right on the jobsite. It was cheaper than bringing in ready-made tanks.

The log cesspools, though, were labor-intensive—requiring the tedious building of square log-by-log walled "holes." Only two contractors in the area did that kind of work. One company came in at four hundred grand for the job; they had a lot of capital behind them. The other outfit came in at half that; they had a bigger labor force behind them.

Alaska was a territory back then—not yet a state. If a contractor didn't complete his work, he could be sued, but could not be followed to the lower forty-eight. It wasn't the safest feeling.

And this job had to be done on time. Weather was always a factor, allowing only a small window of optimum construction environment.

So what Hansen did was this: he gave the labor-heavy contractor their requested $200,000. Then he gave the other company $200,000 just to guarantee the first contractor's work! So for the original quote of $400,000, he now had both games in town on his side.

He also overbought steel for the septic tanks so that more tanks could be sold around the area after the project was complete, saving on shipping and other costs. He was a clever businessman and how he operated stuck with Karl.

But there was still the matter of the unions…

WILDCAT STRIKES would break out weekly, and there'd be Hansen, driving his Cadillac all around the jobsite, blowing dust at the union steward.

In the middle of it all was Karl McMillen, Jr.—wanting to learn, wanting to work, and just wanting to make money.

His work ethic was met with more complaints than kudos.

"Slow down!" the union workers would warn him. "We don't work like that up here!"

It got ugly.

Karl was mindful of these complaints—and potential repercussions. *He walked softly between the houses carrying a big wrench…*

Hansen finally pulled a few steel strings and brought in an attorney from Washington, D.C., who was "close to" the UA (United Association of Plumbers and Pipefitters). The attorney eventually told the UA to either pull off that job or have their charter pulled.

"How the hell did all *that* work?" Karl asked Hansen.

"The Secretary of the Interior has some money invested in this job," Hansen quietly answered.

More education. More of that "connection to life."

Steve Hansen left Alaska after the work was complete and headed for Seattle. He bought three Cadillacs right off the bat: one for the superintendant of the Alaskan project, one for himself, and one for his wife.

Next he headed south to Santa Barbara where he bought a big house in Hope Ranch. He later purchased a sixteen-unit rental property near the college. He bought a bar downtown. Then he made a deal for a lodge and a ranch up on the San Marcos Pass.

That ranch was called Hidden Valley.

Then things started to fall apart financially for Hansen. And in the midst of regrouping, a neighbor came over to the ranch and mentioned that the former owners of Hansen's property used to make and market salad dressing. Hansen *had* noticed a lot of stuff in an old storage room related to that type of production, but he hadn't paid it much mind. After the neighbor's comments, Hansen figured that the old storeroom might deserve a second look.

It did.

All the savory supplies were there to make this dressing into a business. Hansen put it all together, set up a distribution point in British Columbia, began manufacturing the dressing, and then sold the whole works to General Foods—for millions.

It was a very profitable double take.

Hansen also devised a flavorful fabrication around the Hidden Valley Ranch dressing's origin. A tale tastier than finding a bunch of culinary castoffs in a storage shed.

Hansen's tale had him as a guide and a cook for hunting parties in exotic locales. At one point, the story goes, he was out of his usual ingredients so he had to come up with a concoction from what he *did* have—hence this unique dressing.

Hansen may have become versed in some of that tale-spinning and truth-creativity during his dealings with the unions!

SEPTEMBER 1953

Karl was in Alaska for ninety-nine days. It was ninety-nine days of work that earned him enough to buy his first house.

But he flew home the same way he had flown up there: on another cheap up-and-downer. Some of the other contractors who had gotten fat on the job flew home first class and nonstop. Not Karl. That wasn't him.

Thelma had stayed behind in California when Karl headed north to Alaska. She was pregnant—a fact unbeknownst to either of them at the time. It wouldn't remain unknown for long; a miscarriage would come quickly as well. But so would another pregnancy, soon after Karl's return. That house Karl had just earned would come in handy.

Those formative years were becoming more intense, mapping out a life path that was quickly becoming a multilane highway.

Karl graduated from USC with a B.S. in Finance in June of 1954. With a toolbox that now included a USC degree next to the pipe wrenches and toilet augers, Karl immediately went to Kohler, the household name in plumbing supplies, for employment. But their monthly pay offering was what Karl had made in a *week* in Alaska. A "job" like this would no longer work. Karl knew his worth, and higher levels had been reached in his understanding of the things people need in the way of marketed consumables.

It was obvious to Karl now that there was a *big* difference between a "job" and "business." He did get a "job" with Cobabe Bros. Plumbing, where he stayed from mid-1954 until well into '55; but "business" was the never-veered-from destination. He knew it as a finish line that would provide the actual start.

Karl would eventually partner up with Dal and a work associate named Tony to form Alert Plumbing; plumbing is what they all knew and something people always need.

He prepared for it long in advance. But then again, Karl was always preparing—always ready.

An inspector from L.A. whom Dal knew gave five-hour prep courses in his garage for contractor licenses. Karl was there. Few people have a license with a number as early as Karl's. He passed the test and received a classification for C36, plumbing. He was later grandfathered into a lengthy list of classifications because of his partnership with Dal.

He became very well equipped for this *business*.

WHEN KARL WAS PRESENTED with his USC diploma, he was presented with another writ of honor: a poem from his sister Ruth, recited by her at his graduation party.

The poem is cute, clever, and fun. But between the lines of light and loving congratulations can be seen a key dynamic in the mining of Karl's "Golden Touch."

This dynamic is the combining of formal "book-learning" with "tool-turning." It's great to get that finance degree, but it's even more expansively practical if you can also hammer in the nail to hang it on.

Karl had calculations in his brain *and* calluses on his hands.

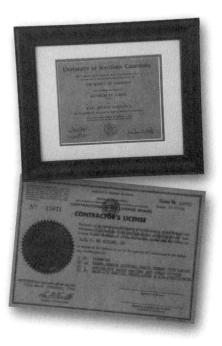

Karl's Golden Touch was ignited by the union of book-learning and tool-turning.

Ode to Karl

BY RUTH MCMILLEN MORROW, JUNE 1954

The campus is quiet, not a sound can be heard,
When all of a sudden, "It's a plane! It's a bird!"
No, it's Big Mac—he made it, with a wrench and a tool.
At last he's a graduate; Southern Cal is the school.
So, tonight, I have the honor to speak
On behalf of my brother who reached this high peak.
And never, no never, did Big Mac get tired;
And always, yes always, he read on, inspired.
Crawling under a house, the spider his main foe,
He learned economics, semantics, and Plato.
A book in one hand, thread cutter in the other,
He could memorize pages, from cover to cover.
While close to the sewer, he'd be closer to Chaucer;
He connected the fittings, and even read law, sir.
Yes, from under the bathtub, with dirt on his face,
He rose up and studied, and now takes his place
With the Southern Cal alumni—his sister is one.
Oh, his mother and father are proud of this son!
He is a Bachelor of Science, so joined by Louella,
We toast this esthete, a brilliant young fella.
And honor is due to Thelma, his wife,
Who helped him achieve this great moment in life.
Yes, now he has a college degree,
And soon they add to the family tree.
Stand up on your feet and offer a plaudit,
To the lad on my left, the King of the Faucet.
So, though the campus is quiet, let us give a loud cheer,
To Karl, the graduate, the Man of the Year!

The years from 1946 to 1954 were indeed formative: the foundation for the triumphs portion of Karl McMillen's life had been laid.

And Karl and Thelma did soon add to the family tree.

On the *last* day of 1954, December 31st, Karl and Thelma's first son, Mark Andrew McMillen, was born.

The foundation for the *other* portion of Karl's life was now laid as well.

CHAPTER 4

Hydronic Harmony & Steaming Stress

"If everyone is moving forward together,
then success will take care of itself."

—Henry Ford

THE TIMING OF MARK'S BIRTH was significant.

Everyone's is, to an extent. But with Karl, there were always more levels. Those business levels.

Thelma certainly did her part to make sure those levels were in order. Her first baby was conceived *and* delivered barely under the wire—a work-structured wire.

Karl had been working only part-time during his final semesters at USC. Because of his non-full-time status, his union insurance policy was only in effect every *other* month. So in processing Karl's medical claims, the union wanted to know just *exactly* when Mark had been conceived.

Hmmmm…

Romance—like any other job on the work list—evidently needed to be charted, graphed, and chronicled. Apparently you *could* put numbers to it!

Karl and Thelma's timing was eventually worked out to the satisfaction of the union and the insurance provider. The new parents were able to enjoy the birth of their first-born son in a less financially fiery framework once their procreation had been chronologically sanctioned.

Mark's birth date also had a special place in Karl's enterprising heart. Mark made it into this world by the skin of his not-yet-teethed-teeth to be used as a tax deduction for 1954!

But it was now 1955. By fall, Karl had left Cobabe Plumbing to start the race toward his own business destination.

Right before establishing Alert Plumbing, Karl and Tony opened up a side project that, if nothing else, doused them in a spray of reality. This first flow of business-bleeding would help them to slide into Alert with some new and necessary grips on how the industry runs.

The two young plumbers took over a tract of about twenty houses. Everything was done except the finish, but all progress had stopped when the first contractor went broke. Karl and Tony jumped in for a ridiculous price, maybe fifty bucks a house.

They were doing the labor only; the general contractor would supply all the material.

That was fine—as was the line they were walking.

What wasn't so fine was that the Karl-Tony team didn't refile the permits; a legal requirement when changing contractor horses in the middle of this dammed-up stream.

Those permits ran about twelve bucks a house, which would render the profit margin as thin as that fine line. All of this information, of course, was lost in the drain trap of inexperience. As they were finishing up the fourth house, enlightenment drove up in the form of an inspector.

From that moment on, Karl and Tony had to find enough "extras" to bill the general contractor for so they could make *something*.

This wouldn't happen again.

Soon after that, Karl and Tony joined with Dal Means, and the Alert Plumbing partnership became official.

Karl would never again have a "job."

It was now *business.*

All business.

Real business.

Alert Plumbing and Karl's family were both evolving, but it was Karl's company that suffered the draining bulk of the growing pains.

Now "alert" to building businesses, Karl would never again have a "job."

At least *then.*

Tony made a quick exit just weeks into the new venture. Partnerships are seldom pure business bliss, but Tony's constant questioning of what the other principals were doing was not making for hydronic harmony. Stress was starting to steam.

And Karl's gut was beginning to ache.

Karl went to see a doctor.

"Well, you've got a problem," agreed the doc.

Still in his early twenties, Karl didn't have an ulcer—*yet.* But the doctor felt it was just a matter of time.

"Okay," said Karl, getting down to *business.* "We've got to correct this thing."

ASAP!

He went straight to an attorney and had an agreement drawn up. The next day everyone met at Karl's house, and he and Dal bought out their disgruntled other third. The drain-valve of discord was over.

Then Alert Plumbing began to expand.

Karl and Dal's company began in a metal building behind a mattress company on Hawthorne Boulevard. In time, the mattress place moved out and Alert took over that building, too.

Dal suggested that Alert should set up a retail business for plumbing goods in the old mattress building. After all, they had plenty of inventory in back for their business; they could certainly sell it retail, too.

"We really wouldn't have to do much in the way of extra work," Dal said.

Karl was all for it; but that "not having to do much" stuff was not proving true. Pretty soon, the front store was carrying screen doors, electrical hardware, and all kinds of things! They were busy!

The plumbing business was gushing and now this retail venture was sailing along with it!

One of their many new customers was a guy named Ralph Todd.

Dal sees that Ralph is a sharp guy who knows this business.

"We need to hire him!" he tells Karl.

So they did. And Ralph was indeed sharp; metal-edge sharp. He could do it all, from setting up phone systems to cataloging any and every type of plumbing and construction supply.

Then Alert hired Ralph's brother.

And Mac—Karl's now seventy-two-year-old father.

Again, Alert Plumbing expanded. They built a new building.

After the move, Alert began buying some materials from a guy who sold out of his station wagon. It was spaghetti tubing—what you hook up a toilet with. The six-feet–long tubes were sold in bulk packaging of two hundred lengths per crate.

Ralph's brother had just handled this sidewalk purchase from the station-wagon guy.

"Did you count the pieces?" Ralph asked him.

"No," he replied. "You don't need to count that type of stuff."

"We count everything!" Ralph told him.

Well, they counted it—and it was short.

And they'd already paid this guy.

Ralph jumped into his car and sped over to Pacific Bank where he knew the guy would be, cashing their check. Ralph pulled him out of the line and brought him back to the shop, to square things up.

The situation got worse, or better, depending on which side of the pipes you were on.

Ralph ran an extensive inventory of everything this character had sold to them and compared it to what *they* had sold to their customers.

Short again.

Like, thirty or forty grand short!

They introduced station-wagon guy to their attorney guy and pretty soon Mr. Sidewalk-Shortage came up with ten thousand bucks not to prosecute.

But business is business, and problems and predicaments are a perennial part of the game. They can burst onto the scene ugly and quick, like a frozen pipe shattering at midnight.

Karl, however, always overcame. It was that Golden Touch attitude: *"Okay, we've got to correct this thing."* No matter what the "thing" might have been.

Whether it was expired permits.

Or short shipments.

Or money.

The maxims Karl heeded about careful management of capital— not foolishly or impulsively overextending, being on time for all obligations, and building a positive reputation of bill-paying respect— are textbook when it comes to models of success.

Neither he nor Dal ever had to borrow from their parents. The closest Karl ever came to that was when his father told a wholesaler that he "would stand good for the boys" when they first started Alert. But he never needed to; Karl always managed to stand good for himself. He always found a way.

On one six-unit job, another contractor they were working with went broke. And like he had done back with Tony, Karl and his team took over the finish. But this time, things were different. And at the end, right at the end, Karl asked the general contractor if he could get his check directly after the inspection was satisfied—not thirty days down the road.

The contractor agreed, which allowed Alert Plumbing & Heating to pay *their* supplier immediately as well. Alert's business reputation began to flow.

During this time, Karl had gone to two banks for a loan. One was a major bank that offered only to extend Karl a second trust deed on his house.

Good business rep or not, the answer was no.

The second bank also turned Karl down, but they were much more human. It was a smaller bank and the vice president spoke with Karl personally. And at least *he* was interested in the dip-tube details of the business Karl was building.

"Come back and see me in six months, and we'll see what we can do," the banker told Karl.

Karl did.

And Karl stayed with that insightful banker throughout Alert's business tenure and well beyond.

Karl's business proved to be good to have.

AND THERE NEVER WAS AN ULCER—just education and experience.

Even the turndown at that bank turned into a slap-awakening of what personal attention and investment in the right people can lead to.

Karl saw that everything—and everyone—needs to mature. At twenty-six years of age, not all the questions were answered yet. But some had been.

Karl was discovering how to find one's niche as a partner—one's most functional place in the whole of an operation. Applying your honed skill while others apply theirs. That's how you grow, with a common goal as the reason for each and every person being there.

It was another essential for Karl as his dealings later expanded into a giant employee roster at Todd Pipe.

That, and his pervading motto: *If there's a problem, you get out there and solve it; and then you move on,* would elevate Alert Plumbing into the top twenty-five companies of its type in America.

With Alert's upward climb, Karl's real estate investments also awakened. Houses, duplexes, industrial property, and other projects— Karl was buying and selling; *fixing* and selling.

Expanding and elevating, however, come with a cost. You can't get to the top without some sacrifices.

> *"If you're working that many hours,*
> *the wife takes care of the kids and this and that,*
> *and maybe you have a dog or two to comfort the family.*
> *And maybe once a year, you take a weekend."*

When Karl made that candid, straight-up observation, he wasn't being cold or cavalier; he was being realistic.

It's just what happens in business.

OCTOBER 31, 1956

Karl and Thelma's second son, Chris Alan McMillen, was born. Mark had been born on New Year's Eve of '54 and now Chris came into the world on Halloween '56. Two "holidays" were covered; but relaxing, *real* holidays were a ways off.

Businesses and children—it's risky leaving either in someone else's care when they're young; but eventually Karl and Thelma tried to do both. For just three days. To a destination just twenty-three nautical miles away—or *twenty-six miles across the sea,* as the song goes—the island of Catalina.

Both Alert partners went, accompanied by their wives. Both were there to get the phone calls—first, about one of their trucks being wrecked, and then about all the other things that "happened" in the seventy-two hours they were gone.

After that, "vacations" became centered around plumbing conventions and other work-related events. The focus paid off—at least monetarily. Alert was progressing nicely.

As Karl's business success progressed, his sons, Mark (right) and Chris, would progress nicely too.

After a few successful early years, however, the world of construction began to renovate itself. In 1958, Alert took a financial hit. But it surged right back as Karl and Dal kept up with the times and tailored their business to meet the specific needs of the new wave of on-your-lot construction.

If there's a problem, you get out there and solve it; and then you move on…

Karl could *always* solve the problems in his businesses—businesses that would never stop expanding and improving.

As long as *he* was there.

EDITORIAL REPRINT:

FEBRUARY 1964

phc
PLUMBING · HEATING · COOLING BUSINESS

STOCKPILE of prefabricated drain, waste and vent trees is checked by Alert's purchasing agent, Bob Martin. Firm keeps about 700 prefab assemblies of both drainage and water supply piping on hand at all times, has turnover every 30 days. Five variations of the plumbing tree serve needs of about 40 builders

HOW TO PLUMP
7,000

PRINCIPALS Dal Mèans and Karl McMillen, both PHCC members, operate 67 trucks. Most vehicles are 1½-ton size ...ve two-way radio for close contact with offices. With ...ice-like operation, firm did 7,000 new houses in '63

In early 1964, the trade magazine *phc: Plumbing, Heating, Cooling Business* published a long, savory success-from–scratch piece about Karl and Dal's company. By that time, Alert Plumbing employed 150 journeymen, operated a fleet of 76 trucks, and was performing 7,000 jobs a year.

Karl had digested overall business instincts and was now chewing and savoring every bite of the plumbing industry.

Karl's business was on track and growing. His sons, Mark and Chris, were growing as well.

SUCCESS BREEDS MANY THINGS. In the rewards category is the ability to physically live well—to own and roam a realm that transcends landlords, overdue rent, shared-wall neighbors with bad taste in loud music, and communal center-courtyard pools that need megadoses of chlorine just to keep the typhoid and ringworm at manageable levels.

Rolling Hills and the surrounding Palos Verdes hills on the southwest Pacific edge of Los Angeles County is such a realm. Karl and Thelma bought a lot on the inland side of Rolling Hills and had a three-thousand-square-foot custom home built.

The McMillens had first bought a home much closer to the beach, but in the confines of the narrow streets and alleys there, a car had brushed Mark. That "brush" with danger was too close for small-child comfort; the wide open spaces of higher elevation seemed like a safer bet.

The McMillen brothers' early life of opportunities included sports and travel.

The new "house on the hill" became the meticulously manicured growing field for the boys. The Alert years from 1955 into the mid-sixties that swelled the rewards of Karl's work ethic and savvy were also the bounty years that weaned Mark and Chris on a life of opportunities.

As each reached two years old, they also reached for the water, becoming expert swimmers. They became stars in the clean, all-American sports of Little League baseball and tennis. They were known as the best of the best in athletics. In whatever they attempted physically, they achieved success.

Mark Andrew McMillen

And, like Karl, they were child entrepreneurs. They'd gather up golf balls from the course down the street from their home and sell them back to the golfers inside the club. They did all the normal things kids do. It seemed that the deep-grain, hard-work, "stand good" push and power of their father and grandfather might even be doubled this generation.

They certainly had it all.

The blue sky over their plush Pacific peninsula was the limit.

And the waves below became the glamour-track for their spotlight success in being the "best of the best" at surfing.

Day after day, Thelma would take the boys down the hill to the shore to surf. Karl hooked up a trailer to her car, and she'd load up Mark and Chris and all their friends.

One of those friends was a kid who moved in across the street, Don McDonald. Don was three years older than Mark, and the pair played

Chris Alan McMillen

together, hung out together, surfed together, and in some ways grew up together.

Don would eventually grow quite close to Karl and Thelma, developing a relationship that grew outside of their own blood families. But for now, it was all about the beach.

Thelma may not have been driving the surf-signature old Ford woodie or VW van, but she was so cool nonetheless. The kids would stack up their "logs," "planks," and shortboards in that trailer—boards with those classic nameplates of Jacobs, Bing, and Dewey Weber. It was a daily beach party on wheels. Paradise was all theirs.

1965

Karl's business interests were expanding into real estate. So at the age of thirty-seven, Karl *retired* from the plumbing business. His partner, Dal Means, took over the pipe-wrenching reins of Alert.

Karl's father had continued to work at Alert. He and Ralph Todd became friends, and Mac would take Ralph and Ralph's son out on trips to his still-loved desert, generating a rock-steady interest in gemstones for Ralph.

Mac worked right up until his death in '65, when he was hit by a car as he crossed Washington Boulevard in Culver City. He was walking to a mailbox to send out a card for Karl's mother. It was a sympathy card to Frances' friend—a friend whose husband had just died.

At Alert, business was slowing down. The Southern California housing industry had overextended and overbuilt. Property was now being seized back by lenders.

Ralph Todd had seen the door to mass construction closing early on. So he'd left Alert to open his own door to a smaller, more personal venture: Todd Pipe & Supply.

When Alert began to downsize, many of the laid-off plumbers became "bootleggers," taking on independent gigs. At that time, you had to have a contractor's license to buy from a wholesaler. But when a bootlegger needed material, he could go see Ralph, and Ralph would lend him a hand.

Already out of the hot water of the plumbing trade, Karl was concentrating on his own flood of property and investments.

He was also heavily concentrating on another type of investment—his sons.

He would now share something new with them, something that defined Karl McMillen, Jr.

CHAPTER 5

¡Olé! We're on Our Way!

FOR ALL OF KARL'S KNOWLEDGE, sophistication, and cleaned-and-pressed businessman abilities, he was always happiest in places like Tobe's crude swaying cabin and the remoteness of the wild and the untamed. Karl would never leave the trail of his *real guy* persona. He would never lose his affection for the challenge and simple-man ambience of basic pleasures like dirt roads.

That was *him*.

So was Baja, California, below the Mexican border—a place with plenty of dirt roads.

The San Diego Natural History Museum describes Baja quite poetically: "A place so remote and compelling, full of strangely beautiful species of plants and animals, Baja California from the earliest times has lured adventurers who later told the tales of their adventures to eager listeners. Books about Baja range from painstakingly detailed accounts by naturalists, who examined every new leaf and cactus spine encountered, to those who treat Baja more as a philosophical state of mind than a geographic and physical entity."

A philosophical state of mind...

The place for father-son bonding.

The place to emotionally fuel up for the family future.

Mark would go first. Chris would follow.

The Baja trips became regular and unifying treks—a dusty-fun family tradition that Karl would use for catching up. And that "catching up" would sometimes extend to twenty days or more, roughing it along those dirt roads.

The old pickup truck was loaded with the boys, boards, and dreams of *la ola perfecta*—the perfect wave. Head south and don't bother to check that rearview mirror.

Baja was therapy. It was that calming slide into the "philosophical state of mind" where Karl was indeed Karl.

And in the earliest trips, Mark was indeed Mark.

The innocent and adventurous nature of Mark McMillen was lived out in the early Baja trips.

MARCH 1966

At age twelve, Mark had already shown how much like his father he was; reflecting Karl's work ethic and drive, and his eclectic look at the world and all that it has to offer. Even at that age, so much of who Mark was—and might become—could be seen. It manifested in the way he interacted with the wild and the untamed. Just like his father.

One winter's-end southbound sojourn served as raw material for a school assignment of Mark's: *My Trip to Baja California*. It wasn't a bad trade: three weeks out of school for the cost of one lengthy report.

Mark's chronicle of that particular southern swing was more than a preteen's standard "What I Did on My Vacation" project. Much more. Mark's work was a self-portrait that begs to have a button pushed to stop the frame.

Hold things right there. Run ahead on Mark's path and realign the direction signs. Keep Mark McMillen forever as the surging super surfer and co-heir to the McMillen family stature—worshipping the purity of dirt roads and integrity in business.

Lock it in; before the tears.

Before the questions.

Dear Mrs. Potter:

The following pages contain Mark's report of his trip to Baja. Mark kept a log each day of their progress. We used his original wording as much as possible and edited only where we felt it was necessary for clarification of the places, etc.

We hope this meets the necessary requirements.

Sincerely,

Thelma B McMillen

Karl B. McMillen, Jr.
Thelma B. McMillen

Mark's formal yellow-HyTone-folder-bound report, complete with captioned Polaroids, lovingly typed and "contributed to" by Thelma, leads off with some expository journalism that reveals how much of Mark *was* Karl. Especially that mind for "data."

MY TRIP TO BAJA CALIFORNIA
March 4th through March 25, 1966
Mark McMillen

OLE! – March 4th, We're on Our Way

I could hardly sleep the night before we left because I was so excited, but 5:30 A.M. arrived and we were on our way. The mileage read 11882. We had 45 gallons of fresh water and 35 gallons of gas loaded.

We arrived at the border in Tijuana at 9:15 A.M. We were unable to get a car permit but were informed we could get one in La Paz. We continued south on pavement for approximately 140 miles.

Evidently you could put numbers to vacations, too. Mark had *his* numbers wired: gallons, odometer readings, precise times and miles! And then it was on to his own "affection for the challenge and simple-man ambience of basic pleasures like dirt roads."

At this point, the road turns to graded dirt and rock. We traveled on a side road to Johnson's Ranch. We became stuck in marshy ground. We were able to get out of the marsh and went on up north to a cove and saw a baby seal. In this area we found lots of driftwood. Johnson's Ranch is located on the beach. We found the best place to camp was behind a sand dune because the wind was blowing so hard. It was quite cold.

We broke camp the following morning March 5th at 6:00 A.M. I went down to the beach before we left and found a dead seal. Traveled on to the Cabo Colnett which is five miles from Johnson's Ranch. The countryside is quite dry and covered with lots of cactus and yucca plants. The highway now is gravel but with large chuck holes. We found it best to travel the old road which parallels the new. Most of the traffic did this. We proceeded on

We shaved every 3rd day!

to San Quentin. We were told that only vehicles with 4-wheel drive could go on. However, our jeep is equipped with the 4-wheel drive so, on we went. We saw crows eating a dead horse at El Rosario. We also saw a mission which was built in 1774. There were just a few adobe rooms left. We made camp at 4:30 P.M. Had steaks for dinner. There were many different kinds of cactus there. Dad says we are in the "Heart of Baja."

They were.

They were also in the heart of something else. The heart of togetherness—stuck in a marsh, exploring the countryside, and witnessing nature at work.

Together...

Accompanied by Yaska, their large part-Lab/part-police-dog pooch, and Karl's pal, Chuck, they were a father-son travel-team ideal.

Last night a pack of coyotes came to visit us. They
left after a period of howling outside our camp. Today we
shot 3 quail, 4 rabbits and saw 1 bobcat. We used a 16 gauge
shotgun. The weather has turned warm and sunny. We made 91
miles today. The road is getting pretty rough now.

"The road is getting pretty rough now." Mark's line leads into a
photo section, depicting a kid-perfect son preparing for and enjoying
this trip.

But it's a tough line to read—a prophesy-haunt of so much to come.
Where—WHERE?—is that pause button?

I saw a variety of country. Typically desert in some
areas and others covered with wild flowers. I saw many
skeletons of animals.

Today, we got up at 6:00 A.M. The air was freezing. Later
we found ice on a pond. We went a record breaking speed of
32 miles an hour, traveling on a dirt road. We saw a rabbit
that would not move off the road. I almost had to pick him
up to avoid hitting him. After lots of honking he finally
moved. He would not move because the air was so cold.
The road is now fair to good and we are at the Bay of Los
Angeles. We made 109 miles today.

Almost every morning there were fresh coyote tracks
near our camp. We had tracks of a baby mountain lion one
morning. This is a beautiful bay.

Mark was ready for anything. He was his father's son with a wide-
embrace energy-grip on life, like that of a fast-growing kitten or a
first-gallop foal.

We crossed a dry lake – pretty muddy and good. Decided
to leave in the morning.

We took a side road to Mission San Borjas and took
Polaroid pictures of a family. They were very happy. We
continued on to Miller's Landing. Sometimes we thought we
were lost but we ended up on the beach and after some cross
country driving found Miller's Landing. On the way we saw
a herd of wild burros. Two of them were white, one a mother
and a baby. One of the burros kept rolling on his back
for us. He must have been wild. We saw a mountain lion's
footprints as big as my hand.

At Miller's landing we really got stuck in the mud. It
took us four hours to get out. It seems the low gear in our
truck isn't working at all and this is creating a lot of
trouble. We camped here for the night.

It was a muddy campsite. After we got out of the mud we
gathered large pieces of onyx which had been transported
from the mountains to Miller's Landing in the old days.
From Miller's Landing it was loaded on ships for export.

Here is that Karl McMillen principle of coping, now shared by
Mark: *If there's a problem, you get out there and solve it; and then you
move on.*

Stuck in the mud for four hours? A long-gone low gear in the
truck? Muddy campsite? *Yeah, we'll take care of it—but, hey, isn't that
onyx and the history of all this so cool?!*

It was a mindset of toughness and success.

After leaving Miller's Landing we continued on to the
south. We stopped at an isolated area and hiked to the beach
(about 4 miles) over sand dunes...Not seeing any nice places
to camp we drove on after darkness and finally camped. In
the morning there was heavy dew on the tarps which covered
our sleeping bags. As we looked around we noticed moss

growing on the cactus. We must have picked a very damp place to camp. Later that day we arrived in El Arco; the halfway point to La Paz. Twenty miles south of El Arco we started having trouble with our water pump, but were able to go on to San Ignacio...I took pictures of the children in San Ignacio with our Polaroid camera. We brought lots of candy with us for the children. They were very friendly and fascinated with the pictures. We go on slowly since there is no place to get the water pump fixed. The next town was Santa Rosalie...The water pump for some reason has stopped leaking. We decide to try for Mulege. At Mulege we sent a telegram to the States requesting shipment of a new water pump. Also a telegram to Mother and Chris.

Mounted with adhesive photo corners at the exact plot-pertinent location in his report, Mark had carefully folded and preserved the *communiqué internationale*. It was Western Union proof that the McMillen men could roll with some pretty adverse *golpes*:

Waiting on the water pump.
All fine.
Enjoying trip.
More positives than negatives by far.
The mindset of success…

We camped on the beach at Mulege. A plane lands once
a day there. One day it goes south and the next day north.
We waited and met the plane hoping our water pump would
arrive—it never did. We went fishing and took a "bath" in
the ocean. We used liquid Joy and it works just fine in salt
water. The water temperature is 70 degrees.

Everything was working "just fine"—at least the important stuff
like a dish-soap bath in the warm ocean. Even when a minor blip like
an imploding water pump was added to the list of the hard-working
Jeep Gladiator's idiosyncrasies. It may have slowed down the dirt-road
progress, but it didn't hinder the hunts, the hikes, and the heart of
being together.

The rest—and all—of Mark's Tigger-springy descriptions of the
trip bring the adventure so innocently alive like only an exceptional
twelve-year-old can. But the *vacaciones* was already so alive. That
was obvious.

At Rancho Buenavista it was very beautiful. We met a
fruit peddler who told us about a road from there to the
Cape which our map did not show. The main road at this point
turns inland. We took his advice and followed the road
nearest the ocean. After getting lost several times and
asking instructions at several ranchos we arrived at San
Jose Del Cabo about 9:00 P.M. It was an interesting road but
we were never sure where we were. We camped off the main

road a short distance since it was dark. In the morning we discovered we had slept in the city dump. Two miles from this point we found a perfect campsite. We stopped and fished. Caught 14 bass, and cooked them for breakfast. We did all our cooking on an open fire.

March 25th, we are going to try and make it home today...

From Magdalena on we saw two accidents. Cars had slid
off the left shoulder. We arrived at San Luis, crossed the
border into Yuma, Arizona. We are back in the "Estados
Unidos". We had dinner and drove straight through, arriving
home at 3:04 A.M.

I had a really fun trip but it was good to get home.

Was this *On the Road* with Kerouac?

On the surface, maybe not. But not far below, it had all the same freewheeling impact. Mainly because it was from the heart of a kid; and this kid had all his sensory-synapses firing. From wild animals to nursing an ailing truck in a foreign land to camping in the city dump to fishing for a Baja breakfast.

He was happy, filled with that ready-for-anything enthusiasm.

MARK MCMILLEN WAS COOL and observant. How he handled all of this, and so loved it, back in '66 would have brought him in as today's runaway winner in *The Amazing Race*.

Beyond "reality," this was *life*—Mark McMillen's life. And that of his father—in all of its noble savage ideals.

These first trips were casual catching-up, good-time, surf-camp-and-lounge-around getaways. However, the purpose of the Baja runs, like most facets of the McMillens' lives, would ultimately change.

Reflecting on the Baja trips elicits some of the most enduring and piercing questions about the paths that Mark and Chris chose beyond those simple dirt roads.

How did we get from here to there?

But none of these questions were on Karl's mind yet. For now, on these early and easy explorations, as the rock-and-hole back trails of Baja led him out to the *playas desiertas,* he could relax, have a drink or two, look toward the horizon, and enjoy *nature's* million-dollar view.

¡La vida era perfecta!

CHAPTER 6

Windows with a Million-Dollar View

IN THE LATE 1960s, a marketing maxim floated around the booming Southern California coastal communities: *"If you want to make real money, buy right on the ocean."*

Karl knew this was true. And besides, Thelma had to drive *all the way* down the hill every day to get the boys to the beach.

The boys were getting older and more athletic; there was little chance of being "brushed" by any more cars.

In fact, there was little to worry about at all.

It was time.

And going down to the shore was definitely a move up.

On this top-of-the-heap turf, it isn't "the house on the hill" that packs the highest status. And it sure isn't the penthouse apartment in the best doorman-enforced building uptown. Or the plush "flat" in Midtown or the Upper East Side or wherever caste is measured in the cold urban meshes that are never mentioned in Jimmy Buffet songs. In the we're-all-so-healthy warmth of this high-life heaven, it's the place closest to the sand that has the most coastal cachet. The place where you can hear the crash of the waves as loud out of your windows as New Yorkers can hear the taxi horns and sirens out of theirs. Where you can feel the saltwater spray on your face when the summer afternoon westerlies kick in, while you're out on the patio barbecuing prime beef and dipping into an ice bucket filled with Coronas.

There are few pale concrete-and-café days in So Cal.

In 1968 the McMillens moved into 2100 The Strand, Hermosa Beach.

"The Strand" in Hermosa was the place—*the* place. It's *so* Southern California. It remains the wallpaper for wish-you-were-here palm-tree postcards and the envied backdrop for a near-endless summer.

Mike Love of the Beach Boys lived along The Strand just north of the McMillen home during his band's hangin'-ten heyday. *That's* vintage surf ambience! And it was an apropos setting for the 1988 Mel Gibson film *Tequila Sunrise*—about a drug dealer trying to go straight.

Lakers, Leno, and lots of other names lounge in the area's "locals preferred" sunshine; it's a pivotal and prestigious part of paradise to claim.

But along with staking claims in utopia comes a high degree of social interaction. There is nothing low profile about the beachfront digs with the million-dollar views or the people who live there. They attract attention.

And if you add something special to the mix, like the star-quality that the McMillen brothers were surfing into, things really jump.

Mark and Chris didn't just "pick up" surfing—they owned it. They excelled at it and began gathering competition trophies and reputations. Especially now, with their playing field mere yards from their front door.

But more was rolling into the shores of the West Coast besides the eternal Pacific waves.

And it was just as relentless and strong.

As Mark (top left, bottom far left) and Chris (top right, bottom second from left) collected surfing trophies, no one sensed the turbulent enemy rolling in with the tide.

We'll look forward to hearing more about what YOUR group is doing!

ence to voters who do not always have eas access to a deputy registrar.

SURFBOARD CITY'S SURFING TEAM

THE very first Hermosa Beach Surfers Contest was held north of the Municipal Pier on Saturday, November 1, with eighty-one surfers competing for the First through Fourth Place trophies. Under the auspices of the Recreation & Parks Department, and open to residents of our community, the purpose of the contest was to determine ratings in several divisions that will represent Hermosa Beach in a number of future contests in many southland beach communities.

Prizes were awarded by the Mayor to the following winners

Minnies Division — Jimmy Brooks, Ty Page, Mark Levy, and Casey Trout.
Boy's Division — Mark McMillen, Chris McMillen, Pat Gannon, and Mike Astone.
Junior Division — Greg Armer, Mike Behnke, Wilson Olbrich, and Mark Johnston.
Women's Division — Laurie Wilson, Pam Fuehring, Dorothy Robertson, and Debbie Place.
Men's Division — John Baker, Dick Page, Alan Bergloff, and Byrle Smallen.

Hoppy Swartz and members of the Western Surfers Association assisted with the judging of this very successful contest, and we can look forward to many exciting surfing events featuring the Hermosa Beach Surfers in the months to come.

THE SEX-DRUGS-AND-ROCK-'N'-ROLL-POWERED "SUMMER OF LOVE," 1967's claim to infamy, had just ended. In its wild wake, the social order of America, most notably the young, had crested and crashed like each "tube" that hit the Hermosa shore.

At fourteen and twelve years of age, Mark and Chris could athletically handle those saltwater tubes with no problem; but they were ripe virgin fodder for the crashes and rolls of that other kind. Those "heavies" were just starting to form and the entire McMillen family would be sucked into their barrel.

There on the beach, the young McMillen boys succumbed not only to normal adolescent life experiments and peer pressure, but to a high tide of social change never seen before in modern Western culture.

Nor since.

Most parents of the era were caught so off guard. Even with the media barrage of music and faces of the "new revolution"—from the Beatles to Timothy Leary—*real* drugs, in the minds of most parents, were still the shadowy staple of jazz musicians and other far-removed cellar dwellers. And those were just the drugs they had heard of—marijuana, cocaine, heroin. The up-and-coming new order of hallucinogens and psychedelics were unfathomable to '68 dads and moms.

While 1968 may have been the evil eye of a one-off perfect storm, what happened back then has transcendent roots when it comes to exploring, understanding, and fighting addiction and substance abuse.

It's an icy and intense case study—for the McMillen family, of course, but universally as well.

Naiveté, "distractedness," and eventual enablement are three major components that help an addict continue along his or her jagged path. A fourth, even more subjective, component is the desire most people have to feel important.

All four were at work during the drug-lifespan of Mark and Chris McMillen.

And that final "feeling important" factor may have been the sucker punch that sent Mark and Chris reeling down their dark road.

The McMillen brothers *were* important. They had surfed their way into prominence and were now starting to enjoy the rewards. Mark and Chris were rising from mere kings of the beach to gods. They were in a world that completely revolved around that water to the west, the sun above it, and the cool clout you could gain by morphing with it all.

Which they did.

Mark quickly grabbed the attention of the older guys on the beach—guys who were already into drugs. And they were more than willing to bring him into their inner circle, a circle that would be *that* much more prestigious if it featured the best-looking and most skilled surfer on the beach.

Like a leaping bottlenose dolphin keeping pace with a leisure boat of admirers, Mark was pulled willingly into the wake of the in-crowd and the importance.

And the marijuana.

And wherever Mark went, Chris soon followed.

Mark had been the better surfer, but Chris caught up. Chris looked up to his older brother. Mark was the protector; he was the guy who looked out for Chris and showed him the ropes—about *everything*.

And while Mark was the powerful, good-looking older-brother athlete, Chris was the warm and soft-spoken communicator. Both had been born and raised as pure as the driven tide, balanced in the solid and innocent baby-boom morals of their parents.

The younger McMillen was a great reader, constantly absorbing knowledge. From early on, Chris could brilliantly convey both life lessons and objective facts from his reading. So when Chris talked, people listened. And with the listening came further respect.

Chris's loyalty was also recognized. He was known for having "the back" of those close to him. "If you had Chris on your side you knew you were going to be okay," said his friends. "Knowing and having Chris and Mark with you was great. They had that social magic, like Butch Cassidy and the Sundance Kid—charming and mysterious."

The brothers also had the attention of the girls. As the brothers' teenage years unfolded, it wasn't rare for the most beautiful girls to make nighttime pilgrimages, climbing in and out of the boys' bedroom windows.

Certainly, Mark and Chris's importance was expressed to them by their loving parents too; but it was offered with more consistency and a closer generational hand by the buds and chicks on the beach.

Those hands consistently offered them drugs, too.

DURING THIS TIME, Karl and Thelma were also enjoying that feeling of being important.

Karl was reentering the daily overtime workforce in a venture that would prove to be his all-time greatest business achievement. And Thelma was an increasing part of the beach community's "social interaction."

Parental naiveté and distractedness fell right into place.

In those few years, essentially no one was watching Mark and Chris, in a parental sense. It wasn't that Karl and Thelma were negligent; it was more that they had genuinely good kids who they didn't think *needed* watching. So their attitude was to be more friends than parents and to just let the kids have fun in this incredible and beautiful environment.

Plus, while no one on earth was more possessed of dignity, an attitude of success, values, and doing the right thing than Karl McMillen, the truth was that the time-space continuum was one commodity Karl could not conquer. There was only one of him to go around, no matter how he stretched and bent. It was a fundamental law of physics.

Karl wasn't always around to physically see what his kids were doing. But, okay. Wasn't that normal for a guy out making a good living? Karl didn't have any guidebooks or counselors or philosophers weighing the merits of working hard to get a lock-tackle on the best of the American Dream versus needing to sit directly on top of his kids so they didn't climb into the muzzle of a cannon.

THE HOME AT 2100 THE STRAND was now party central, for both generations.

Thelma was everyone's best friend. The younger partiers kept her position alive from the surf-trailer days as "the coolest lady there was." And when Karl returned from his long days at work, he would join in the party.

Karl and Thelma's generation had its own vice—an accepted escape that was part of everyday life. From the cocktail-holding Rat Pack to the array of ads on TV and in magazines, everyone drank.

And everyone knew what Manhattans and highballs would do. It was okay. This LSD stuff, this "acid" and beefed-up "grass" and "hash" and other strange concoctions being touted on the news— what the hell were they? What would *that* do to you?

It didn't matter, though; it wasn't here. Not on *these* sacred shores. *But it was.*

So while Karl and Thelma continued to party in "traditional" ways, the beach-important brothers were rising from the sea level of the Pacific to "Eight Miles High."

The difference was in the choice of kicks.

It was a social juxtaposition demonstrative of the giant 1960s generation gap; Karl and Thelma were but two of countless parents oblivious to the influx of drugs. But the scene also exposes how maybe too much closeness takes the tough-love parent out of the mix, replacing it with a forgiving, anything-goes buddy.

Karl and Thelma were just a part of the party scene at that moment. They didn't think anything was wrong at that moment. They had no thought that anyone or anything was going to get out of control.

It really *was* all good fun.

At that moment.

MANY YEARS AFTER "THAT MOMENT," Karl would refer to Hermosa Beach in the late 1960s as the "marijuana capital of the world," a fact that he and Thelma "didn't understand" when they moved down to the sand from the sunny overlook of Rolling Hills.

Hermosa may not have been the exact center of herbal commerce in '68, but it was indeed a stop along the trip-trail that became a well-worn drug path between Los Angeles and San Francisco before swarming back East, and then into the heartland. And along any trail, the rest stops, watering holes, and settlements spring up where the resources—and the people of action—are.

If there had been a "Map to the Stars" for that trail, it might have read: Hollywood and the music scene of the Sunset Strip; down into the South Bay beaches of Redondo, Hermosa, and Manhattan, and up into Venice; the hippie hitchhike hub and hemp hostel of Santa Barbara; the land of the lost up through State Route 1 and the surreal Big Sur; further north to Monterey and the holy site of the pre-Woodstock supernova that was the 1967 Monterey Pop Festival; and then the furious final approach into the Emerald City of San Francisco with its wellspring of wizards behind curtains of pharmaceuticals and walls of Marshall amps.

But while the vice-slam and daily drugs of the sixties seemed quite at home eating away at the tenderloin sleaze of a decaying inner-Hollywood and 'Frisco's run-down Haight-Ashbury, it felt so out of place in the Shangri-La of sand and salt water. Its taint was as appalling as greasy fast-food litter scattered among the Hapu'u ferns in Eden.

The stuff of postcards: Hermosa Beach may not have been the "marijuana capital of the world," but its sixties surf scene had its own drug-dominated subculture.

A lot about those days wasn't right; that shade of darkness should never touch that special sunshine. That warm and soothing light had shined with such bright potential on the handsome and talented Mark and Chris McMillen. But it was on target to be so heavily eclipsed by the black hole of substance abuse.

And substance abuse is a darkness that can cover the entire land. The destruction of addiction has no parameters or barriers— economic, ethnic, or otherwise. Fair or not, many would say that the crack baby born in a filth-hovel room at Third and Main has a built-in, just-what-you'd-expect future. But again, fair or not, when that sad, one-way destination is punched into the ticket of those who look out windows with a million-dollar view, the mystery and the head-shaking "Why?" become more intense.

So does the search for answers. A search that for Karl McMillen has produced a lifetime of hindsight, looking ahead, and pouring out of resources—fighting to make sure that what happened to *his* sons and *his* family is not repeated in the lives of others.

In '68, the Beatles and the Stones and The Who may have commanded the "British Invasion" music charts here in the States, but the lyrics to a 1966 all-American Beach Boys tune were what echoed in the salient and crisp salt air of the South Bay. "Caroline, No" was the ultimate innocence-to-experience lament. It was the eulogy for fun-gone-wrong and a cutting example of how those no-limit blue skies can so easily be "painted black"—as so much was, as the decade progressed and regressed. It was much more than just a song; it was an introspective dissection of how life was dramatically changing on the beach.

It was about "sweet things" dying and an inability to bring back an essence once it was gone.

Sadly, it easily applied to Mark and Chris.

But another tune from '68 captures a more upbeat essence, one that fits the business energy-drive of Karl and the opportunity coming up for him. "Time Has Come Today," in its title and take-charge sentiments, points to what Karl was about to undertake.

Every business and life skill Karl had developed since those early days under his father's work-ethic wing were on the line.

It was the beginning—and the beginning of the end—of so much.

CHAPTER 7

A Man with Two Families

IN 1968, POLITICS AND THE DAILY NEWS churned with the Vietnam War; the murders of Martin Luther King and Bobby Kennedy, the Chicago Democratic Convention riots, and the protest groups' persistent uprooting of traditions, mores, and morals. But even with the faddish chaos, America's infrastructure needed to keep humming. The silent majority below the headlines continued to enjoy having hot and cold running water and proper sewage. So despite the "drop-out" ethic of the few free radicals with loud voices, the businessmen below those headlines were keeping the economy going.

Karl was certainly one of them.

He was a part of "normal" and traditional America and was a businessman through and through. Amid all the long-haired hoopla about anti-capitalism, communes, living off the land, and mankind facing the "Eve of Destruction," Karl stayed the course. For him, earning an honest living and providing goods and services was always more stable and satisfying than joining the boisterous bedlam of bandwagon anarchy.

KARL HAS BEEN RETIRED for a couple of years—except for the time it takes to make real estate investment after real estate investment, that is.

He's out looking at property and stops in to see Ralph Todd at his still relatively new Todd Pipe & Supply business.

Karl is shocked by how small and crammed-in the business is; operating out of what is essentially a house and garage.

Ralph needs help.

Karl offers to buy Ralph a building and lease it back to him so that the business can grow.

Ralph counters with an offer of a partnership in the business for Karl.

Karl comes back with his mentor and advisor, Dr. Ken Trefftzs from USC.

Analysis…

The professor tells Karl, "Yes, it's a good, going business. So, first of all, to join with Ralph, you will owe him half of what the assets are, plus, because he took the risk of starting the business, he should have a bonus of like fifty thousand or so. I would suggest that the first fifty thousand the business makes goes to Ralph, and then you're full partners from there on.

"Sounds fair to me!" says Ralph.

"And besides," Dr. Trefftzs says to Karl on their way out, "you're thirty-seven years old; it's time we get you off the street anyway!"

Karl was actually ready to get back into the industry saddle and become a partner in Todd. He was ready for a return to the staid sanity of structure—the "time had come today."

Ralph was a sound businessman, but adding Karl's name to Todd's door was a dream coup d'état—like when a good team signs the league's top scorer as a free agent. This squad was now a long-term contender and a force.

Ralph Todd had developed his business muscles just as Karl had, right there in the sweat of the game.

Back in 1956, before the Alert Plumbing days, Ralph worked in sales for the consumer auto-parts pioneer, Pep Boys. On the weekends he was repiping his own home, inch by inch and piece by piece. Even then, at the Pep Boys counter, he was taking in what it was like to make customers happy, gain their confidence, and most importantly, bring them back! Ralph brought all of that to Alert and then to Todd in 1966.

Ralph was the best salesman you could have. Companies conduct surveys and mail them out; they spend a lot of money on research. Ralph Todd stood at the door with his "Hi, how are you?" when the customer came in. By the time the customer got done, Ralph was asking the guy, "Is there anything I can do better for you, or is there any help you need?" Soon, they were old friends.

He also brought with him a winner's rare fearlessness and determination. Ralph started Todd with a small yard, zero forklifts, one truck, three employees, and foresight that coached Karl McMillen onto the team.

Karl arrived at Todd with his own A-game and Golden Glove leadership.

From the will-to-work instillings of his father at the mines and the hot days in the farm fields, to the doctrines of detail cultivated at Alert, to the rules of negotiation sharpened through real estate jousts, Todd was the beneficiary of a bona fide MVP.

Within two months of Karl's arrival, Todd *did* move into a bigger building—it was a lease and wasn't yet the headquarters they wanted, but it gave them some room to get "uncrammed."

Within a year, they applied to American Standard to become a dealer. Karl wrote bios on all of their employees and found some who had worked at other wholesalers that were American Standard dealers; Karl's history search helped Todd get the dealership.

They told American Standard all the pertinent details, except that the company was on a month-to-month lease in their four-thousand-square-foot steel building. That may have been a tad too *temporary* for the bigwigs at American Standard.

But those four thousand square feet were shrinking daily. The office was too small, so they brought in a trailer and cut a hole in the building to line up with its door. *This works. Neat.* A short, cool step from the building into the new trailer-office.

Then there was Karl's camper.

He takes it off his pickup truck, backs it in, puts it on sawhorses adjacent to the trailer, and there you have another annex!

A second deck is added to the metal building. Then a third—the roof had a crown that provided a little more space. Just as long as you could climb the ladders up to it.

Karl even started talking up the idea of getting miners' hardhats with the lights in them to replace the flashlights they had to carry up to the mezzanine.

Finally, Todd could afford its own new building.

Karl again brought in Dr. Trefftzs for guidance.

The land they decided on was going to cost $350,000, but Karl could prove by the numbers that it was worth only $320,000. Still, it was a key location with freeway off- and on-ramps right there.

Karl told Ralph that when they bought this property, Todd Pipe & Supply would become an institution of where to buy in the South Bay.

He was right.

Dr. Trefftzs agreed.

"Don't worry about the price difference," he advised Karl. "You have the location; that's what's important. And we'll have the owners take back a second mortgage and we'll get the differential on the interest rates to recoup on that extra that you're paying!"

Certainly.

Let's do it!

Todd Pipe's popularity took root at its Hawthorne Blvd. location. But it would far outgrow those early fifteen-hundred-square-foot digs.

RIGHT FROM THE GATE at Todd, Karl developed a well-founded reputation as "the good guy." Leo Durocher's axiom about where nice guys finish just didn't fly here. Karl's winning theory was simple: *Treat your customers as people.*

That theory was now an assay-proven part of his Golden Touch. How could combining common decency and kindness with practical "book-learning" and "tool-turning" fail?

It couldn't.

But simplicity and basic human values in business are too often overlooked or overcomplicated in favor of deep management-psychology seminars and other mundane meetings and pretentious brainstorms that are more about conjecture than what actually takes place in the trenches.

Not at Todd.

The "Legendary Service" that is now Todd's motto began immediately.

They knew their customers' names. That was based on yet another simple theory: *If you go to a grocery store and the clerk knows you, you'll go back to that grocery store. If you go to a bank and the tellers know your name, you'll go back to that bank. It makes you feel important, and you ARE important as a customer.*

"Feeling important" is such a vital component to *anything*. Karl would analyze customers' needs and how Todd's competition wasn't meeting them. When Karl discovered that customers were waiting for their suppliers to open at eight a.m., he opened Todd at six. And then at five-thirty.

Todd's mobile supply trucks were finally loaded at night instead of in the morning, so that they, too, could be on the road before the competition.

Todd trucks would also pick up back-ordered supplies around town rather than wait for them to be shipped, in order to fulfill their customers' needs.

Over-service the customer was added to Golden Touch playbook.

As was *Treat your employees as people...*

That same personal detailing that shined on the Todd customers was extended to the Todd employees. Karl knew all of *their* names, too, and the names of those in their families. Sure, he would have his notes, but they weren't just cold cheat-sheets; they were working "blueprints" to the real lives of the real people he employed. They were the schematics that showed the foundation of their families and, in turn, the family that pushed Todd to success.

The relationship was personal. That is key.

Even something as subtle as t-shirts. Lots of companies promote themselves with logo Ts, but Karl knew plumbers need pockets.

So Todd's shirts had pockets.

And Karl knew it would look good having customers wear the Todd togs into another wholesaler's place. So if a plumber came in wearing a competitor's shirt, Todd would trade him *two* of theirs for that one. Then they'd put the bounty up on the wall as a trophy.

It was some serious scalp-collecting!

Many studies have been conducted about those who have become successful and the methods they have used. There are guidebooks and workbooks, novels and exposés. You have your Anthony Robbins–style big-smile here's-how-to-do-its and your Zig Ziglar–like motivational management strategies. But so much in life and business goes back to those often-overlooked basics that are built into the genetics of Karl McMillen.

While someone, somewhere, was conducting a seminar on complex "skillpaths" that will help to "fast-track" careers and advancement, Karl's idea of corporate success was to warmly build a family that loved where they worked.

While someone, somewhere was sending employees off to *Assertiveness Training; Coaching, Mentoring, and Counseling; Conflict and Change Management;* and *Prioritization,* the Todd staff was enjoying a morale-boosting bounty of very personal perks.

As the company grew and branches were built in various locations, a massive Christmas party became a yearly introduction and renewal for the Todd family to "put faces to the names" that were talked to on the phones each day. Buses brought in the Las Vegas branch to party with the L.A. headquarters—and to stay in a hotel there. San Diego and Garden Grove would roll in. The bonuses would be passed out. Sales staffers would handpick gifts for their customers.

Everything was *always* personal.

Karl's sincere appreciation of his staff, his desire for all of them to succeed, and interactions like the family parties went a long way in eliminating unnecessary complexity and accomplishing workplace goals—without seminars.

And there was more.

The company had a beautiful vacation trailer at Capistrano Shores for employees and customers to use. One end of the mobile home was completely glass, therapeutically looking out at the waves.

Todd also had two plush condos in the sun-soaked high-class ambience of Palm Springs. The resort-rest retreats were used by employees on the weekends and customers during the week.

There were double bonuses for the employees if they got their monthly statements out early. There were bonuses for on-time deliveries. It was a family and a team who would all benefit together from their combined efforts, top to bottom.

A 2002 article by Jim Olsztynski, *Todd Pipe & Supply—The Streetwise Wholesaler,* highlighted another basic in Todd's, and Karl's, success: *A major reason* [for Todd being selected as 2002's Wholesaler of the Year] *has to do with "street wisdom"…with few exceptions, the people in charge of this company have tenure measured in decades. Even more pertinent, almost all of them worked their way up through the ranks. The vast majority started out as warehouse workers, counterpeople, truck drivers or plumbers.*

It was even more recognition that Todd was a family maturing together. But good, stable families of any type take up a lot of time; the Todd kindred was no exception. Karl was always there, ever extending himself to his business. Like when he went to Mexico to bring back the body of one of his employee's sons who had died down there.

And Karl would provide personal loans to employees who needed them. It was a family, and everybody at Todd knew they were part of it.

This above-and-beyond personal care was another giving aspect of Karl and who he is. You can't be the MVP sitting in the locker room. He had a major-league business, with complete dedication to it and to his power-aptitude of data. Todd started with zero in 1966, acquired Karl in 1968, and took off! Under Ralph and Karl's combined leadership, Todd Pipe would increase in sales volume every year—never dipping.

Dedication.

And time…

FROM 1968 INTO THE EARLY SEVENTIES, Karl was fathering *two* families—the ever-expanding Todd tribe and the young household in the home with the now *multi*-million-dollar view. This second household, like Todd, would also expand.

The "neighbor kid" from up in Rolling Hills had a family, too, but it was imploding. After the McMillens all moved to Hermosa, Don McDonald's world collapsed. His brother and sister were both sent to foster homes, and Don, at age seventeen, found his way to Karl and Thelma's.

They took him in.

Don could see what was happening with Mark and Chris. There is no parental naiveté and distractedness among peers. Don had already spent three years of high school surrounded by the sixties; he had seen the damage and the arrests and the filling of juvenile facilities due to drug use. So he could see what Mark and Chris were falling into. He didn't want any part of it.

Instead, *he* was the one to go to work for Todd Pipe; part-time until he graduated from high school and then full-time. He swept floors, cut box tops, cleaned toilets, and looked toward the future.

Another juxtaposition of priorities and possibilities and potential; now at the home level.

But while Don disconnected from "the scene" and the sixties, at 21st Street and The Strand, the parties increased.

As far as the drinking went, Karl knew he could handle his liquor. He had a pretty unshakable and optimistic theory that seemed to back that up: *When you start work at six in the morning and you never miss a day, it shows that you can handle your drinking!*

And the ever-mounting rewards of being the boss let him occasionally leave the office early—maybe at two o'clock or so—and enjoy that million-dollar view.

And the parties.

Occasionally…

But the norm was long hours—the twelve-hour work days that always ended with the unwinding via booze. It was a schedule that had a hard imbalance—which "family" was getting the biggest share of Karl?

CHAPTER 8

Bars on the Million-Dollar Windows

"It is easy to get a thousand prescriptions
but hard to get one single remedy."

—Chinese Proverb

KARL HAD NO IDEA.

Thelma began to sense something.

She even began to casually ask neighbors about *their* children and how *they* were doing. But there's a lot of sand along the rich Hermosa shoreline, offering plenty of places for people to bury their heads. Everyone's kids were just fine.

It took a reach from another of those "closer generational hands" to finally uncover *exactly* how Mark and Chris were doing.

Jeff, a ten-year-old cousin of the McMillen brothers, walked into that Strand garage one day as Chris was hiding something in the old couch.

"What are you doing, Chris?"

"Nothing…nothing…"

That wasn't a good enough answer for adolescent curiosity—Jeff came back later with his older brother, Fred.

Fred found the foil-wrapped package.

"What is it, Fred?" Jeff asked.

"Firecrackers," Fred quickly told his kid brother.

"No, it isn't. You're lying!" Jeff insisted. "What is it?!"

"It's marijuana…"

Marijuana is not a "gateway" drug that predicts or eventually leads to substance abuse, suggests a twelve-year University of Pittsburgh study. Moreover, the study's findings call into question the long-held belief that has shaped prevention efforts and governmental policy for six decades and caused many a parent to panic upon discovering a bag of pot in their child's bedroom.

—ScienceBlog.com

Well…

Maybe panic isn't so bad—in spite of what some neatly wrapped, mathematically precise studies may say.

The tip of this herbal iceberg that surfaced in the hidden folds of that couch was certainly a gateway for Mark and Chris McMillen. Call it what you want, but *their* Titanic voyage *did* start with pot.

Mark and Chris didn't grow up with demon personalities and a predestined crime-greased slide to early deaths. They were sweet, good kids. They knew right from wrong. They loved their mother and father, surfing, and having fun.

But something happened.

And maybe reasons and answers can be found in *another kind* of study—a study about the effects of drugs that isn't conducted by white-smocked researchers with clipboards.

Plenty of "studies" come directly from the street. And those studies tend to pack more punch.

They are so terrifying in that they are real.

"Voices from the street" may be uncomfortable, but they are vital to any serious look into addiction. The voices from the street presented here and throughout this book are the combined wisdom of addicts: some who knew Mark and Chris, some who did drugs with Mark and Chris, and some who lived and breathed fire with their own personal demons elsewhere:

The Power Angle

There's a definite power in being high. Mark and Chris were already getting to enjoy natural power and attention through their surfing and good looks, and now they'd found a booster rocket.

And when you move up to selling the drugs, you've really got the power. And that move comes fast. Nearly from day one of using, you're dealing. From day one, you're selling to your buddy, trying to make a freebie. You're the man. And that in itself is such a drug.

It consumes you.

Your ego starts building.

You're the one "in charge."

Everyone's looking up to you.

Endorphins start firing in your brain. All of a sudden if you were feeling good about yourself, you're feeling ecstatic. You look in the mirror, and you're proud of who you are. Dopamine's going off. Yep, you're the man, and one thing leads to another.

Now, if you step even further up to selling cocaine or heroin, you're <u>really</u> the man. It's the difference between dabbling in junk bonds and working the best blue chips on NASDAQ.

You're on fire with this new investment. You're seeing just how "successful" you can be. Free money, free this, free that—and you don't have to work hard for any of it.

In fact, for many dealers, the lifestyle is as enticing as any high.

It's a quick-shift marketplace with some <u>very</u> serious entrepreneurs. But both dealers and customers can easily transform into victims. And that can happen quickly, too.

These studies—these voices from the street—are far removed from the sterile think-tanks that downplay drug-use evolution.

It simply has to start somewhere.

For all of its Southern California earthy and economic eliteness, you can still occasionally find the random long-haired white-bearded homeless throwback roaming the Hermosa shore. Surrounded by stained bags of salvaged aluminum cans or absorbed in a vacant stare—these few represent that gray area of folks who *sort of* survived the drug "marketplace."

Most didn't.

A big part of those studies from the street involve the objective truth about this environment: *You die or you get sober*—with that small unbathed shadow bunch wandering around in pitiful purgatory.

But it was so cool being cool.

Mark and Chris were definitely cool.

The problem comes when that coolness turns into a hard icy skid. Before you know it, you're addicted.

That homeless guy with his filthy shaking hands in that trash dumpster, scooping up treasures of cans and food, was very cool at one time too. He probably doesn't remember.

And the dead are no longer concerned with image.

The ones who sobered up are the ones who finally have their definitions in good order.

Even the most street-naïve realize that Mark and Chris didn't wake up one day and say, "Hey, I'm going to turn into a drug addict and I'm going to die from this disease of substance abuse."

No.

They didn't think that way. They thought they were just getting some kicks, being all-powerful, being the man, being important, and having fun doing it.

That's what they thought.

But power has a way of shifting—ebbing and flowing amid wind and season changes like the Pacific tide. If you're not quite in that top-tier dealer category, well, there are bills to pay.

> *Cocaine is God's way of saying*
> *you're making too much money.*
>
> —Robin Williams

The McMillen boys had money, or at least access to it.

When they needed capital, they got it. Only now, the needs went from investments required for some good clean fun to needs that were genuine *needs.*

And here's where Thelma's sensing turned into a horrible, hard awareness—laced with some of that "panic" so scoffed at by the university's study.

It wasn't the start of the problem, of course. That had settled in long before.

The boys' need for money grew.

It became desperate.

Something had happened…

But an in-depth analysis still wasn't there.

Why? and *What's happening?* were questions not really asked, and certainly not answered.

But finally a hard bottom line couldn't be ignored. All this money was going *somewhere.*

No. This can't be.

A wicked sun started to dawn with some agonizing answers in its heat.

Drugs…

But wait—*we can fix this.* We'll just back off giving them money. Problem solved! *Now let's pour another cocktail…*

So THE MONEY FLOW STOPPED. But the needs, of course, didn't.

One night, Karl and Thelma were coming home from an evening out—coming home to the prestige of 2100 The Strand—and they just happened to run into their sons.

While their sons were carrying the family television set down the street.

To sell.

For drugs.

Needs…

The boys' plan had been to fence the TV and set it up to make it look like the house had been broken into and robbed.

It was a blueprint that would be followed in many plans to come.

The windows with the million-dollar view soon had bars on them, anchored into place to keep valuables *in.* The Pacific panorama wasn't quite the same.

Things had changed.

It was a little like breaking your leg. One day you're running the track; the next, you're on crutches. It may not be pleasant, but you adapt quickly to what you must now do to get around—to survive. Coyotes who chew themselves out of a trap also know the feeling.

Karl and Thelma were right there.

Emotional blood was freshly dripping from *their* trap when they heard another dull, excruciating snap. You see, the issue of Mark's and Chris's needs lingered on. And it didn't stop with the money cutoff or the bars on the million-dollar windows.

Plenty of other nice places were around that *didn't* have those bars.

Other homes had television sets.

And here is where everything in the lives of Karl, Thelma, Mark, and Chris McMillen *really* changes. Here is where the cold objectivism of a university study into the clockwork inner mechanics of a drug addict becomes just words on paper.

Here is where you start to shake your head and wonder why the million-dollar view, the girls, the surfing championships, and a pretty healthy back-up of capital wasn't enough.

Here is where that true power of drugs is seen.

THE FIRST CRIMES were considered "just little burglaries."

Little, maybe, but their frequency increased—as did the number of times the boys were caught. They were apparently better at surfing than they were at sneaking in and out of houses. The never-ending ins and outs of juvenile facilities—and later, jails and prisons—joined this family's changes.

All of it added up to more than enough to slide the McMillens irrevocably toward a lifestyle they'd never conceived of.

Over time, new routines would begin for Karl and Thelma. Saturday agendas would be set up around *visiting hours.*

A continual parade of court appearances would commence.

Phone calls would signal ordeals and bad business. *What had happened now?*

Even from the beginning—like when the youngest McMillen was placed in a correctional facility camp on the other side of Mount Wilson in Southern California's scenic Angeles National Forest. It was a thirty-day stay, but that was too much for Chris. Near the end of the sentence, at around the fourth week, he and a fellow inmate split. They escaped. They hiked out the back way, over the hills to the highway, caught a ride, and Chris simply came home.

It was the first of many "I'm sorry's," too.

I'll change my ways.

I'm done.

I saw the right of my wrong.
I'm on the straight path.
I'm not a kid anymore.
Please give me another chance.

All parents *so* want to believe their kids. So Karl and Thelma let it go…

More phone calls.

Wrecked cars begin to pile up.

Trips to pawn shops are added to the agenda—attempts to buy back what Mark and Chris have stolen from their home. Quests from one "loan establishment" to the next, trying to retrieve drug-fund bounty, from ever-replaceable TV sets to prized possessions like Thelma's cherished turquoise necklace.

It was a horrible wave that just couldn't be held back by four loving hands. And it hadn't even begun to crest yet.

Thelma's sensing had been so right. She sensed a future, but now she was rethinking the past. That social interaction and attention and importance were paling in the Hermosa sun. It was an unbearable realization.

Anyone who knew Thelma knew she would go to any lengths to protect her kids. She was like a viper when it came to ensuring no harm came to Mark and Chris. But harm did come. Tangled into all the importance and attention, the damage was done.

WITHIN ALL THAT DAMAGE, Karl still had to maintain his "other family." His efforts at Todd Pipe always transcended merely building a business. It was about helping thousands of people have a *life.*

From the managers to the shipping-and-receiving force to everyone else on the payroll, Karl gave so many a chance to have a place to go to work and be treated like family, and each employee felt connected to Karl personally. They had careers and lives and homes because of Karl. Just like Don McDonald.

Yet in Karl's immediate family, those personal connections became harder and harder to maintain.

BUT THE CONNECTIONS and those visits always came full circle with the boys eventually returning home.

Fines and lawyers were paid.

Karl wrote checks.

Mark and Chris knew that their connections represented power apart from the drugs. Unlike the old-beard "victim" at the dumpster, the brothers had a wide and multi-tiered safety net.

The soft web of cash and attorneys was the first buffer; the second was Karl's business-negotiation, problem-solving, we-won't-do-it-again "deals."

The employees of Todd were given a chance at life; Mark and Chris were given *many*.

The problem-solving had begun with the cutting off of the money, which had led to the first television "heist."

Then came the pleading and the promises.

Next came the deals.

If you'll just get off the drugs, we'll do this...we'll do that...

Bargains were made, bargains were broken.

And it would never stop.

The boys were given countless chances to turn things around. But that full circle always cycled back around to junk and juvenile facilities. That personal bond was always taking a hit.

Karl's logic-negotiations weren't working. It's one thing to reason with a person—especially a person you love, like a son. But it's impossible to reason with a drug. And those drugs and their influence had now become fully entrenched into the guts and daily mix of the McMillens. The view, the house, the ocean, the wealth to comfortably enjoy every drop of life—it was all a complete wipeout, like a longboard pearling in a twenty-foot North Shore swell.

The whole family was being hurled end over end into deep water, smothered and suffocating and choking, not knowing which way to even attempt to swim once that wave crashed down. Not knowing which way was up into the light and oxygen, or down into even darker depths.

CHAPTER 9

You Can Run...

1970

A lot of collateral damage surrounds an explosion of drug use.

Normal living is the obvious overall casualty.

But there are many, many specific ones as everyday life goes all to hell.

The normal that the McMillens had known was not remotely connected to something like this.

You expect to find roaches running around the baseboards in *some* homes. You expect greasy dirt on the sheets and under the fingernails of *some* families. A narcotics menu is standard fare in *some* strata.

Not here.

The lifestyle detonations that Mark and Chris were setting off completely crushed the idea of normal for this family and redefined it with shock.

For so many within a hot collateral drug circle, simply trying to go to work each day becomes a part of normal that is now a burden. The user probably isn't even capable, but for his or her family, friends, caretakers, enablers, and sometimes-enablers, going to work is like running a four-hundred-meter hurdles race in the dark, with weights around their ankles and the barriers to leap getting higher all the time. They feel a constant drag on their entire being and a futility-fueled fear of what may come next.

Karl McMillen *had* to go to work. He was in command of a multi-million-dollar company that he had a major hand in building. His decisions meant the difference between success or failure.

But the decisions at home were now the truly tough ones—and "success" there varied in its definition. Success could mean a short-term staying-out-of-jail for his sons; or it could mean yet another perhaps promising look into long-term, permanent solutions.

Both ends of that spectrum were on the vital daily to-do list.

Decisions like which nice restaurant to go to for a relaxing evening out or which new car to buy were not even making the backside of that list.

Things had changed…

Karl still had to go to work, and in theory, Mark and Chris still had to attend school. But education was another part of normal that the drugs were burying.

In 1970, Chris was fourteen; Mark, sixteen. Both were attending Mira Costa High School in Manhattan Beach.

Like everything Karl provided for his sons, beach-close Mira Costa was topflight. Various agencies have perennially rated the facility as one of the "100 Best High Schools in America." With esteemed alumni ranging from athletes who went on to play for teams like the Chicago Bears, Dallas Cowboys, and San Francisco Giants, to famous musicians who fronted bands like Pennywise and the legendary Black Flag, to the infamous surfing legend Dewey Weber, "Costa" was always polished in notoriety and varying degrees of upper class.

But for Mark and Chris, Mira Costa quickly became part of the scorched earth of collateral ruin. Education just wasn't working for the boys within the staid structure of a mainstream achievement-oriented school. They had "other interests" that took their time and energy.

At about the same time Chris went to the juvie camp in the mountains, Mark left the we-expect-too-much confines of Mira Costa for the you-need-help unruly remedy of Pacific Shores Continuation School.

"Continuation schools" come along with the rocky territory of drug abuse. When you drop out of the type of society that can go to a normal school and attend normal work at prescribed hours and meet all of their normal everyday requirements, you need to take a step back.

And down.

Pacific Shores, which operated less than a block downwind of Mira Costa from 1965 to 1993, was known for taking in "problem students" and "students who had attendance or behavioral issues." In 1970, the McMillen boys unfortunately met all of those criteria.

But when Mark began attending continuation school, he impressed one of the teachers there, Terry Devitt. For all of Mark's outside distractions, he was still able to ask pertinent questions about lessons. He could easily talk politics and other subjects. Devitt and Mark bonded, and the teacher became an enduring friend of the family—extending into a closeness with both Thelma and Karl, and ironically becoming part of the party scene at 2100 The Strand.

It was a unique relationship, to say the least. As the years and the situation with Mark and Chris progressed, Devitt would be pivotal, becoming extended eyes and ears for Karl's businesses as well as his sons.

Along with their scholastic routine, the McMillen boys' surf-passion was also drying up. A year earlier, in 1969, Chris had won the prestigious, long-running La Jolla Shores Surfing Association's Menehune Contest. But the heavy cry that had become the McMillens' theme in the seventies drowned out those glory years on the waves.

A lot of time was still spent in the water, but the competitive power drive was gone.

The boys, however—through all the current-churning and crashes—retained their status within the inner clique of famous surfers. Layback legends like Mike Purpus and Tiger Makin would hang out in Hermosa with Mark and Chris—*and* Thelma.

But when the drugs came in, Purpus distanced himself from that group. Like that "neighbor kid," Don McDonald, Purpus was looking toward the future—*a* future. He was determined to be the world champion that he eventually became. It was a destiny that demanded a clear head.

Mike Purpus and Tiger Makin would both nosewalk into big-time surfer history and media; posterizing blockbuster waves and being inducted into Hermosa Beach's Surfers Walk of Fame.

Mark and Chris didn't make it that far.

They were on a different kind of ride—a ride to a part of this scene that could have ended so many different ways. Karl, Thelma, Mark, and Chris were all standing at individual and collective crossroads—and paths had to be chosen.

THE BAJA TRIPS RESUMED—that was one path. Karl felt that any time away from the Hermosa environment would help. Besides, his sons always loved those trips so much.

> *"I could hardly sleep the night before we left because I was so excited…5:30 A.M. arrived and we were on our way…"*

But Mark wasn't twelve anymore.

Things had changed…

Karl kept feeling that the trips held a drug-free, escape-only purity; but those brutal studies from the street raise the odds against that. Drug addicts will tell you emphatically that when they are going somewhere for, oh say, three days, well, they simply pack three days worth of "stuff."

And not allowing "authority" figures—especially not parents—to see them smoking, dropping, shooting up, or in any way ingesting *anything* is the number one rule in the playbook.

But the Baja stage-setting stood intact—the boys would surf and Karl would cook in camp.

Before that, though, the fourteen-hour driving days and the back-road bouncing into the heart of Baja's coast usually required some unwinding.

While the boys did their own *unwinding,* Karl would have a cocktail or two, or more, while cooking in the beach-impromptu Dutch oven. He'd wind up fried and the dinner would be burned. He'd come to, smelling the smoky remains of his own collateral damage.

Occasionally, he and Thelma would wonder: *Did the boys do drugs because we drank, or are we drinking because they do drugs?*

1972

In the early seventies, Mark's high school career was winding down, but his substance abuse was riding high. Karl tapped into the early-twentieth-century ideas of whatever suitcase-philosopher first hooked up travel with educating one's mind, and decided that Mark should see some of the world far removed from Hermosa Beach.

"Travel broadens the mind"

—Unknown

In fact, a complete relocation might be just the ticket.

Couple that with some serious forced self-sufficiency, and there might be a way out of this drug problem.

Mark found himself a little over twenty-five hundred miles away from The Strand, on the Hawaiian island of Maui. He could surf.

He could go to school. He'd be safe from the haunt of Hermosa and its influences. He was enrolled at the oldest American post-secondary school west of the Mississippi: Lahainaluna High School, established 1831.

This change was big.

It was an experiment that could work!

Mark's only job over there was to stay clean.

That was it.

It was another of the bargains: *We'll set you up in paradise; you stay off drugs.*

Paradise was Mark's, if he would just stay clean.

Mark was there and Chris would soon follow. Maybe this *was* working. Life seemed calmer.

But there was that twenty-five-hundred-mile distancing.

After a sabbatical-like semester at Lahainaluna, the boys are brought home to finish up their high school requirements at Pacific Shores.

1973

Now it's time to turn up the heat on the experiment. If twenty-five hundred miles was good, seventy-six hundred would be better. Karl and Thelma prepare for an extended "holiday" to the South Pacific with their sons.

This would be more than a family vacation—Karl was in full analysis mode. Maybe they could *all* relocate here. Maybe the kiwi fruit and New South Wales prime beef could take away the bad taste of Hermosa hemp.

Maybe this was working…

But Mark had already developed a taste of his own. He had *really* enjoyed Hawaii.

Right after his graduation from the continuation school, Mark had headed back to the Valley Isle. Then Chris went back too, another *visit* with his older brother.

Karl and Thelma could swing by and pick their sons up on their way Down Under.

"He can run, but he can't hide"

—Joe Louis

WHEN THE FORMER CHAMP made that comment about an opponent way back in the 1940s, he was talking about a quick, hard-hitting heavyweight. But drugs are the baddest heavyweight of all—with a long, long reach.

The move—Mark's run to Maui—had in fact put the wolf in the Hana henhouse; with a full selection of condiments and fine china thrown in to make the feast even more delectable.

Mark was quickly becoming "established" in the island drug scene. But there was another run ahead before he could truly settle in.

> *"Robert wondered what was in store for them.*
> *Would they find surf? Would they catch malaria?*
> *Would they be speared by a native?*
> *He didn't have any idea."*

> —From *The Endless Summer,* 1966

In Bruce Brown's existential escape-epic film, *The Endless Summer,* a couple of surfers travel around the world, following a continual solstice sun. If you stay in the right place at the right time, you're never touched by cold or the cuts of winter.

Sometimes it pays to run.

Sometimes…

The McMillens were going on an epic of their own—six months out, with a hoped-for eradication of a more personal strain of chill.

MAY 17, 1973

Karl and Thelma touch down on the Big Island at 11:30 on a Thursday morning. By 6:30 in the evening, they make it over to Kahului, Maui. They find Chris and they all have dinner.

Mark finally meets up with the rest of the family at 10:00 p.m.

The group departs Hawaii the following Tuesday. They're booked through to Perth, Australia; but with open airline tickets that allow them to get there and back via stops almost anywhere in the region.

Tickets anywhere for six months.

For all four of them.

First stop: Pago Pago, the capital of American Samoa.

Then Western Samoa.

The plane out of Western Samoa departs only once a week, so they head out on its next hop and zigzag around before ending up in a rented house in Fiji.

If only they had Bruce Brown and his camera along with them! *Endless Summer* meets yet another episode of *The Amazing Race*—and *Celebrity Rehab*—long before the tide of reality TV shows came rolling in.

In Fiji, they meet a "holy man" with a long beard, adding an island philosopher to the epic's cast. It's the early seventies in Fiji, and here they are with a Dalai Lama–flavored Ratu-guru—a perfect post-sixties transcendental trip!

Sitting on the floor, they all share a fresh fish dinner while the sage of Suva expounds upon many esotericisms. Of course, our mathematically-minded power-patriarch, Karl, is thinking: *What the hell is he talking about?*

From Fiji, it would be on to Brisbane. The night before their departure, the family stayed in a hotel. It wasn't quite as peaceful as the ethereal evening with the holy man, but it was more logistically practical.

In the morning, the boys erupted into total chaos, running all around the hotel. Karl chased, but he couldn't catch them. The only thought on his mind was another important thing that needed to be caught: the plane to Brisbane!

The odd hustle didn't escape the hotel personnel. This wasn't normal, even given their daily dealings with a harried-and-spinning tourist clientele. Dead center in the chase, Karl finally resigned himself that all this had something to do with drugs—using them, hiding them, *something*. He now only hoped that whatever the boys had, they'd just "use it up" so that they could all make that flight.

Whatever did happen—or get used up—everyone finally calmed down and the plane was met on time.

The group landed in Brisbane. The planeload of people quickly cleared customs—except for the boys. Did the hotel call someone? Were drugs stashed in some secret cavity in one of the surfboards?

It was a nervous time, but Mark and Chris were finally cleared, and it wasn't long before they were in the east Australian waves.

Here, the *Endless Summer* free-drift aura really kicks in (even though in the counter-clockwise whirl of the Southern Hemisphere, it was rolling from autumn to winter!).

The McMillens head from Brisbane to Sydney, about a thousand kilometers (six-hundred-plus miles) south. It takes them thirty days. There are stops, places to stay and see. Follow the surf, hope for the sun. Run. Hide.

Coffs Harbour, Newcastle, Dee Why, Narrabeen, Cronulla, Bondi…

Living a true *Endless Summer*, regardless of the season.

Karl is beginning to worry about the number of miles being racked up on the rental car. The fitting where the speedo cable connects into the drive train is sealed. This is one odometer that won't be fooled.

Sydney then Melbourne.

From Melbourne, the McMillens take a long flight over to the west coast and Perth. They rent another car: 277 kilometers (172 miles) to Margaret River and Main Break (a.k.a. Surfers Point). With its left and right breaks and fifteen-foot waves, it's called the "jewel in the crown" of west coast hot spots.

But it's June—winter here! And it's cold! Long underwear joins with wet suits as part of the everyday uniform.

But in Perth, a standoff begins. Mark wants to leave—to go back to Hawaii. He has *needs*.

He is also now eighteen years old; an adult. And after all, it was the family who got him "settled into" Hawaii in the first place. This is what *they* wanted, right?

Mark wins the argument; Karl lets him go.

THE THREE REMAINING MCMILLENS head over to New Zealand. Another run—and a final analysis.

When the family was together in Fiji, they met a young man from Wellington, New Zealand. The guy had traveled the world as bartender on a cruise ship and also owned an *almost*-legal after-hours bar in an industrial part of his hometown.

He was well-connected and knew "after-hours" processes for more than just bars.

When Karl mentioned that they were going to be touring his country, the guy was more than happy to refer them to a friend of his with a used car lot.

"He can be of great help…"

When Karl, Thelma, and Chris hit Kiwi country, they looked this friend up. He explained how insurance in the country must be in the driver's name. So if you're going to be there awhile, it makes more sense to *buy* a car than rent one. Once you add in the insurance, mileage, and all those assorted waivers and hidden fees, a hitch in a Hertz can cost you a Mount Cook–sized pile of that colorful Kiwi currency.

So Karl buys a car from the bartender's buddy, striking a deal that includes a fixed buy-back price.

The numbers worked.

In their new used car, the trio motors through both the North Island and the South Island—*analyzing*.

And they have other *connections*.

An old friend of Karl's, one of Chuck's former partners from the fishing-boat days, had emigrated to New Zealand and set up a lobster business. He had an oceanfront house that backed up to the forest.

Maybe we could do something like that, too...

But as they travel, Karl is hit with some of the ramifications of the socialistic government of the time. The post office is on strike, museums are closed, the public economic sector is ugly. Karl is forty-three years old and a powerhouse of a business man; he's wondering how he can possibly make a living *anywhere* here—especially after meeting the half-million-dollar bond-like requirement to emigrate from America.

And what about the culture? What about "blending in"? Chuck's old buddy had the common ground of fishing, but *Karl*?

And the real estate—well, let's just say the market wasn't like Southern California.

Karl had started his property analysis in Brisbane. The construction of oceanfront condos in the area was rolling in 1973. It was a new concept. And they were going for eighty grand.

But it was a high price when you looked at it, and Karl definitely looked at it. The area around Hermosa Beach had millions of people (3 million in the city of Los Angeles alone). Those numbers could "back up" prices like the $77,500 Karl had paid for 2100 The Strand. But in 1973, Australia had only about 13 million people spread out over the entire 2,941,299 square miles of the giant island-continent. *Something's wrong,* thought Karl. *Either they're too high Down Under or we're too low up in Hermosa.*

These numbers *didn't* work.

Karl's thought processes were on fire.

Are we really considering moving here?!

What the hell am I doing here?

It's beautiful, yes, but all the real business is in Los Angeles.

I feel like I'm in jail.

How long can you drive around on the roads and look at the sheep crossing? You've seen one, you've seen them all. It's like living on a rock!

The only way you can make it down here is to have a business and commute!

Karl knew business and he knew real estate. He and Thelma had bought, sold, turned, and flipped, and they had done well. Todd Pipe was on its way up. *In California.* Here, well, this was something else. This experiment and analysis would go no further.

The idea just wasn't economically sound.

It was only halfway into the six months, but it didn't matter; the numbers were in. Time to go home.

BACK IN HERMOSA, it's all business. The Down Under odyssey has been cut short by half. Mark is back in Hawaii *"settling in."* Chris is "doing his time" toward finally graduating from Pacific Shores. Todd Pipe is expanding.

The first item on the agenda is to find a place to stay. The Strand castle has been leased out for the full six months of the McMillens' intended international introspection, and the new residents are enjoying their Northern Hemisphere summer on the sand. They still have three months to go, and they aren't about give up any of *their* time with that million-dollar view.

Karl pays for a nearby overlooking-the-shore apartment— adjacent to one of the beach's finest surf-and-turf restaurants.

Ocean-view or no, the McMillens now also fall into the category of temporary tenants. It's a strange feeling.

Like having their reunion with their beloved Yaska delayed. Their new apartment set the rules: "No Dogs Allowed"! But they would smuggle him up in the elevator late at night for visits.

It won't be long, old buddy…

The next item was the growth of Todd.

Expanding businesses, like those high-profile beachfront homes and the people who own them, attract attention. Todd Pipe had already attracted some very *unwanted* attention—from the labor unions. It was another matter that demanded analysis.

Terry Devitt had impressed Karl. He was educated, perceptive, and detailed. He had all the credentials to conduct a study that just cried for perception and detail: *How do we keep the unions out of Todd Pipe?*

Right before the McMillens left for their stroll through the South Pacific, Karl had enlisted Devitt to actively address some specific questions:

What is the most difficult type of business to organize unions for?

Why does that particular type of business make a union stronghold difficult?

The answers were vital, especially considering that for labor unions, 1973 was to become an exceptionally hot year.

The United States vs. Enmons case settled in '73, causing public outcry as it exonerated union members from prosecution for violence carried out "in pursuit of a legitimate union objective."

Also in 1973, former Teamsters boss Jimmy Hoffa was enjoying a year of freedom after his prison stint on a jury-tampering conviction. He was also enjoying a $1.7 million "welcome home" in the form of a lump-sum pension from his international brotherhood.

Nineteen seventy-three was also the battle year for the Teamsters as they engaged in a violent civil war with California's United Farm Workers.

Unions were a multilevel burning topic, particularly for owners and managers of big businesses. Karl wanted to turn *down* that kind of heat at Todd.

Devitt goes to work.

He calls the local chapter of the Teamsters.

"I'd like to make an appointment to talk to your business manager," he tells the guy on the other end of the phone. "I'm doing a thesis on business organization and I know you'll be able to give me the best and most truthful answers."

The guy on the other end *was* the business manager.

"I'm especially interested in what type of business is the hardest to organize, union-wise. Could I come down, say, tomorrow?"

"Well, hell, you can come down today if you want," the loyal-to-the-local tells him. "I'm jus' sittin' here!"

I see…

"No, I got a class this afternoon," Terry explains. "How about eleven o'clock tomorrow? We can talk over lunch?"

"Fine, fine…"

Devitt rolls into the appointment with a list of questions.

The Teamsters manager has answers:

The hardest labor nuts to crack are those businesses owned by a family.

And the ones with good managerial-employee relationships already established.

And the ones who supply side benefits that create good employee morale—you know, exercise machines, things like that.

Maybe even vacation trailers…

What that union boss was *really* telling Devitt was that the hardest labor nuts to crack are the ones made solid by a Golden Touch.

Imagine that.

Todd Pipe's labor force was happy and healthy, and business was booming!

CHAPTER 10

Heroin:
The Kalani & the Convict

BY 1974, THE MCMILLEN FAMILY TREE had taken on a new shape. No longer were the branches healthy, natural, and winding along easy and normal path-seeking turns.

Now the branches were straight and clinical, forced into objective parameters through legal wranglings and the stark up-and-down results of substance abuse. These branches were stretched tight like the sides of a badly skewed obtuse triangle, with two long sides extending out to a ready-to-snap thinness across the Pacific from Hermosa to Maui, where Mark now lived.

The other long side of the triangle connected Maui and Mark to Hawthorne, California, and the headquarters home of Todd Pipe: his father's triumph of business and an institution that could have been Mark and Chris's future.

That branch of the tree was even thinner.

The small side of the triangle hooked that Hawthorne HQ to 2100 The Strand, rounding out the triad of life centers for the McMillen family.

At those cross-points in Hawthorne stood Karl. He stood in his brand new mammoth company building. He couldn't help but think back to the first Todd "business hub," in all of its rough-worn sheet-metal glory.

He thought of his business growth.

He thought of his youngest son.

Chris was twelve when Todd Pipe was at its fledgling level in the old building. He and his cousin Jeff would go with Karl on weekends to work, sweeping floors, putting up tools.

The drafty warehouse was filled with makeshift mezzanines and decks. On one of those weekend days, Chris had been walking across the plywood flooring, when it gave way. He "surfed" the floating four-by-eight sheet all the way down to the bottom floor without missing a beat—or breaking anything!

But times had changed…

Soft landings were no longer a part of these once-charmed lives. Anecdotes and smiles were replaced with trying to keep track of what was occurring at the end of each of those lines in this new-shape family tree.

And so much was occurring.

Before Mark left for Hawaii, during the McMillen boys' *evolution* into drugs and "feeling important" star-life on the beach, a lethal landmark was hit.

The sharp fangs of heroin bit and ripped their way into the bodies and beings of the boys.

A marijuana-driven penchant for getting high doesn't compare to being tightly tethered to the maniacal blood-dragon of heroin. "Lighting up" ignited into being burned alive.

If Karl and Thelma and the entire parent-collective of the 1960s were baffled by the new "cultural" offerings of grass and acid and uppers and downers, then they were sure as hell thrown into blind confusion when the screaming full darkness of heroin hit.

That little foil bag of behind-the-couch grass had metastasized into a monster.

The older kids who fed Mark the initial "recreational" drugs and the attentive lifestyle of being "the man" had pushed this terrible sharp edge much, much deeper.

Recreation turned terminal.

This was darkness as heavy as the tidally locked backside of the moon and every bit as permanent.

But that secret side of the moon does see the occasional light from other heavenly sources—it's just that we never see it from where we are.

We can't see the random flashes of *something* that brighten the day there.

And most will never know—or see—those drug flashes that kill the pain in the addict for even a moment. Most will never know the vile quick-light of a rush that has become a need that overpowers all else in life.

Like that freezing darkness and that sometimes-light hitting the backside of the moon, it's a sensation that can't really connect with those who are grounded elsewhere. Something that's occurring on and in a highly different world.

But we have gazed up at the moon and the stars and the heavens for as long as humankind has existed. We have grown to comprehend, at least, the rock and gas that make up the hardware of the universe; but to get a complete grip on how infinity was hung and staged there and how all of this exactly works falls into a folder marked "Mystery."

How did all that *really* happen?

How *does* that happen?

And how did two young men with world-class athletic talents, surfer-god bodies and appearance, intelligence, morals, and loving, well-to-do parents drift into the lair of that most horrible of beasts?

ONE OF THE MOST POTENT VOICES from the street comes from one of the McMillen boys' closest friends, Richard "Richie" Davidson. Like the McMillens' cousin Jeff, Richie was with Mark and Chris every stumbling step of the way. His recollections of their rides beyond the waves are more chilling than the Pacific in winter:

The Dragon Lair of Heroin

I was also a part of the surfing scene in Hermosa. I was a bit older than Chris, same age as Mark. And I remember so well the first time I tried heroin. I was sixteen. I had just come in from surfing. A "friend" of mine came to the house and asked if I wanted to get high. I asked him what he had.

Heroin.

It kinda freaked me out, but I had smoked some weed a couple of times...tried a couple of bennies. I was experimenting. I was inquisitive. So he crushes up a little line and I snort it.

I remember it like it was night and day.

It had an impact on me.

Impact...

There's a reason heroin is the most addictive drug in the world. I lay down, and for me, it was heaven on earth. Like when you go into the hospital and you're in terrible pain and they give you a shot of morphine. You just go, "Aaahhhh..."

It provides an indescribable sense of ease and comfort. Where everything is totally perfect and you feel sooo connected...

That's before, of course, your entire life becomes <u>disconnected</u>.

When those fangs drew that first blood of Mark and Chris McMillen, and the venom shot into their veins, the unknown effects and the unending questions surged. Not even that all-powerful rising dragon could conjure up what the final results and answers would be.

THE EARLY TIDE OF HEROIN EFFECTS, added to Mark's and Chris's already hefty drug consumption, was as expected—waves of even more disruption and more destruction. But it moved much more quickly than the cyclic waters along the shore. All of this was happening fast.

This is the most explosive period in the timeline of drug addiction. That middle period in the three-stage progression that a user's family has to endure.

The first stage is when the initial discoveries of what is happening sink in. That's when family and friends can look at the tangible bite marks of truth and know that, yes, drug addiction is now a part of their lives.

The third stage is the grinding, winding-down period of damage control, of rehab, of promises, tears, repentance, and maybe even death.

But this stage, stage two, is the *action* ground. This is when the bloodiest battles occur.

Cousin Jeff, who had seen the first stash in the couch, was now old enough to emulate his role models in ways other than the surfing and fun they shared. One Christmas morning, he noticed Mark "nodding out" on heroin, twisted and bent in an image far removed from the towering power surfer who dominated world-class waves.

It was another of those nauseating backward holiday moments when joy and family interaction was being redefined.

But it didn't matter.

Jeff, too, was introduced to many of Mark's and Chris's demons. All Jeff ever wanted to do was to be like Chris. In every way.

Nothing was holding back the pull and draw of this deadly crosscurrent, although some were trying.

The police and the court system were increasingly involved in the boys' action ground.

The early-on crude attempt at stealing the family television, the subsequent cutting off of money, Mark's first arrest for drug possession, and a head-to-head with the law during their maiden voyage into breaking and entering had rolled into a routine.

The local cops knew the McMillen brothers and they knew them well. During one particularly rough detaining, they had run and tackled Mark right there on The Strand.

Mark and Chris had built juvenile records reaching arm's length. Their regularity had worn on the beach-beat police; law enforcement is never overly happy when their end runs of "lock 'em up and throw away the key" become a repetitive and irritating game of fox and hounds.

When Mark was experimentally exiled to—and then permanently perched in—the humid warmth of Hawaii, the badged heat in Hermosa had one of their prime crime teams reduced by fifty percent.

This was indeed the action ground for all involved.

On the home turf, Chris was now a singular focus for the police, and they made the most of it.

Chris's record would unfurl far beyond that arm's length. He was the only McMillen boy left within reach, and the truth was that he just wasn't as slick at crime as Mark was. He was never as heavy a user as Mark, either.

Chris was a "chipper"—he "chipped away" at heroin. Mark was into it full-tilt from the gate.

But that may be like comparing two victims of drowning—one found in a bathtub, the other planted at the bottom of the Mariana Trench. One situation may have involved more pressure and intensity, but the end result is the same.

The fangs of heroin are beyond razor-sharp. There is no such thing as a flesh wound. These bites always go clean, clear through. And the bleeding, whether fast or slow, never stops.

THE INTENSITY AND PRESSURE in Chris's life came from the double play of having to feed his habit *and* having to do so under the bloodhound noses of Hermosa's police force.

And his parents.

Mark didn't suffer those same factors of intensity and pressure. His were different.

Deeper.

Hawaii in the early 1970s—especially the isolation of Maui—was not even close to any corner of metropolitan Southern California in terms of civilization. It was a tough frontier, only a handful of years removed from territory status.

Stateside, you had mobile carloads of cops to work the fifteen-by-forty-block, 1.5-square-mile beachfront of Hermosa Beach. The 727-square-mile jungle that is the island of Maui was free of that concrete congestion, making certain "opportunities" easy.

And Mark immediately became aware of those opportunities.

That thin line stretching all the way back to the giant Todd Pipe and *its* opportunities was getting thinner and thinner, fading with each needle Mark put into his veins. But what this island presented in the way of opportunity was immediate, and it helped keep his needs satisfied.

A wide opening gaped for someone to venture into the field of supplying narcotics to this newest of the United States.

Mark was the man for the job.

He had focus.

The hippies who drifted and drugged around the islands provided a big built-in clientele. These lost souls were pretty "hang-loose" and freewheeling, not too concerned with the business of drugs, just the results.

Notes from a city board meeting of the era portray a festering form of island fever:

> *The perennial topic of discussion—the "hippie problem"—*
> *cropped up again at last week's meeting of the Maui Chamber of*
> *Commerce directors.*
>
> *The discussion was prompted by a letter from A.J. Huddleston*
> *of Lahaina, who claimed that the island's long-haired visitors are*
> *"adversely affecting real estate values, the tourist trade, and life, as*
> *we have known it, in the island of Maui"... The letter sparked ten*
> *minutes of talk in which "hippies" were accused of trespassing, taking*
> *advantage of public funds, and violating building codes.*
>
> —The Lahaina Sun, sometime in the seventies

Mark was not hang-loose or annoying, or "trespassing" around. Or anything else that might be associated with the happy, frolicking fantasy-factors of the hippies. Mark was *very* concerned with the serious side of business.

So while being an unwashed annoyance to the "straights," the hippies fed right into an underground customer base for Mark.

While Chris kept close to home struggling with cops, institutions, what was left of school, and supplying his ever-mounting habit, Mark was digging in.

Mark's intensity and deepening pressure came from his establishment of a business where customer relations can have many levels of meaning. The overhead can be staggering, the competition more than fierce, the complaint department has to be manned by Smith & Wesson, and product development follows phantom phone calls and meetings in remote fields at three o'clock in the morning.

Mark took on an executive partner: a like-minded entrepreneur named "Preacher." Together, they took it upon themselves to freely bend the laws against monopolies. *Their* business, too, was booming.

Mark's action ground was constantly shaking.

And the tremors were felt all the way back to Hermosa Beach, where Thelma, too, was shaking.

CHAPTER 11

Deal or No Deal

THELMA KNEW.

She knew just what was shaking in that action ground of her oldest son. A thin-line family tree and twenty-five hundred miles of distance means little to a mother suffering her own brand of intensity and pressure.

Her trips to Maui began immediately after Mark was relocated there. Her understanding of what her son was going through was becoming just that, understanding.

Thelma McMillen was absorbing a great deal about what these years of the late 1960s into the '70s were producing in the way of social turmoil.

And she wanted to help. She wanted not only to help her own sons but to help others caught up in the spaced-out spin of the sixties as well.

She volunteered at the South Bay Free Clinic in Manhattan Beach, spending seven of the era's most crazed years aiding in directing that turmoil's traffic.

Thelma described her Free Clinic guidance work as "lay counseling with young people concerning birth control methods, social diseases, and drug abuse and family problems...keeping constant contact with every available halfway house and engaging in continual discussions with professionals about methods in which these very troubled youngsters might be helped...These were very trying years for many of our youth with the promiscuous use of drugs and sexual behavior."

This was pioneering.

This was history.

This was society shifting into gears that modern America had never witnessed, the low gears of extreme drug abuse and the high gears of rehabilitating energy.

But in the decades and decades since the anti-drug, anti-life's-social-ills pioneering of the 1960s, nothing has ever replaced the instinctive human desire to cure any downturns with basic love and compassion. That kind of caring, coupled with business-deal reasoning, *has* to turn things around, doesn't it?

In 1975, Mark was on a bit of an island hiatus back in Los Angeles. Between ever-looming drug possession charges, recurring DUIs, the resulting car wrecks, and sustaining the hard-honed habits he'd sharpened in Hawaii, he wound up spending that more-than-memorable Christmas morning at Wayside alongside his constantly "in" brother.

Something simply had to give.

Something had to change.

Karl again hired Terry Devitt to do a study. A case study designed to be what case studies are: an "intense analysis." Karl wanted an intense analysis of Mark and Chris's *problem*. The union situation that Devitt had helped Karl with previously was small potatoes compared to the complexity of drug rehabilitation psychology.

At this stage, Karl had solicited in-depth examinations of "all of this" from doctors, lawyers, counselors, and law enforcement personnel. As with his business, Karl always sought help from the best of the best. Devitt's new study was to give Karl and Thelma McMillen insight into precisely what they needed to do to eliminate any more requisite visits—on Christmas or any other day—to both of their sons behind bars. This new study would put this problem into *data,* into numbers and a structure that Karl could more easily digest.

Business...

Ever hopeful, Karl and Thelma delved headfirst into doing whatever it would take to help their sons.

It was an important study then, and it's an important study now. It represents what you get when you attempt to reason with a drug. It represents trying so hard to get a rational perspective on something that has gone so far out of control and has affected so much and so many.

And it represents love.

It represents a first step into that third realm of drug abuse—the foggy, thick realm of "winding-down damage control." That grinding, exhausting cycle of "rehab, promises, tears, repentance, and maybe even death."

JUNE 1976

Terry Devitt hands Karl and Thelma his multipage *Final Report and Recommendations.*

Perhaps, with its pioneering punch, it should have been given a title more icy and tough, like, *A Handbook to Halt Enablers.*

Or maybe it could have taken on a softer heading: *Why Do "Love" and "Help" Have to Be Such Different Words?*

The report contained much of both.

Devitt began with his goals:

> Goal A: Getting the boys healthy, drug-free, and legally clear. That is, functionally independent and able to care for themselves.
>
> Goal B: Removing from your lives the constant strain and tension that has now been present for more than half a decade.

Then came the lessons to be imparted.

The report contained many:

> It is my conclusion that the establishment of a conservatorship is not practical or attainable. Furthermore it is not desirable from this standpoint: The future of the boys' lives is not, and has not been for some time, in your hands or subject to your wills. The boys' future is their own. It is only through their own efforts that their lives can be as good and full as their own

capabilities allow. Further aid, interference, inducements,
bribes, etc. will only delay that time when they recognize
that the consequences of their acts are their own...

Devitt obviously felt that being given free rein in paradise, having
wrecked cars paid off, and enjoying access to a bottomless bail bucket
just wasn't working. Even the contracts designed to motivate the
boys could be doing more harm than good; keeping them, and Karl,
"hooked" into an unceasing cycle.

In Mark's case, he must decide whether to give up a life
filled with crises, POs [parole officers], jail, and drugs,
and go after the rich future that lies ahead of him. Again,
it can only be his choice.

But that "choice" can be influenced.
Intensely and with pressure.
That blood-dragon of heroin is such a damned strong persuader.
It's an enemy that even the armed forces didn't want any part of.
The possibility of military service for Chris was analyzed in
Devitt's report—*could Chris receive disciplining and straightening out by
Uncle Sam?* But it appeared that ship had sailed—and sunk:

We have spoken to numerous attorneys and recruiters
in attempting to aid Chris. The uncomfortable fact that
emerges from my discussions with recruiters is that there
is little if any possibility that Chris will ever see a day
in uniform...
Air Force—no way.
Navy—no way.
Coast Guard—no way.
Army and Marines—These are the only two services that
give any encouragement at all. In both instances, we would

need moral waivers on Chris's juvenile record. Of course,
even with the recommendations and references, should the
recruiter call the Hermosa Beach PD we are sunk.

Devitt also jumped into a little private investigative work, discovering a local pharmacy and a community doctor who had served as drug pipelines for the boys. Both were reported to the authorities.

But most of all, Terry Devitt tried to explain to Karl and Thelma that some very basic—and again, pioneering—"tough love" would have to be at the heart of any "deals" they made to get the boys back on the straight and drug-free narrow.

Tough love, of course, fits nicely into the "easier said than done" box.

Proposed Agreement

KB [Karl] and Thelma agree to provide Mark with a car on
condition that Mark resume work at Todd Pipe no later than
the day after Memorial Day.

Mark works a regular 8 hr. day, forty hours per week
except for medical and legal appointments only and
understands that he will not be staying with parents while
he is in the South Bay.

KB and Thelma will provide first month's rent and any
small expenses to set up a place.

Car will be provided two weeks after beginning regular
employment.

Mark agrees to check with KB and Thelma before coming
by the house as per restraining order.

Car is given to Mark on a six-month loan basis after
which he may purchase it from KB or buy a car of his own.
Price of buggy, should Mark wish to buy it, is subject to
negotiation.

This all sounded reasonable, even the part about the restraining order. But that was a bluff, and the whole agreement was about as binding as a shopping mall parking ticket.

The problem proved to be that just as it's impossible to reason with a drug; neither can you enter into an *agreement* with a drug.

Junk [heroin] *is the ultimate commodity. The merchandise is not sold to the consumer—the consumer is sold to the merchandise.*

—William Burroughs

All the "working of an 8 hr. day," and the cars, and the car payments, and the apartment setups, and the paychecks, and the paybacks, and the promises, and all the rest meant little when the need for the soothing sweetness and the "leveling" power of diacetylmorphine started to sweat and surge in the bodies and veins of Mark and Chris.

BUT DEVITT AND KARL *did* anticipate how unenforceable these agreements might be.

Long before the term "I'm going to rehab" became as common and accepted as "I'm going to the dentist"; years before music artists like Brad Paisley and the late Amy Winehouse sang about celebrity addiction and drying out; decades before "Dr. Drew" Pinsky started broadcasting detox and withdrawal in high-def. Karl McMillen commissioned Terry Devitt to study and evaluate treatment centers in the area.

The specter of therapy would be added to the agreements.

Devitt delved into many of the Southern California facilities operating at the time. Again, this was back in decidedly dark ages when it comes to the development and proliferation of rehab clinics and programs. Still, the teacher-turned-investigator went from one end of the area to the other, rating and describing places like Via Avanta, Pacifica House, UCLA NPI, and Reality Therapy Institute.

He even knocked on the door of the infamous Synanon compound.

Synanon unfortunately exemplified much of the ignorance of the period when it came to functional rehabilitation. The program and facility in one form or other had been around since 1958; but as the tumult of the sixties and seventies unfolded, Synanon began to be looked at as cultic.

The infamous Synanon reflects the crudeness of some early rehabilitation programs.

Criminal activities from attempted murder to tax evasion became more associated with the facility than did rehabilitation successes. Communal child-rearing and many of the sexual aberrations of the "free love generation" also defined Synanon.

Devitt's report on the place was clinically concise, if not a hint understated:

> It's surprising how many people will recommend this program—it must be their good PR. Not satisfactory in any respect for our purposes.

Terry's analyses of the other programs ranged from lukewarm to optimistic. But his comments about the Via Avanta facility in the West L.A. area were again quite telling of the time:

> First [program] to point out the difficulty in finding
> any good program for someone with Mark's experience
> and background. Suggested that best course might be
> to let things just happen without parental support or
> interference. Said he had seen too many parents go down
> with their children behind the mistaken notion that they
> could be helpful.

THE REHAB SCENE IN THE MID-1970S was indeed grim. But even as rehabilitation and understanding and professional methodology developed, the voices from the street spoke up, explaining the addict's feeling about "coerced" help and intervention—being forced into treatment before the addict is ready to surrender.

I'm Just Not Done Yet

A lot of times you come into the treatment programs because your family is saying over and over and over that you need it, but in the back of your mind you're thinking, "Hey, I can still make this work. I'm going to move my mouth and say what you want to hear. I'm going to make you guys think I'm okay." But in the back of your mind you're just not done yet.

This is especially true when an addict is young.

Maybe at mid-thirties or forty or so, the need for help becomes more obvious and desperate—that's common among addicts—but it's very, very hard for someone at a young age to hit bottom.

It's easier when you're older, after years of abuse, years of devastation, years of tragedy every single day caused by drugs and alcohol, and then to realize, "Wow, this is really going on in my life. And yeah, I can't beat it on my own—I do need some help." And then take it seriously and turn your life around.

People who are twenty, they haven't had enough yet.

They haven't had enough of a bottom.

They haven't partied enough.

At that age, no one is going to tell them what to do.

"I'm not going to let someone tell me I need to stop—I'll tell you when I need to stop."

It's rare for the young ones to come to their senses and obtain permanent sobriety at an early age. It's so unfortunate, but it usually takes years to hit that bottom.

And that makes it even more of a hell to see them cross that line at age thirteen, fourteen, fifteen. Then it takes them twenty years to understand that this lifestyle isn't working.

And they can never get back those wasted years.

Maybe this answers yet another question that has hung over every part of Mark and Chris McMillen's lives and actions.

They were the Kings of the Beach—young, good-looking, talented kings.

And kings have egos.

And a strong ego is going to reaffirm the "I'm not going to let someone tell me I need to stop—*I'll* tell you when I need to stop" attitude.

I'm just not done yet…

AT THE END OF HIS REPORT, Terry Devitt throws in a personal note to Karl and Thelma:

> You two are among the finest people I've ever known, and your love and strength in dealing with all of these problems is an inspiration to me and to others.

Terry Devitt had no idea as to the power of his prophesy.

Chapter 12

Locking the Door
on the Sand Castle

December 1976

Chris is in jail.

Again.

He is due to be released February 2, 1977. He has spent nineteen of the last thirty-one months in confinement.

Terry Devitt's report goals have not exactly been playing out. Particularly for Karl and Thelma, the part about *"Removing from your lives the constant strain and tension that has now been present for more than half a decade."*

The 1960s were hazy history and the backside of the seventies was speed-spiraling to an end. Time was flying, and flying high. The sickening progression in the *regression* of Mark and Chris was moving so quickly. "Strain and tension" had easily jumped the "half a decade" point, and those gaping realities joined in with the parade of daily downers.

Mark was free and back in business in Hawaii.

Both McMillen brothers were now more than full adults in the eyes of the law, and the juvenile records that had grown and grown but had eventually been sealed gave way to the indelible, forever brands that could rise into the "three strikes" strata that California lawmakers were getting close to enacting.

Twenty-five to life…

Chris had been arrested twice in 1976. In January, he was caught driving under the influence of drugs; in April he was apprehended during a burglary.

Right there in Hermosa Beach.

His sentence for the break-in was 270 days in jail with thirty-six months probation.

During the Christmas season, Karl was, as always, thinking about his sons.

December 30, 1976

Dear Chris:

Well, son, you are getting close to your release date...we are making plans even though we are not sure you want us to or if you appreciate the help we can give...Son, you are now at a major cross road of life as you are now an adult in early manhood. All your mother and I can do is present the problems and seek solutions as we see them... Through the years, Chris, we have given you a free hand (i.e., Pacific Shores, Hawaii, work at the shop when you wished to). Now we are going to lay it out. We hope and pray for a productive and happy life for both you and your brother, sons which we can speak of with pride.

Dad

PART OF THE "SOLUTIONS" that Karl described was to make plans to lock the doors at 2100 The Strand and move south to Orange County, into the exclusive Dana Point/San Clemente coastal area.

The McMillens could be looking at the same Pacific Ocean, but they would finally be out of the drug contagion that infected Hermosa Beach.

Karl and Thelma's "plans and help" didn't include Chris moving back in with them after his latest release, but it did open their new door for visits and stays. However, those visits and stays would not be in a home surrounded by Chris's old friends and associates.

You can run…

Meanwhile, some things *could* be hidden. Unknown to Karl and Thelma, Mark was firmly the drug *kalani* on Maui. He and Preacher ruled the island with a *kekoa* spirit.

Their business was successful.

So was Karl and Ralph's.

Todd Pipe opened its second huge branch, this time expanding its wares and reputation north to Buellton, into the beauty of California's central coast. With more business responsibilities, the twelve-hour work days didn't let up much for Karl.

Neither did the unwinding with cocktails. The partying of The Strand may have become part of the collateral past, but the drinking had not.

For Karl *nor* Thelma.

EARLY 1978

Chris has been released from prison, and everyone's time is spent weighing the latest series of wishful, future-altering options and alternatives. Maybe, just maybe, things will finally turn around, and Karl and Thelma's hopes for a "productive and happy life" for Chris will come true.

This time.

And part of that *might* be a nice trip to Hawaii for him to see his brother.

On March 1st, Chris boards Continental Airlines Flight 603, bound for Honolulu.

The DC-10 never makes it beyond the runway.

DC-10 Crash Kills Two at LAX

A Continental DC-10 on its way to Honolulu with 197 passengers and crew crashed on takeoff Wednesday killing two passengers and injuring at least 40 others, five of those critically.

These were the first fatalities at the LAX proper in its 50-year history.

Two tires blew out, collapsing the landing gear and causing the plane to skid off the runway, tip over, break the right wing and catch on fire.

The entire left side of the plane was burned.

The 9:25 a.m. crash occurred on the east end of the north runway, near Sepulveda Boulevard in Westchester.

The burned and blackened hulk was removed within hours to the runway's "threshold" where officials of the Federal Aviation Administration immediately began to go through the wreck, looking for the tragedy's cause.

An earlier report from the FAA said there had been voice communication with the pilot, Captain Gene Hershey, who decided to abort the takeoff.

Hershey was on his final flight before retiring after 37 accident-free years.

"He did a beautiful job," said one LAX official of Hershey.

"He has nothing to be ashamed of. He saved a lot of lives."

—*Culver City Tribune,* March 3, 1978
Karen Davis, Staff Writer

Chris was fortunate to be among the shaken-and-singed but essentially unscathed. For his pain and suffering, he received a settlement that allowed him to buy a brand new Chevy El Camino.

His life had been spared, and he had cool fresh wheels. Things were certainly looking up.

AUGUST 14, 1978

Chris is back in court. This time he's before a Torrance, California, judge on yet another aspect of the 1976 burglary charge.

It does not go well.

NOVEMBER 28, 1978

Chris is received into the California Department of Corrections facility at Chino, where he will be housed until well into 1980.

A lot happens to an inmate in prison.

And a lot happens to those outside.

Karl and Thelma McMillen had to again add visiting hours to their busy agendas.

Around that same time in 1978, Thelma left her participation at the Free Clinic and took up volunteering at the South Bay Hospital in Redondo Beach, a place of particular interest to Thelma because of its Alcohol and Drug Abuse wing and programs.

Meantime, Karl was involved in perhaps the most far-reaching business decision of his life. As 1979 arrived, Karl and Ralph Todd decided to amicably split their partnership. Karl would take over Hawthorne, and Ralph would keep the pastoral business site in Buellton.

Just as when Karl and Ralph came together back in the late sixties, Dr. Trefftzs was there to advise on this new entrepreneurial era for them both.

The business-money end of the spilt was complicated, with trusts and percentages and many numbers.

But there were subjective considerations too.

Karl stressed to Dr. Trefftzs that Ralph would be up in splendor-surrounded Buellton with clean air and a beautiful landscape while Karl remained down here with all the smog and congestion. Wasn't that worth something in the negotiations?

The good professor, however, didn't lose any sleep over Karl's hardship. No moaning violins were heard lamenting in the background.

"No matter where you are," he told Karl, "neither you nor Ralph is ever going to miss lunch!"

Trefftzs had a way of putting things in perspective.

Ralph was comfortable with settling into the hilly harmony of Buellton; Karl had an itch to expand. And that's just what each would do.

Karl McMillen's Todd Pipe & Supply would grow and grow. A giant new installation in Garden Grove, California, was the first branch to augment Hawthorne.

Ralph Todd (right) and Karl have remained personally close, long since the divvying up of their business bounty.

But inside of Chino, a *life* expansion was occurring: an expansion of Chris into a veteran prisoner. This was a longer stint inside for him than "taking a nap," as inmates refer to short sentences and stays.

This was an education. And hard time behind bars has a hyperacute introspective learning curve. Being in and out of *botes* becomes an all-expressive way of life.

This was now fully a part of Chris and who he was.

The tattoos took form. Karl hated them—the all-black easily recognizable prison ink.

Then came the bulking up.

Chris always had an athletic body. But now, with the tattoos and Chris's prison-yard pumping, the athleticism took on the heaviness of intimidation.

That, too, became a part of who he was.

Chris would claw his way through the predatory landscape of the GP—the general population—where emotions snap like bullwhips and "anger management" means *winning.*

Rule Number One: Never Show Weakness.

Tattoos and prison-yard pumping equipped Chris (left) for life in the GP.

Throughout his twenty-two years, through all of the horrors and ups and downs, no one ever denied that Chris McMillen was basically the nicest guy in the world. A guy who would do anything to help a friend—or even a stranger. But that trait doesn't score a lot of street-cred in the joint. And it's never part of a prison poker game.

Chris wins and the loser refuses to pay.

Decision time.

Never Show Weakness…

Chris *had* to pummel the guy; he *had* to take him apart. Otherwise it would have been *him.*

Chris's jungle was now rivaling Mark's.

And the drug trafficking in both wildernesses was equally active. Drugs "inside" are never difficult to get.

Especially at Chino. It's a prison with a long shady legacy and history.

> In the decades since it opened, poor management, indifference and neglect have transformed CIM [Chino Institute for Men] from a low-security sanctuary into one of the deadliest places in the state...

—From "Years of Indifference Turned Chino Prison Dream into Nightmare" by Mason Stockstill, *Inland Valley Daily Bulletin,* 2006

The article goes on to describe the violence, the drugs, and the guard corruption at Chino.

But Chris manages to create a couple of silver linings among the gray of the bars.

Before Chino, on one of his visits with Mark in Hawaii, Chris had met Sally Turpin. Their relationship grew, even with Chris in lockdown.

APRIL 29, 1979

Karl and Thelma spend a beautiful spring Sunday attending the wedding of their youngest son.

Chris Alan McMillen and Sally Jane Turpin.

Married.

In the Chino Institute for Men.

The prison *somehow* lacked a wedding chapel, so the ceremony was conducted by a local clergyman in the warden's office.

The whole thing was conducted in conjunction with the "basket lunch" visitors are allowed with a prisoner—the big decision being whether to hold the wedding before or after the lunch.

The toast had to be done, of course, with Coca-Cola.

It wasn't quite the high-dollar, fun-social nuptials that Karl and Thelma had envisioned for their youngest son. Still, they thought this might be a step in the right direction.

Optimism.

A hope that never dies. That glass-half-full outlook reaching all the way back to that Christmas at Wayside—*Isn't it great to have both our sons together, side-by-side...*

More high-stepping hopefulness like that followed.

Sally began work in the office at Todd Pipe.

On March 20, 1980, CIM celebrated the "R" Class Graduation from the Commercial Diver Training Program. Chris was included in that proud group.

The McMillen family felt proud and hopeful when Chris (standing, fourth from right) graduated from the Diver Training Program at Chino. *Maybe, just maybe...*

With a new wife and a viable skill in his let's-change-this-life arsenal, Chris's latest release date looked to be more than just another recess between incarcerations.

When the warden's signature hit his exit papers later in 1980, Chris and Sally headed for Louisiana. That's where the work for commercial divers was.

You could almost hear the front porch Creole jazz playing as they rolled in and settled into Morgan City.

Eighty-seven miles from New Orleans, Morgan City is the home of the long-running Louisiana Shrimp & Petroleum Festival. The city achieved a slightly dirty degree of note when it was featured in the movie *Easy Rider.* And Kris Kristofferson wrote "Me and Bobby McGee" when *he* worked in bayou country, flying helicopters for Morgan City's Petroleum Helicopters, Inc.

It's quite the place.

On December 12, 1980, a baby boy was added to the population of the town. Chris and Sally's new son, Ty, would complement a new job and career, 1,844 miles away from Hermosa Beach, where Karl and Thelma had now shut the door to 2100 The Strand for the last time.

Maybe, just maybe, things will finally turn around…

CHAPTER 13

What Kind of Enemy Is This?

EARLY 1981

For all of Morgan City's quaintness and history, and its proximity to the "Big Easy," the town wasn't quite in the same *Better Homes & Gardens* class with Hermosa and San Clemente.

Chris, Sally, and their son Ty's home was a seventy-dollar-a-month rented trailer.

Chris was working for Oceaneering International, a well-known gulf oilfield and deepwater provider.

Things were okay.

Karl and Thelma came to visit.

Among the things *not* okay were the rotted-out floor in the bathroom and the creaky floor throughout.

Karl wasn't happy.

He wasn't happy with the toilet that was about to completely fall through that rotten floor, either. *That* little necessity was replaced right away.

It was another example of Karl's if-there's-a-problem-we-need-to-fix-it mindset.

And the analysis of the trailer had just begun.

Karl concluded that the entire "mobile home" was a disaster and a firetrap—with or without that teetering toilet.

Falling back onto his ability, and enjoyment, of dealing in real estate, Karl decided that this trailer wasn't going to work for his son's family—definitely not for Karl's innocent grandson—and that he would do something about it.

Karl assessed Morgan City and its surroundings. He found the Bayview area and laid down 70K for a house right on a lagoon. Now, one of those "Pelican State" lagoon-looks doesn't exactly translate into a Pacific Ocean–Hermosa Beach panorama. Really, a lagoon is a bayou; and a bayou is really a marsh. Marshes have alligators so you don't swim in them, and a lot of them are contaminated, mosquito-mobbed, and smell. But...all of that is *still* better than another run-of-the-swamp tract house, for making money.

This close-to-nature, not-so-bad, quasi-desirable investment was an improvement, at least, to throwing rent money into a rundown flammable trailer.

But Karl *did* want Chris and Sally to be responsible; to rely on their own self-sufficiency. So he took fatherly license and didn't tell them the house was free and clear. He wanted them to think they were paying on a cold, legally-binding mortgage, as opposed to "paying back Dad."

He didn't want to be the enabler anymore.

He was *trying* to heed Devitt's advice from that report four years earlier.

With the ownership of the house cloaked and clouded, Karl set up a secret account at the bank for the monthlies to be paid into.

It was another plan that was going okay.

Until the payments began to be late.

Chris came into the bank to plead for more time.

"No problem," Chris was told. "The money is just going back into your dad's account, anyway. There's really no due date."

What?!

The "Loosianna" swamp cat was out of the bag. The enabling was back out in the open, again.

And marsh-muck deepened.

Rent checks began to bounce regularly—regardless of where they were going.

There was a reason.

Chris's tenure with Oceaneering International had been going well. He'd been working as a third-class diver with a next step of becoming first-class and then a supervisor.

But drinking and taking pills don't mix well with a high-risk job like underwater welding.

And it's hard to disguise "recreation" like that in an industry like that.

He was fired.

And for Sally, it was too much.

She wanted to take her son and split.

It was hard not to reflect on more of Terry Devitt's words from back in '76 as Karl drove his new Cadillac down to Louisiana to fetch his grandson and daughter-in-law, while Chris, once again, tried to cope and come to grips:

> ...the boys will fail or succeed entirely upon their own.
> It is the only way, the only fair way.

> —Terry Devitt,
> *Final Report and Recommendations,* June 1976

Devitt included that word "entirely" in there for a purpose; his report outlined no caveats concerning hush-hush secrets with a bank.

LATE 1981

As gently as he could, Karl clamped a roof-rack to the top of the Caddy. But the rack, as well as the entire rest of the car, was not-so-gently loaded to the breaking point with Ty and Sally's belongings. Even with all its big-block power, the car was struggling.

It was a Cadillac, yes; a Peterbilt, no!

But the drive-train torture didn't last long. They weren't far west when Sally started crying. She broke down before the roof-rack did.

"I can't do this!" she sobbed.

The Cadillac made a U-turn, and Sally and Ty went back to Chris.

They unloaded the big car, Karl rolled the Caddy back on the westbound I-10, and everyone wondered, *What's going on now?*

What was going on was what had been going on along the entire of the McMillen family branches for what seemed like forever—drugs.

Prison, a wife, a baby, a career, more last chances, more money, more help, more love, more of everything had zero power against them.

What kind of enemy is this?

This isn't a Trojan Horse that slips quietly inside; this is a white-hot foe that burns into you, *becomes* you, and then forces you into the torment of battling *yourself*!

Chris's battle escalated. Pacing and sweating and clawing weren't solving anything. And there was no money and no drugs.

But there *was* pain—such pain.

And there was a pharmacy nearby. And it had drugs.

After business hours, Chris decided to enter from the roof. He was two stories up and just dropping in when the cops arrived. It was the same old choice as back in juvie: get caught or run for it. But running for it here—a daring escape from a rooftop—was more movie script than reality. But no. *This was reality!*

Chris's reality.

He had always been an athlete.

Two stories down.

Jump!

But this wasn't the movies. And Chris wasn't twelve years old in Karl's shop, scooting along shelf edges on that four-by-eight piece of plywood.

Soft landings were no longer a part of these once-charmed lives…

Chris's leg shattered.

Shattered.

Like the burning hulk of flight 603 on the LAX runway back in '78, this was *not* going to be fixed. Like the tattoos, the arrest records, and the torching of so many social and family bridges, this was permanent.

It was rough insult to real injury as the legal proceedings began.

For starters, Louisiana isn't a good place to be if you have to go to prison. California may have Chino, but down where the Confederate flag still flies, they have Angola, the Louisiana State Prison.

The Alcatraz of the South.

The Farm.

The prison has its own cemetery right on the grounds, for those unfortunate inmates who might happen to suffer "back-door parole."

Angola is bedlam with conditions that even the American Bar Association has described as "medieval, squalid, and horrifying."

If Karl didn't want Chris sitting on a swaying toilet in a rented trailer, he damn sure didn't want him in LSP.

It is they who must make decisions and it is they who will live with the consequences of those decisions.

—Terry Devitt,
Final Report and Recommendations, June 1976

The money and the machine is set into motion.

Chris's bail is ten grand.

Karl writes a check.

Now, get him the hell out of there. Get that leg looked at by a real doctor. Fix this.

Chris is flown to California.

Karl calls the bondsman back in Louisiana with a proposition. He's more than aware that across the country there's U.S. law, there's Texas law, there's French law in Louisiana, and a lot more twists and turns and *opportunities* as you get to know a particular territory.

Karl offers to add, oh, say, another ten grand to the bail payment.

The bondsman tells him that the judge assigned to Chris's case is not like most Louisiana judges. This guy isn't going to go for that.

Okay.

Neither are we.

To hell with the bail money, Chris is here and we're going to fix that leg.

Sally is from Hawaii and wants to go back. With Ty. Mark is over there, too. So Chris and family are flown to the islands. He can have a decent operation on that leg over there.

He does.

But the island humidity isn't kind to infection. The leg worsens.

Back to California for Chris.

Sally and Ty stay in Hawaii. Karl buys them a house there—to be comfortable.

But Chris is *not* comfortable.

He is about to lose his leg.

More doctors.

More money.

The leg is saved.

But here come the marshals from Louisiana; jumping bail is never an endorsed exercise.

They see Chris. They see his leg. They see the medical bill potential. They take pictures. They make phone calls.

You can keep him, Mr. McMillen. Louisiana doesn't need this.

Chris is home.

Mark is not.

CHAPTER 14

Were His Therapist, Attorney, and Public Defender People We Could Count On?

MAUI, 1982

A Pan-Am jet touches down in Honolulu. A couple of just-faces-in-the-crowd tourists make their small-plane connection to Maui. They have their luggage; they have their surfboards. And they have something else.

Drugs.

In the security-slack days of the eighties, the stuff would slip into the islands in suitcases rolling down baggage claims, in the passenger holds of cruise ships, and in many other inventive ways.

Not to mention the lush, home-grown varieties.

From all those clever supply sources came the dealing for the demand. That's just the way this process works.

The way this process also works is that nothing is ever simple and smooth. If it's not dark and dangerous, then we must be in the wrong place. Drugs are not a clean commodity at any level. If you're not looking over your shoulder, then you're not doing your job.

Success comes down to who is looking over their shoulder with the sharpest eyes. And what they're ready to do if something back there isn't going quite right.

The "tourists" head for their final destination: a meeting with the island's dominant dealers.

Mark and Preacher.

As that pair heads to the rendezvous point, their mood is all-business.

They have a straight-forward negotiation strategy—one that leans more toward strength than shrewdness. Take the drugs, don't buy them. Beat the hell out of the sellers and warn them never return to *our* island.

Done.

A successful acquisition.

Business as usual.

Until one day Preacher finds Mark passed out—catatonically loaded on their wares.

You can't argue with a drug, you can't reason with a drug, and you damn sure should never become vulnerable in front of it.

Exposure like that isn't healthy.

Preacher steals Mark's stash.

It isn't a smart move.

Mark gets it back—and more. But the partnership perseveres. A booming business like theirs was too lucrative to throw away over a *disagreement*.

But damage was done—in more than one way.

For Mark, the business of drugs was giving way to how the substance affected him personally. Through it all, Mark had never been the "chipper" that Chris was. Mark's using was like his business dealings—all in. And now it was doing *him* in.

The older McMillen's new distrust of Preacher certainly weakened their partnership, and heroin was weakening Mark—both to the point of a quicksand struggle. Something to grab onto was needed, fast.

Mark found his lifeline in Renee.

But Renee wasn't without a little *'ope 'ope* baggage of her own.

Mark and Renee had met on the mainland, and Renee still had some *hemo* ends to tie up. Like wanting to take—literally *take*—her two kids, Cai and Chaz, from their home and their drug-using father in San Luis Obispo.

Karl was good at loose-end tying, so he was enlisted to help.

Karl, Thelma, Renee, and Renee's father beat a stealthy path for the Central Coast.

Renee's father handled the physical end of the operation. The posse snatched the children and headed south. But on the way out of town, they stopped at the police station to "explain" what they had done. They had just saved these kids from a bad situation; they didn't need an angry tail on them heading back to L.A.

Karl put Renee, Cai, and Chaz on a plane to Hawaii—and to Mark.

E hoomau maua kealoha.

In the early part of '82, Mark and Renee were married. The couple, along with the kids, were looking at a new life, individually and together.

Renee had fought substance abuse problems of her own—maybe Mark would be *her* lifeline as well.

Maybe, just maybe, things will finally turn around…

ACROSS THE LINE FROM MAUI TO HAWTHORNE, Karl's Todd Pipe is only about a year away from its major expansion into Orange County; this looks to be the time of renewal and upside, all the way around, for the McMillen family.

Karl cashes in on another of his in-the-know investments. Some stock he owns has developed into a bonus-bounty, enough to fund Todd's new Garden Grove facility.

Again, Todd and Karl are on the move. New California locations in Sepulveda, El Monte, and beyond are planned.

The company branches are growing and the family tree branches seem to be thickening as well. The thread-thin line to Mark is getting stronger. Thelma's visits are producing optimism and brightness beyond Maui's high mid-Pacific sun.

With Renee's help, Mark is trying to pull himself up and out of the drug mire. At twenty-eight years of age, he looks to this first and only marriage as something he can get *all in* to.

Maybe, just maybe…

Mark's marriage to Renee might be just the spark to turn things around.

But there are prices to pay for the past. Another "I'm sorry" isn't going to dredge away the quicksand this time.

But Karl and Thelma can help.

They always do.

Mark and Preacher and their lifestyle of bare knuckles and power has left its scars.

Legal *issues* are pending. Traps are poised to spring. Drug charges on Maui and a gun possession charge on the Big Island are wrapped around Mark's ankles in that quicksand.

And then there's that blood-thirsty craving in Mark's veins, in his head, and in his soul. That isn't helping his escape.

As 1982 ROLLS INTO '83, the optimism for a new warm sun of peace and renewal has cooled considerably, hardening in icy chaos.

Regardless of all the high hopes, just too much is happening right now. Too much all at once. Too many repercussions from the past. This last stage of drug-decimated lives—this stage of damage control—is, in so many ways, the worst for family and friends.

That first stage—the discovery phase—is a quick kick-in-the-groin shock.

The second stage—that action stage, when those you love become unrecognizable people doing unrecognizable things—is like dizzy wandering through blasts of a strobe light. Events happen rapidly and in flashes.

But here in damage control, the pain and torture is so lingering and all-encompassing. It's the difference between being shot between the eyes and being staked out in a pit of fire ants to be eaten slowly. It's not quick, and there are no flashes. The strobes have stopped and the light has risen to a low gray; just dim-bright enough to see your loved ones dragging themselves back into those gnawing processes of "rehab, promises, tears, repentance, and maybe even death."

This is where life has progressed to for the McMillen family.

Chris has returned to California from Hawaii after his latest leg operation. Of course, one of the addiction-searing side effects of each operation and treatment on Chris's leg is the medication—the pain pills. It's hard to quell cravings when they're being legally fed and sustained by the black magic in those little orange plastic bottles.

The fire ants are crawling...

Mark, however, seems to be doing well with Renee and his challenges and changes in Hawaii. But Karl and Thelma need some reassurance. Maybe some of those ants can be crushed before they begin their march.

SEPTEMBER 1983

Terry Devitt is enlisted for yet another report. And again he begins with some goals:

> When I left for Hawaii two weeks ago, I went with several purposes in mind. I wanted to know how Mark was really doing. Was he happy with the family? Was he working and attending school? Had he given up the drugs that caused us all so much grief? What was his legal situation in Maui? In Kona? Were his therapist, attorney, and public defender people we could count on? Most importantly, had Mark begun to become the person we all know he can be?

Those were good questions. And like Devitt's first report, they are telling.

The last line especially is the marquee banner for those with loved ones who are drug addicts. It's the up-in-bright-lights ever-hopeful shout about their potential.

They just aren't who they are under the spell of those drugs.

But those drugs are who *they* are, and the spell they cast is like nine-inch nails through your arms and hands, pinning you to a tree. You're in agony, locked in, and bloodied. It's that spell that makes official people like "therapists, attorneys, and public defenders" a part of the normal traffic in and out of your life.

Regardless of your potential.

Mark's potential ranked far behind Karl and Thelma's resolve and resources when it came to the "rehab and promises" part of this phase.

Karl and Thelma were ready for Devitt's report, and they were ready to go to work.

By now, Mark and Renee and the kids were living in Hilo on the Big Island:

> I arrived in Hilo on Friday and was met at the airport by Mark and Renee. We spent the first day shopping for groceries and having a really nice family dinner at their house. It was a home. It was a family.

Devitt went on to break down his observations of Mark and his playing-it-straight rebirth into "Personal," "Family," and "Finances" categories. The first two were chock full of the "reassurances" that Karl and Thelma needed:

> Mark looked well, clear-eyed and energetic...much like his old self...Not once in that week did he raise his voice or cause a scene...The kids call him "Dad"...He and Renee have a good thing going and they're both proud of how well the kids are doing...There is no doubt in my mind that the family has made the difference in Mark...

The "Finances" category, however, lamented Mark's lack of money. His "business" was no more, and Karl had cut off any aid. For now.

But Devitt had a few suggestions. And apparently he'd softened somewhat since his last report:

> I think it is very important that financial pressures
> not be added to those Mark already has. They need a little
> help from time to time and I think it's an excellent
> investment. Mark and I also had a long discussion of
> his trust funds...He even knows now and cares about the
> opportunities that await him.

"Await" was a key word. The "opportunities" wouldn't kick in until some debts and obligations had been paid.

Another section of the report described Renee as "a good mother and wife" and Devitt noted warmly that "it is the love Mark and Renee have for one another that has made possible the wonderful growth I've seen in Mark."

But the meeting of those legal obligations was a looming kiawe thorn aimed at everyone's side:

> One of my greatest concerns is how Mark and Renee will
> be able to cope with the separation that seems inevitable, at
> least for some months. Renee is concerned she will fall apart.

The concerns were legitimate. Two matters were outstanding and both were serious. Mark's lack of fluid finances had forced him to use a public defender, and Devitt's description of the man tempered any optimism for success in the cases:

> This public defender is like most I've met—young,
> overworked, and a little cynical. He and Mark had not hit it
> off well...

Devitt did not have a particularly sunny outlook about the nuts and bolts of the crimes, either:

They have the goods on Mark and all we can do is hope for some mercy on the part of Judge DiSilva, a man not known for kindness...We have to be ready to accept some very bad news.

Terry Devitt and Karl went to work to do whatever it would take to ease the outcome of that "very bad news."

They petitioned to get all of Mark's time, for both cases, served in Hilo. At least he would be close to home and Renee.

They worked on getting any sentences to be served concurrently.

Even a work/education furlough while doing his time was a possibility. Mark would "sleep at citizens' expense" in that scenario, according to Devitt.

Still, the stark possibility loomed of a full sentence of five years in the state penitentiary.

Hawaii may be paradise outside; but inside an island prison, tribe mentality takes over. Ethnic animosity and racial polarization are sometimes worse than in mainland institutions. The bloom definitely goes off of the white kukui blossoms when that iron-barred cell door is shut.

Devitt recommended a therapist for both Mark and Renee, to help them now and to prepare them for the possibilities in the future. He also endorsed hiring an outside attorney—not to completely take over Mark's cases, but to work with the public defender.

So Karl added two more professionals to the Hawaiian payroll. But Devitt did not recommend that they have free reign—especially with Karl's resources:

The professionals out here seem to like Mark but we and his family care about Mark. I'm willing to listen to them but I think it's time to listen to our own feelings

and instincts. My feeling is that [the attorney and the
therapist] are way too optimistic and don't mind spending
your money. I'm willing to do anything to help Mark and
I know you are too but I don't think throwing away money
does anyone except lawyers and doctors any good. I mean to
keep an eye on those boys.

Devitt then took a hop over to Maui, meeting with Mark's parole
officer involved in his cases there. She was on board with all that
Terry and Karl were proposing, and she did what she could to make
it all happen.

One final portion of Terry Devitt's study pulled the long branches
in the McMillen family tree a little tighter, and it threw a touching
lasso around Mark and Chris's core of carers.

After leaving Maui and Mark's parole officer, Devitt went back to
the Kona side of the Big Island to see Chris's wife and son.

Sally and Ty had been in Hawaii since the failed attempt at a
new life for all in Louisiana. But they were still a part of this ever-
expanding "family" of people and responsibilities in the Aloha State
that were direct and indirect dependents of Karl.

Mark.

Renee.

Renee's two children.

Sally.

Ty.

Mark's lawyer.

Mark's psychotherapist.

Pending criminal charges.

Children to raise.

Bills to pay.

Mounting obligations and complexity.

All of which went right back to the sour source of drug abuse.

Hawaii was a busy place for Karl and Thelma; and a place generating much concern.

Sally, however, caring for Ty in the island house that Karl had bought for them, was a part of Devitt's overall optimism:

> I asked Sally bluntly if there was anything she needed.
> I asked the same question of Mark and Renee. All of them
> said, No, Thelma and Karl have already done too much. I
> told them all that I was over here to see how the family was
> doing—the whole family. I told them that I would tell you
> both what I saw and if they needed something I'd pass that
> along. Naturally, I told them that I would give my honest
> opinion if I thought for a minute they were looking for a
> free lunch. They're not.

But...

> As I mentioned earlier, Mark and Renee need some help
> with bucks.
> Sally would like to send Ty to preschool. It's
> reasonable (all day for $135.00 per month). It would give
> Sally a little space and be of benefit to the kid...We can
> talk about this too when we sit down. Naturally, if that
> school move looked good, you could pay the school directly.
> Why take chances?

CHAPTER 15

Thoroughbreds in the Mud

LATE 1983

The machine kicks in.

Mark is *not* going to jail.

The barrage of letters begins.

Mark's psychotherapist implores the attorney to become even stronger in his legal attempts at reducing Mark's penalties:

September 15, 1983

[Mark's] relationship with his family is excellent. His openness to psychotherapy is also excellent and this is the first time that he has ever allowed himself to "become a patient" and to seek out help in an honest way. He is presently working laying carpet every day. His work is usually in excess of 8 hours a day and is often up to 10½ hours a day. He is also attending school and in this area has perhaps taken on more than he can handle in the number of credits that he is trying to earn...His wife Renee and the

children appear central to the rehabilitation
process along with the psychotherapy he is
receiving. He is very concerned about his
family...because incarceration would remove
him from these supports and his continued
rehabilitation, I am of the clear opinion that
society would be best served if this man were to
continue to work, continue to go to school, and
to perform whatever number of hours of community
service the court sees fit.

Terry Devitt addresses the probation officer directly:

September 23, 1983

Dear Ms. Mountcastle:

It was in his senior year [of high school]
that Mark first began to exhibit the behavior
that would characterize his life for a decade.
His first arrest was for possession of marijuana.
Then followed a series of arrests for drugs,
burglaries, automobile accidents; resulting in
frequent incarcerations. His crimes were always
drug motivated and, in my opinion, drug induced.
Mark told me some years ago that he couldn't do
any crime if he weren't loaded.

Those years between 1970 and 1980 saw an
incredible deterioration of a once gifted young
man. He, his family, and those of us who cared
about him suffered mightily. Repeated attempts
by all of us to help Mark fell on deaf ears.
His addictions, cynicism, and lack of regard
for anyone but himself led to increasingly
long periods in jail. I saw him in jail several
times in that period and always came away with a

profound sadness. He had not changed. Every time he went in, he came out worse.

Some seven years ago his mother and father asked me to write a report on Mark. My recommendations were simple. I told his parents they should never give him money, bail, legal fees, a place to live, jobs, or any other form of support. I also told them that any attempt they might make on his behalf simply paid for his drugs and perpetuated his criminality.

For the most part, they heeded my advice.

As recently as two years ago, while Mark was in Los Angeles, I told him I never wanted to see or hear from him again. Such was my anger and contempt for him.

It was not until about a year ago that I thought there might be some changes taking place in Mark. I have always been, and continue to be, very close to his parents. They are kind, thoughtful, and loving parents who have suffered in the most cruel and undeserving ways. About a year ago...they commented that Mark seemed to be doing well and attributed it to his marriage to Renee...Still we were all wary, having been conned by Mark on numerous occasions. I called him in Hilo and we began to exchange letters. From our conversations and correspondence, I too, became sure that something positive was happening.

Mark's parents and I talked long and hard about the wisdom of my coming over here to see firsthand how he was doing. Finally, we agreed that such a trip was worthwhile.

Indeed, it has been worthwhile. I know that because I've known him for fourteen years and I think I know him better than anyone else in the world...

Regardless of the disposition of this case,
I shall continue to believe and work for that
day when Mark reaches his full potential. He's
about halfway there now and moving in the right
direction. Given the opportunity, Mark Andrew
McMillen will enrich his community.

Karl and Thelma were right there with Devitt, personally addressing
the probation authorities, showing that "kindness, thoughtfulness, and
love" that Terry had spoken of:

We now see a dramatic change in Mark, a
complete turnaround. He no longer cares about
drugs but cares about himself and his family.
He is going to school and working every day
and doing well in both. He is a kind and loving
husband and father...Needless to say, we are
ecstatic seeing these positive changes taking
place in his life. A possibility we knew was
there. Mark is ashamed of his past life and
openly admits it. This is certainly a very
positive note and one of the first steps to
rehabilitation...
We are hopeful the Judicial System is aware of
these outstanding changes in Mark and will grant
him a work and/or educational furlough in Hilo
allowing him to be near his family.

But other weapons were needed in this battle for Mark's freedom.
The lawyer wasn't working out. He wasn't strong in his approach
and he didn't seem to care. Even Devitt questioned his focus in a
letter to Karl and Thelma:

I am not impressed...He did not plea bargain
this case. He has not made plans for the

> eventuality of Mark's going to jail...He continues
> to tell me, "Well, I have to think positive, I'm
> trying for a suspended sentence." I don't think
> that is remotely likely...The prosecutor will want
> some of Mark's hide and this defense lawyer is
> telling me he's looking for probation.

Karl analyzes the situation; he does some research, and another attorney is brought in. This guy has power and clout—and he will gladly exercise it. For a deposit of seventy grand.

Karl writes a check.

One phone call later, and the charges against Mark are dropped.

And a big part of the deposit is refunded to Karl—after all, how much could one phone call cost?

Mark is now headed to rehab, not jail.

AUGUST 8, 1984

Mark enters into the program at Habilitat, a rehab center on the island of Oahu.

Habilitat was founded in a two-bedroom house in Kailua on the Big Island in 1971, by ex–heroin addict and author Vinny Marino. Like Marino's drug diary of a book, *Journey from Hell*, Habilitat's program is tough and to the point: "We do not subscribe to the notion that addiction is a disease. We teach people that addiction and alcoholism is a choice."

And the program at Habilitat has a vocational-training focus: "We have understood for many years that long-term drug rehabilitation alone is not enough to ensure long-term success. People need marketable skills and work ethics if they are to be competitive in today's workforce. Our vocational training programs are second to none in the substance abuse treatment community. We motivate the unmotivated and often succeed where other programs have failed."

Mark went into the rehab's construction department, studying and working in the landscaping division. The "long-term" part of the program was integral to making this work. Mark, Renee, and the kids would all just have to accept and cope until Mark returned, healthy and reenergized as a husband and a father.

They knew they could all be strong.

Back in California, the "obligations and complexities" faced by the rest of the family weren't quite as optimistic and rosy, but some signs of "motivating the unmotivated" could be seen here as well.

Karl and Thelma returned to the Todd Pipe proximity of the South Bay, selling their home in San Clemente and moving to Hermosa's even more upscale neighbor, Manhattan Beach.

Chris had been arrested again, twice in 1984, for theft, fraud, and receiving stolen property. Thirty more months of probation; thirty more days in jail.

This was getting old.

But maybe, just maybe, things will finally turn around…

Like Mark, Chris now seemed ready to change his life. After this latest round of survival in the general population, maybe, like that wisdom from the street predicted, Chris was finally "done." Maybe he had "partied enough."

Maybe he had finally hit bottom.

APRIL 20, 1985

At twenty-eight years of age, Chris enters the Impact House program in Pasadena, a facility listed in one of Terry Devitt's son-saving studies. Devitt found that Impact House had been treating drug addicts since 1959; with the added bonus of an exclusive in-custody program in partnership with the Los Angeles Sheriff's Department.

For the first time since the three undermining stages of drug addiction began for Mark and Chris, and at the flashpoint of this final stage of damage control, Karl and Thelma McMillen witnessed both of their sons take their first committed leaps into clinical rehab.

Things *were* turning around.

June 13, 1985

Dear Mark,

It has been some time since we have seen you and longer yet since I have written to you.

Your mother and I are very proud of you—going through the program. Your future is definitely on the uptrend. We love you, Mark...I saw Chris's counselor last week at Impact House... Very nice man. Program is probably the best on the mainland—would prefer Habilitat however. Thank you for writing your brother—good to keep a close-knit family.

Mark, always outwork everyone—BE THE BEST!!!

I love you, son.

Both Mark and Chris were under care now. They were being treated. They were at excellent facilities in extensive programs and were on their way to being healed. Karl and Thelma could sleep better than they had in years. The deep heart of the night brought comfort rather than fear. The tortuous ravenous ants were retreating and some of the wounds were closing up. It was finally time for sleep without the wrenching restlessness, like lying under soft thick covers and hearing the rain outside, knowing that everyone from the big lovable collie to the purring cat to the kids were safe, under the warm dry roof and out of harm's way.

For now...

But rehab and all the buzzwords and buzz-realities of disease, choice, motivation, vocation, counseling, skills, ethics, and all the rest are so subjective. They are so dependent upon the raw and real causes of what makes addiction victims keep doing what they do.

And those causes can be many.

Another voice from the street offers an inside look at an addict confronted with rehab. It's a voice that expresses understanding about Vinny Marino and Habilitat's claim that "long-term drug rehabilitation alone is not enough to ensure long-term success." It's a voice that expresses understanding that there's no clear-cut answer as to what exactly *will* ensure that long-term success. Except that it must come from within.

The Addict's Choice

There's no magic pill or magic trick that works for one person or another when it comes down to truly getting rid of addiction.

An addict's parents and loved ones might be enablers or they might go the other way—beating them, drug testing them constantly. Instead of allowing the behavior, as an enabler would, that kind of harshness can result in making the addict feel worthless. That kind of harshness can make the addict feel responsible not only for making himself happy but for making the angry parent happy, too. All while struggling with the drugs.

It puts the addict in a real bad place.

In the end, addicts have to take responsibility for their own actions; it's part of taking responsibility for making the decision to do drugs in the first place. It is the addict who must be ready to decide: "I've got to deal with this; this isn't getting better. And it's never going to get better until I deal with it."

Because that's basically what drug addiction is: You don't want to deal with feelings. You don't want to deal with what you're carrying around. And when you do drugs, it's the one time of the day when you totally forget about everything.

But once the drugs wear off, it's back tenfold; and it gets worse and worse and worse.

Getting sober is a tough decision to make, but once you make it and stick with it, you get some tools and some understanding. That's when it starts getting better: when you're ready to deal with your own issues.

But as long as the addict keeps placing blame on other people and finding excuses, they're never going to get better. They never are.

So many programs—I mean, four days after you're out, you're partying again.

And the pattern can so easily spiral. "I've done this, and I'm ashamed of that, so to alleviate the pain of what I've done I'm getting high." It just keeps building.

Thirteen weeks into the program at Impact House, Chris is kicked out for gambling, a side addiction that seemed to logically follow the drugs. From the prison card games to extending the social ambience of using, Chris loved to gamble.

But gambling was not part of the social ambience accepted at Impact House.

July 31, 1985

Chris McMillen entered the Impact program on April 20, 1985, and was terminated on July 31, 1985, as a disciplinary action.

Upon Chris's admittance into treatment, he adjusted to the structure in a normal time frame. He complied with staff directive on a functional level, but had some difficulty internalizing the program philosophies into his daily living situations. With the counseling efforts given him, Chris began to show progress and was advanced into the second phase of the program...

However, Chris was evaluated...for two separate
incidents. He was dephased in the early part
of the week for breaking a major house rule,
which consisted of gambling during his job
assignment, and he was involved in splitting up
his second phase pass while in the community.
When questioned in regards to the above incident,
Chris lied several different times, in regards to
what exactly happened. It was a management group
decision to terminate client as a disciplinary
action, for the part he played in breaking major
house rules.

It is our opinion that until Chris has a
change of attitude, his chances for recovery
are poor.

Stuart Tooredman,
Clinical Director

At twenty-eight, Chris was not yet in that "mid-thirties or forty" bracket of revelation and aged awareness that the strung-out street people see as a landmark. Was Chris—and everyone else—wrong about his finally being "done"? Had he not *really* hit bottom?

Or maybe those "major house rules" at Impact House were just too much for Chris. Maybe the switch from the down-and-dirty pressure zone of prison to the clean, well-lighted parameters of clinical rehab was the *real* "too much" in this part of the battle. Maybe all of these factors had contributed to this latest sorrow-struck setback.

All these factors plus the rage and fire of that "white-hot" enemy of drugs, of course.

And by now, that enemy had proven itself to transcend time and place. It wasn't just Hermosa and all those homes and windows with the million-dollar views. It wasn't just in Baja and international airports and hotels. It wasn't just in Morgan City's *Easy Rider* scenes. It wasn't just in the hippies-on-the-Hana-Highway with their "Maui-wowie."

This enemy was everywhere. Even the cities of refuge, which were now the sophisticated rehabilitation clinics and programs, couldn't build walls high enough to keep all the invaders out.

About six weeks after Chris's eighty-sixed exit from the Impact program, Karl and Thelma received more official news:

September 19, 1985

Dear Mr. & Mrs. McMillen,

I am writing to formally notify you of the circumstances surrounding your son's departure from Habilitat on September 4, 1985.

Mark entered the program on August 8, 1984, due to his inability to manage his life. During his residency of 1 year, Mark accomplished a few of his goals such as making friends, advancing to the re-entry phase, and reestablishing his relationship with his children.

Mark was receiving his vocational training... where he was learning a viable skill.

Although Mark appeared to show a desire to change his lifestyle, he refused to listen to the direction and suggestions given to him by his peers and the staff. On September 4, 1985, while at work, he left the jobsite without telling anyone.

Hopefully, Mark will come to realize that he cannot continue to run from his problems.

Sincerely,

Danny Katada
Family Director

As with Chris and his situation, the court and the authorities had to be notified.

More obligations.

More complexity.

The machine needed to kick in again.

Mark was not going to jail...

Karl and Thelma addressed yet another probation officer in Hawaii. Mark needed to stay in treatment. He needed to return to Habilitat. He needed to stay out of prison:

October 24, 1985

Dear Ms. Tavaras:

Our son, Mark, has been a resident at Habilitat...for the past fourteen months.

We last visited with Mark at Habilitat the first week of April, 1985. We were overwhelmingly delighted with his progress. Mark readily admitted that the in-depth soul searching therapy applied at Habilitat had allowed him to really see into himself and his problems. We believe that Habilitat is the best program available and without a doubt the most difficult. He showed remarkable signs of positive growth in maturity, morality, and accepting responsibility.

Mark will be 31 in December and is desirous of putting his life in the proper perspective. He would like to do the following:

1. Return to college.
2. Work in our business, Todd Pipe & Supply.
3. Plan for the succession of management in our business.

Mark would also like to reestablish his marriage. He feels his marriage was not given a fair chance due to the problems both he and his wife Renee had. With a clean, clear mind and body on both their parts, a wholesome marriage could be consummated.

We believe that the previous turbulent years of Mark's life are behind him and that he can become a productive and honorable citizen.

We respectfully hope the court will give consideration to these facts.

Karl B. McMillen, Jr.

Thelma B. McMillen

Now what?

What next?

But wait, maybe Mark's and Chris's aborted time in the programs *did* have an effect.

Maybe even with the boys' aversion to the cold and clean parameters of rules, at least some of what Impact and Habilitat had to offer took.

Maybe this was working…

Mark decides he wants to start a legitimate landscaping business. Karl sets him up.

A&A Lawn & Gardening Service
•Yard Maintenance

•Rubbish Disposal

•Gardening Services

•Lot Cleaning

•Reasonable Rates

•Free Estimates

Mark "Andy" McMillen "Owner"

A new truck is sent over from the mainland.

In the short time the business existed, Mark did finish some work.

And he seemed so satisfied. It wasn't a temporary-high-satisfaction; it was an accomplishment-satisfaction.

He would call Thelma when he turned the last shovelful of dirt or laid the final piece of turf to tell her what he had created and achieved.

Mark asked Karl to set him up in a landscaping business.
Maybe this was working...

But the reformed and well-worn drug users are always right there to share their cynical wisdom. Their been-there-done-that voices from the street see right through the island colors in those flowers:

Let's See If They'll Swallow This

That's one of the cons of an addict, to try to work. That's what drug addicts do. But what they really work are their parents and loved ones.

"I'll get better."

"Just send me money."

"Set me up."

That's the normal of any drug addict: "I'll get better if you just give me this chance."

A month later, Mark wrecks the truck by running it into a tree. Again, now what?

FOR KARL AND THELMA, the nights of torture return. Everyone is no longer safe, warm, and dry under protective roofs. The corral gates have been sprung open and the magnificent thoroughbreds are heading for the mud. And even over the sound of the gallop, those words—those terrible words—from the street are screaming along with the wind:

It's very, very hard for someone at a young age to hit bottom... They haven't had enough yet...They haven't had enough of a bottom...At that age, no one is going to tell them what to do.

"I'm not going to let someone tell me I need to stop—I'll tell you when I need to stop."

And they can never get back those wasted years.

Mark tries rehab again—this time at Maui's Aloha House. But Chris...

Three months after leaving the Impact House program, and just four days before Christmas 1985, Chris is once again arrested. Halfway between Hermosa and San Clemente, the Long Beach PD nab him for violating California Vehicle Code number 23512(A): *Driving under the influence of alcohol and/or drugs.*

"Petitioner convicted."

Three more years of probation.

Another Merry Christmas and Happy New Year.

FEBRUARY 2, 1986

Thirty-three days into '86, the sleepless nights are not getting any better.

The phone rings.

Chris has been arrested yet again. Another DUI is added to his record.

The year has not started well, and numbness sets in.

Aloha House is trying to work with Mark; and Mark is still trying to make a go of the gardening business, with or without the wrecked new truck.

Spring becomes summer, but the warmth and the brightness isn't even close to what it once was, at least not for the McMillens. Looking out at the Pacific from Southern California or from the various shores of the islands ceased being an exercise in the appreciation of nature. It was more of a blank stare in '86, just a space-filling backdrop while whoever was doing the looking thought about loved ones or themselves and pondered why all of this happened.

JULY 27, 1986

A peaceful Sunday in summertime So Cal.

Things have been fairly quiet.

Karl and Thelma's phone rings.

It's Renee in Hawaii. Her son, Chaz, has discovered Mark collapsed in the garden of their apartment complex. Overdosed.

Action is needed within the numbness.

Now.

Within hours, Karl and Thelma are on a flight.

The top speed of a Boeing 747 is nearly six hundred miles per hour; still not fast enough for the McMillens. The trip drags on, anchored and weighted down by sick-worry and a final fear.

At the hospital, Karl and Thelma find Mark on life support. Over the next three days, the doctors continue to pump Mark's stomach, remove the toxins, assess the damage, and try to bring him back.

Nothing is working.

And Mark's *real* life support is standing there looking at him.

For thirty-one years, Karl and Thelma have been there with love and comfort. They gave birth to Mark, and Karl gave birth to a life for his sons that should never have included a scene like this.

What was going through Karl and Thelma's minds?

Everything.

Everything that went right and everything that went so wrong.

The last line of Mark's report on that Baja trip when he was twelve…

I had a really fun trip but it was good to get home.

It was the perfect thought to have. That innocent boy enjoying the back roads of Mexico was Mark. The surfing champion was Mark. The best-looking kid on the beach was Mark.

This ravaged young man was *not* Mark.

It can't be.

Where is that sky's-the-limit potential?

Where is our son?

Karl pulls the main doctor aside.
We can't take any more of this...
You need to shut this down.

Mark Andrew McMillen
1954–1986

CHAPTER 16

A General and a Martyr

As the machines of life support were turned off in that hospital, another life support system was starting up.

The enemy that attacked Mark was now more defined. It was time to defeat it.

Expose it.

Uncloak its evil to any and all who might be tempted—or already infected.

Within two years, Renee would also be dead from an overdose.

This has to stop!

Mark's ordeal and his passing would become a weapon and a gift, to and for so many. Terry Devitt's prophesy from back in 1976 about Karl and Thelma utilizing their "love and strength" to be an "inspiration to others" was now truth carved into the enemy.

Karl and Thelma began with Mark's life-insurance money; dirty money they did not want. Instead of burying it in the bank, they used it as the first seeds of battle for the good guys.

$5,000 to Maui Memorial Hospital.

$5,000 to Ty's school, Kahakai Elementary.

$30,000 in scholarship funds for students at Pacific Shores.

$15,000 to the Lokahi Pacific community development organization on Maui.

$5,000 to Aloha House.

$5,000 to the Maui Special Learning Center.

And a memorial wall plaque with each donation:

Mark Andrew McMillen
"Andy"
1954–1986

It was like a battle flag. The army was on the march.

Since the 1960s, the entire concept of rehabilitation centers had evolved. The drug situation that had caught so many off guard was now being recognized for the plague that it is, and that was helping the help. Getting the facts is high-caliber ammunition. The generation that grew up on alcohol rather than drugs was opening its bloodshot eyes.

Everyone was learning.

Looking into the first rehabs—Synanon is a good example—is like looking at photos of early dental tools.

It's painful.

All that crude experimentation may have accomplished *something*—maybe even cured some—but at what price?

Even Habilitat, where Mark spent over a year, has an "interesting" story behind its development, and an equally interesting founder. It was common for the time.

When Vinny Marino started Habilitat, the surrounding community was "uncomfortable" about it. Vinny had to somersault through an obstacle course of bureaucratic harassment and legal hoops to battle their efforts to get him out of the neighborhood.

Marino "had a hard head [and] a big ego," according to his daughter, at his funeral in February of 2000. "He was very controlling, but he had a big heart."

When Mark walked out of Habilitat, the program owed Karl a refund for advance payments towards Mark's unfulfilled treatment.

Karl was paid off in copies of Marino's book.

Closer to home, Thelma's volunteer work at the Free Clinic, the South Bay Hospital, Al-Anon, and at women's centers had given her so much personal insight into the problem.

So had Mark and Chris.

So it was once again time to go to work, but with a magnified mindset.

The objective work began with the donations to the Hawaiian organizations; the subjective work began at Mark's memorial.

Mark was brought back home to Southern California; to the other end of the Pacific. To the other end of the waves that never stop. To the mainland sets where he and his little brother first stood up to the swell. *And* where they both fell to the crush of a force far less imposing but much more deadly than tons and tons of rolling salt water.

He came home to the love of a family that was as perpetual and relentless as that ever-churning ocean.

Chris was on probation between jail stays, so he was able to be at the memorial unencumbered—by legal restraints, at least.

He was, however, encumbered by something else.

At my brother's funeral, I told myself that I would walk thru this sober. Two hours before the service started, I took a drink. And then more. I attended the service, but I was three sheets to the wind.

—Written by Chris McMillen, twenty years later,
during an assignment at rehab

Chris hadn't gone to Hawaii with his parents when Mark overdosed. And he hadn't had a voice in the decision to cut the life support. The reason for his absence is lost among the twists, turns, detours, and secrets of drug abuse. But not participating in the emotional meditations to end Mark's life was added to Chris's deepening dismal reflections of his past. Reflections that stalked Chris's memory like a fast-moving, faster-tempered shark.

The same reflections that stalk his childhood friend, Richie:

The Delusion of Cool

It easily spirals—you do drugs because of what drugs have done to you. As much as you might want to stop and want to get help, you have to face it sometimes that maybe you're just not ready. Maybe God isn't ready for us yet. We have to be pretty mangled before we're ready for help.

I was low bottom.

Chris was low bottom.

Mark, I stayed away from. He was into some seriously bad stuff. Worse than us. I heard one rumor that he'd gone in to rob a house and one of his buddies got hit in the head with an axe, paralyzing half his body. Scary s—t like that. I had known him as a kid and he'd become a different person. He became the drugs. We all do. And you don't want to turn your back on drugs.

But when you're in it, you keep looking back on when it was sexy and attractive. Well, it wasn't so sexy and attractive as we got older. And even the image from back when we were kids was an illusion. The delusion was that we were cool, solid dealers.

It wasn't cool.

At the end of the day, we were nothing more than nickel-and-dime drug addicts and scammers and takers. We annihilated anything that was good. We stole from our parents and friends. We took and took and took.

Down there on the beach in Hermosa, we had it all; we were the best surfers.

Then we all got caught up in the same things, and we ended up doing bad things. We missed the mark.

THERE IS A CUSTOM within the surfing world that when a member of their community dies, all his or her friends hold a "paddle-out."

A paddle-out is like a surfer's version of a funeral. Everyone paddles out beyond the person's favorite local surf break and they arrange themselves in a circle.

Many times leis or flowers are tossed into the middle of the circle. Then each person in the circle says something about the person who has died and a few prayers are said and everyone paddles in and heads to the party, which is a surfer's version of a wake.

In cases where the deceased has been cremated, it is the custom to spread the ashes in the circle as the prayers are said.

—Corky Carroll, surfing pioneer and champion

Some time after the services, Chris, sober or not, led the paddle-out to scatter his brother's ashes off the shore of Hermosa Beach. That great white of reflections and memories was surely right there with him.

Grief-gripped flashbacks were the blood in the water on this day.

This was where the boys' classic photo was taken in 1970 after they placed first and second in the first annual Hermosa Beach Surfers Contest.

This is also where the boys were first pulled into the riptide of drugs.

But Chris did what he had to do on this day—what he wanted to do—in the face of that monster's biting and thrashing.

He completed the circle for Mark.

No kau a kau, kaikua'ana...

For eternity, my brother.

MARK'S MAINLAND SERVICES were a memorial, certainly, but they were also a rallying cry against the enemy. Local newspapers published the eulogies:

> We all recognize that drug use in the South Bay is rampant and, perhaps, the publication of the eulogy might dissuade some young person from following the inevitable, tragic path our boy took.
>
> —*Karl McMillen*

> At 15, Mark could have been on the cover of *Newsweek* magazine. He was the epitome of the Southern California surfer: tan, lean and good looking...Few kids had as solid a foundation upon which to grow. Few kids had the vast potential and great promise that Mark had. He literally could have been anything he wanted...So, what happened? Why are we here today? In a word: drugs. Drugs ruined and eventually ended Mark's life. Drugs stole his promise and devastated his family. Then wrecked his character and destroyed his self-esteem.
>
> Mark is not the first young man to lose his life to drugs, nor, sadly, will he be the last... there is an epidemic in this society. Those of us here today cannot end drug abuse but we can make a difference. Mark's family asks that each of you, in your own way, in your own families, help fight this terrible scourge. If we could save but one

person, it would give added meaning and purpose to Mark's life. That would be the most fitting memorial imaginable.

—*Terry Devitt, teacher*

It was not a choice of your own, but an unguarded moment in time when drugs and this disease of addiction caught you...you will always be a message and reminder of how deadly this disease of addiction really is. The pain and despair we all feel will be a strong force in our quest for a better way of life.

—*Richard* [Richie Davidson]

The message was exploding. This war was more than a tearful, desperate threat—it was real.

The enemy was on people's radar; addiction was indeed being thought about. No longer were heads buried in the beach sand—although there *were* differing strategies. And viewpoints:

Mark was responsible for what he did. For what he did to himself, for which he paid his dues; and for what he did to his family, which will pay their dues for his actions for the rest of their poignantly scarred lives...The sooner we understand and clearly state that each of us is responsible for what we do and somewhat willingly accept the consequences of our actions, the sooner will we become self-reliant and self-respecting... and the sooner we stop lying to folks about who is responsible for what we do, the sooner will our society start to mend itself.

—*Dave, Manhattan Beach*
[in response to Richie's eulogy]

The "responsibility" question may be up for debate; but the mounting collective fight against drugs is not. A general and a martyr came to life with the death of Mark McMillen. Empowered by the spirit of Mark and what he had endured, Karl began leading a very passionate charge. Karl could and would help so many.

But was it already too late to help Chris?

OCTOBER 1986

Todd Pipe & Supply opens its newest branch in the San Fernando Valley town of Sepulveda (later renamed North Hills).

Business is booming…

Still.

Todd would now not only serve its customers, but its profits would join Mark's insurance money, his spirit, and Karl's leadership abilities in an all-out assault on drug use and other attacks on the good in life.

Karl was the ideal commander in chief for this. His perfectionist bent is a trait that has always been lovingly recognized and embraced by those closest to him: *You cook something; he's going to re-cook it. If you sweep the floor, he's going to re-sweep it. That's the way he is. It's got to be perfect in his mind. That's why he's successful.*

That perfection translated into a reaffirmation of Karl's belief in formal rehabs. Even though Mark's forays into organized recovery were ultimately unsuccessful, the structured order of the increasing number of facilities was what Karl was most comfortable with. Their technology and skill levels were improving all the time.

They would improve even more, and more quickly, with Karl's help.

And he was ready to give it.

But along with the energy-push for a war against this now-murderous narco-enemy came the aftermath asides of Mark's death.

The letdown.

The introspection.

Karl's and Thelma's increased drinking.

And Chris's new position as the only son. It was a position with a lot of spotlight and exposure; but that of neither a general nor a martyr.

CHAPTER 17

"I Hope You're Not Still Upset About the Guns, Credit Cards, or the Three Grand I Blew."

August 13, 1986

I know, Chris, how very much you must be hurting inside with the loss of your brother…I know the hurt will always be there for your mother and dad, too. Chris…they need you now more than ever, for you are all they have now. If they were to lose you in the tragic way Mark's life was taken, I know it would destroy them both completely…I don't think you and Mark really realized how deeply it hurt all of your family to watch two beautiful boys being destroyed through the evil of drugs.

Love,

Aunt Grace

BUT MAYBE CHRIS DID. Maybe he did have that realization—a realization that was not only held down and suffocated by the craving in his veins but a realization that was lost and buried under a maze of emotions and pressure.

This voice from the street knew Chris—and Mark—well:

I Don't Measure Up

So often there's a lot going on prior to putting in that needle, other than just wanting a quick kick and a not-so-cheap thrill.

Some kids might feel an obligation to live up to some standard that is or isn't there. And that's pressure.

If a parent is incredibly successful—especially by making it with their own hard work and hands—well, maybe the kids feel they can never measure up to that.

Mark and Chris never had to pick potatoes or anything, like their father did. Maybe that's why they never did—or had to— develop the same work ethic as Karl.

Somewhere down the line, Karl came across a note from Chris that said, "I know my father wanted me to get into the business, but I think it's too late now."

And at that point, it was true. Whatever the reason, and which- ever came first—trying to meet the expectations or not being able to meet the expectations—Mark and Chris did fail.

Now, it's not that these parents are telling their kids: "You have to do this or that; you're a loser if you don't." But through day- to-day living and seeing a successful, hard-working father and not having that same drive inside of them, that's where a lot of that shame and guilt can come from—feelings like "I don't measure up."

And sure, it might be only in their head, but to them it's very real.

IN THE THREE STAGES OF DRUG ABUSE, another phase—call it 3A— seems to follow. It's a stage that further anesthetizes the already-numb limbs of damage control. The stage in which little is left in the way of new horrors and surprises. Even the head-shaking and eye-rolling have given way to a mute head-hung-down acceptance.

Mark's overdose in the bright sunshine of Hawaii left a long shadow of shock as this entire opiate-opera peaked. And in that shadow is where Chris McMillen was caught after his brother's death.

This poisonous pattern and its all-too-inevitable results had already been established; Chris was now simply living out the prescribed nightmare.

But one area of acute feeling lingered within the numbness—*Karl and Thelma never gave up.* Through their harsh years of enlightenment as to what addiction was and what it could lead to, they never ever gave up.

Chris would be saved.

Yes.

We still have the strength and influence of love and caring.

There are better and better programs.

Chris is now the only son.

More focus can mean more help and maybe more getting through to him.

Try.

Try!

Now the only son, Chris is the sole focus of the family's love and healing. *Please try!*

MARCH 3, 1987

Seven months after Mark's death.

Chris is arrested in Costa Mesa, California, for a violation of section 148(A) of the State Penal Code: Falsely representing himself to a peace officer. Two days in jail.

NOVEMBER 28, 1987

Chris is arrested in Manhattan Beach, California, for a violation of sections 459, 4143 B&P, and 11550(A) of the State Penal Code: Burglary, attempting to sell hypodermic needles, and under the influence. One hundred twenty days in jail to begin in June 1988.

THREE DAYS BEFORE CHRISTMAS, 1987

Chris is arrested by officers of the Los Angeles Police Department for a violation of section 11550 H&S of the State Penal Code and sections 23152(A) and 14601.2(A) of the State Vehicle Code: Under the influence of narcotics, driving under the influence, and driving without a license. Three hundred sixty days in jail and an additional fifty days in jail to begin in July '88.

Another Merry Christmas and Happy New Year…

SIX MONTHS LATER, in the summer of 1988, right before his other sentences are to begin, Chris is arrested in Long Beach, California, for a violation of sections 11550(A) and 11550 H&S of the State Penal Code: Under the influence of narcotics. Ninety days in jail.

Summers used to be the best time to surf and to meet beautiful girls; just like Christmas and the holidays were a time of joy with family. All were now part of the deadened senses and had been for a long, long time.

Photo albums filled up with family moments shared in prison yards.

This summer, Chris would see no sunshine and no ocean. The endless part of an endless summer was now defined as plodding and excruciating, not heart-pumping and euphoric. What he would see this summer were the inside walls of a prison cell.

Again.

But by now his attitude and his definition of normal had shifted.

He was hardened.

I can do it.

I can do my time.

I'm not afraid of this.

I'm okay with going out in the yard and pumping some iron and defending my life.

Hell, there's drugs in jail.

Chris had developed a prison mentality.

He had to.

What he was *really* thinking and feeling in that haunting hollow of the life he and his brother led, few could ever know.

Chris's definition of normal shifted. He developed a prison mentality.

He, however, had little else *but* his thoughts in that cell.

Twenty-four hours a day.

All day every day.

All day every day to reflect, regret, re-step, and try to outsmart the craving in those veins.

And to again endure the jungle of GP.

It's uncomfortable to think that being buried alive might become normal for anyone. But that was the cold hole Chris was in.

Some air got inside, however. Some light and warmth crept in at the edges. Right before Chris's bust-blitz of '87 and '88, he had met another woman. He and Sally were now legally divorced and Sally was still comfortably in Hawaii—courtesy of Karl—with their son, Ty.

Chris's new relationship moved along well and in late 1988, his daughter Shannon was born.

Ty and Shannon were a big part of those solitary-cell thoughts. So were Karl and Thelma.

IT'S LATE AT NIGHT. There is light, but little clean and direct *working* light. And it's never really quiet in a prison. Jails and local lockups have their own type of noise: the constant hustle of comings and goings. Prison noise is different. It's not so much of a din; it's the occasional shout or yelling. The occasional crash or thud of *something*.

So there, in a less-than-library environment, Chris would do his thinking—and his writing.

His "stationary set" consisted of only a crude pencil and some notebook paper, but that didn't matter. Whether written with a quill on parchment, a state-of-the-art 1988 "word processor," or in wet beach sand with a driftwood branch, his thoughts were in bold capital letters.

What do you write to your parents when you're lying on a thin prison mattress at midnight? What do you write to your parents after they have done everything possible to keep you off a mattress like that and in a home where you should be, comfortable and looking out at blue ocean water through those windows with the million-dollar view?

What do you write to your parents when you're in a state prison, just two years after their only other child overdosed on the same kinds of drugs that were part of your brotherly bond?

November 21, 1988

Thought I'd drop you a few lines to let you know what's running through my mind. You know, when I talk to you folks, I never really know what to say. When Mark was alive, you guys always had an open line of communication; something I think we never really had. When Mark died, that really sent me for a loop. That was something I had to go through myself. Now that a new daughter…a new family…are in my life, it complicates things for me—being one that doesn't handle new possibilities too well. But on the other hand, maybe it's the foundation that I need when I get out.

Only time will tell…I do know that I have new responsibilities and hopefully I will be able to fulfill them…It's kind of like a second chance… In the last ten years I really haven't spent too much time on the street… I have a release date of February 10th if things go right. I guess what I'm trying to say is I hope you'll be in my corner when I do get released. I hope you're not still upset about the guns, credit cards, or the three grand I blew.

It's getting late so I'll close for now. I've enclosed some pictures of the baby and $40.00 (just joking about the forty!).

Love you both very much,

Your Son

These thoughts are not the grunted ramblings of a homeless drug burnout. These thoughts represent the feelings of an intelligent man—an intelligent man who happens to be a serious addict.

They are thoughts, like every thought Chris seemed to have, of optimism and of turning all this terror around. Maybe this time the strength for acting on that never-too-late optimism and desire to change would be there.

Or maybe this was yet another drug-driven scam.

After the poignant "Your Son" closing, Chris signed his note with the alias of "Sindberg." He had used the name Kristopher Andrew Sindberg from time to time while dealing with the law; like when he needed a "clean" driver's license. Or when he had bought a used truck that was eventually abandoned and impounded in Inglewood. He followed the signature with a smiley face...

Chris's intelligence, optimism, and sense of humor shone through the gray bars of his prison cell.

OKAY...

But what do parents think about in those deep hearts of the night? How, with all the love and patience and help that has been given, do you answer your now-only son when he talks about yet another "second" chance? When he talks about new responsibilities and the desire to fulfill them?

There is love.

There is tough love.

There is that unkillable optimism. That never goes away.

But there is also truth and reality that helps to harden and viciously vulcanize that final phase where the head-shaking and surprises have stopped. When you have been played, worked over, tricked, disappointed, hurt, and betrayed time and time again.

December 28, 1988

Chris,

Yes, Mark and your dad and I had an open line of communication, because he was open with us. Especially after his months at Habilitat. Mark, I feel, was very close to me. He sought my advice on many matters, particularly after his marriage to Renee. [Mark's coworker and friend] often asked Mark why he had to call his mother after they had completed a job and were paid. Mark would reply, "My mom would want to know and be proud of me." You, on the other hand, Chris, never really wanted to be open with Dad and me. When I tried to talk with you, you were always in a hurry and had to go.

Please don't misunderstand me. As far as you and your brother are concerned, I feel you shared equally in the shitty things you did to your dad and me. In some respects, your brother was worse. Offing my jewelry, trying to off my furs, etc. The furs he could not pull off because my signature is sewn in them. My jewelry is gone, as well as I don't know how many TVs.

Also, Chris, you know how many times Dad and I asked you and your girlfriend to join us in Palm Springs for the holidays and other times. You both always refused. Instead, you often went to her family or your so-called friends. That hurts.

We have always been there when the chips are down with money, etc.

Upon your release, if you elect to set up housekeeping with your new family, that is fine. However, I don't know how you will manage... Can you handle this? The only way I can see it working is if your girlfriend goes to work...and you are working...If after a reasonable length of time, there is a light on the horizon, I will be in your corner.

Let's talk about Mark. I know it was a horror for you to lose him...I know you loved each other as only brothers can. Rarely a day goes by that I don't think of him and of you, especially when I hear certain songs that you both reveled in. Be happy you did not see him lying there and knowing he was dead. Remember the good times. That is what I do, and I often laugh about the bad times, thinking about his capriciousness. He is always with us...I love you with all my heart and want only the best for you.

Love always,

Mom

Those are heavy words from a loving mother. But more chances and more "responsibilities that hopefully can be fulfilled" require some weight behind the punch.

It's tough on both sides of the razor-wired fence to face down some of the more biting "hurts"—even beyond death—in a scathing scenario like this.

The stealing from your own parents.

The televisions, the furs. The guns...

Karl had collected Trapper model Winchester rifles. They were valuable. Chris stole one of them.

Karl tracked his Trapper to a pawn shop where the counterman had given Chris BB-gun-level cash for this fine specimen from Karl's five-grand-a-pop collection.

But face-offs like Thelma and Chris were sharing were therapeutic and necessary.

Maybe, just maybe, things will finally turn around…

THROUGH A COMPLEX ENTANGLEMENT of jail sentences, time served concurrently, parole, and other judicial variables, Chris's early 1989 release date did "go right" and he was on the street once again, trying to fulfill responsibilities and build upon that fresh foundation of a new family.

SEPTEMBER 1989

Chris is arrested in Redondo Beach, California, for a violation of sections 459 and 496.1 of the State Penal Code: Burglary and receiving stolen property. Two years in state prison.

More judicial variables and Chris is freed.

JUNE 1990

Chris is arrested in Santa Monica, California, for a violation of section 459 of the State Penal Code: Burglary.

This time he doesn't even get into the house. The cops come as he is busy opening the window.

And this time, *judicial variables* don't go quite as right as before. Chris is given seven years in state prison, with a mandatory forty percent to be served.

MARCH 8, 1991

Back to Chino.

A YEAR INTO HIS SENTENCE, Chris's physical and emotional crash-landings approach a terminal point.

Chris and Sally may have been divorced, but you never completely stop thinking about the mother of your child. And Chris gets the news that Sally is dying in Hawaii—another collateral victim of a disrupted and destroyed lifestyle that bounced from a prison wedding to a house on a Louisiana lagoon.

Sally moves back to Honolulu from the Big Island to be closer to the hospital there. Karl and Thelma are once again on a jet back to Hawaii, to settle matters with Sally's house and make sure their grandson will be cared for.

Back in Chino, Chris is losing it.

One of the worst parts of prison life is the torture-in-restraint of being locked up while your family suffers. And you can't do anything about it.

Back to a cell full of thoughts.

Back to the deep heart of so many sleepless mind-tortured nights.

But now he can't even pace the few square feet of his world.

Along with all the emotional wounds that aren't healing, neither are the physical ones. The leg that Chris long ago shattered during the Louisiana pharmacy break-in is not getting any better. All the prison infirmaries where the leg has been *looked at* over the years haven't exactly been in the Mayo Clinic class.

And the prison docs all seemed to take the easy way out with those pain pills.

Again, Karl goes to work. His letter—his *plea*—to a medical professional he's associated with is another example of hope that never goes away. And of love:

March 8, 1992

Dear Dick,

Chris's situation in prison is deteriorating rapidly. In twenty years I have never seen his morale so low. He feels that everything is being done for Sally and nothing is being done for him. Rightly or wrongly, he feels abandoned.

Part of his sense of being abandoned may be my responsibility. Five months ago, I shared with him the discussion you and I had regarding his possible transfer to an NME [National Medical Enterprises] psychiatric lockup for the balance of his term. That gave him some hope. But with the passage of time, that hope has turned to frustration and anger. That anger has him in constant trouble with the prison authorities. I'm terribly worried that unless we can do something to restore his hope, and do it quickly, he'll do something that will extend his time and ruin any chance he has to put his life in order.

So, Thelma and I very much hope that you can begin to put into motion an attempt to have him transferred. That transfer represents his best, and perhaps last, chance at a productive, drug-free life.

In all sincerity,

Karl

IN 1992, SALLY LOSES HER FIGHT.

Eleven-year-old Ty is in one of the canoes as the traditional Hawaiian funeral sets Sally's ashes free with a raising of all the paddles.

She is given back to nature, to the ocean, by friends and family in flowery "Aloha attire"—no black.

Not here. Not in Hawaii.

No kau a kau, makua hine…

Ty stays in the islands, to be raised by Sally's best friend there. An allotment of four thousand dollars from Karl's trust is sent to the friend each and every month.

THE REST OF 1992 THROUGH 1994

Chris remains in Chino.

Karl and Thelma's routine has long consisted of agendas scheduled around visiting hours, and they see Chris regularly.

Always pumping up the hope.

Always expressing the love.

Try.

Try!

Todd Pipe & Supply is expanding the agenda. New facilities in El Monte and San Diego have been added. Twelve-hour work days are still common for Karl—work days and hours that are never without the added pressure of what will happen next with Chris and the law and the hope.

Chris is now thirty-seven years old. His release date is set for June 9, 1994. Karl and Thelma compose another plan—another *deal*.

February 26, 1994

Dear Son:

All things considered, the decision is yours.
What do you wish to do with your life?

The plan as I see it:
    1. Welding—get licensed.

2. Work for one of our competitors—learn the business
3. Work for Todd Pipe—Hawthorne
4. Work for Todd Pipe—Garden Grove
5. Work for Todd Pipe—San Diego (in a new environment)
6. School—college. We can afford whatever you decide.
7. Parole to Hawaii—you can be close to Ty.

Perhaps the best plan is:
1. Welding—always a backup trade.
2. Parole to home.
3. Have Ty come over—reacquaint with him, take trips.

At this point, make a final decision.

Chris, your mother and I believe in your potential.

It's the spring of 1994, closing in on Chris's release date. It's time to enact a plan that will finally take Chris away from life in the prison system.

That same year, California passes Proposition 184, the three strikes law; the swinging doors are closing for good.

Last call.

Thirty-seven years old.

Potential.

Reacquaint with your son; take trips.

Go to school, to college—*we can afford whatever you decide...*

CHAPTER 18

The People of the State of California vs. Chris Alan McMillen

JUNE 9, 1994

Chris is paroled as scheduled.

Karl and Thelma's latest plan/deal is being considered.

Thought about.

Analyzed.

What is the best decision to make?

At this point, make a final decision...

DECEMBER 9, 1994

Sixteen days before Christmas, Chris rides his bicycle along the sidewalk on Crenshaw Boulevard in Torrance, California, in the vicinity of El Camino Junior College. (His driver's license has been revoked.)

On parole, Chris is attending classes at the JC, not far from the apartment where Karl has set him up.

Chris is shirtless as he pedals the bike, the wild map of prison tattoos that Karl has always hated displayed in their full glory as a beacon of who he is.

And a beacon of who he *might* be.

It is a beacon not easily missed by law enforcement.

Deputies from the Los Angeles County Sheriff's Office stop Chris. They have astutely noticed that he does not have "a light affixed to his bicycle as prescribed by law." The officers have pulled Chris over in order that they might "warn him regarding these violations."

The rest of the police report describes the incident:

Chris's prison tattoos expressed who he was—and told the law who he *might* be...

> While deputies were speaking with the defendant, he displayed objective symptoms of being under the influence of a stimulant and was placed under arrest. Defendant was searched, and during the search one of the deputies found a wadded up piece of tissue in defendant's left front pocket. The tissue paper contained two cocaine rocks containing .08 grams each and defendant was additionally arrested for 11350(A) H&S [Possession of a controlled substance]. When deputies found the contraband, defendant allegedly said, "That's mine—can you give me a break?"

The .08 quantity of each cocaine rock had, at that time, a street value of approximately ten bucks. The .08 quantity of each cocaine rock had, at that time—after the passage of Proposition 184—a penalty prison value of twenty-five to life.

Not long before *this* "situation," Karl's longtime employee, Carol Campbell, had seen another encounter in the area between the cops and Chris. As she returned to Todd Pipe after lunch, there they all were, by the side of the road, discussing Chris's "bumping" of another car with his own. (He was still driving at the time; the question of a valid license being another matter.)

She rushed back to the office.

But she didn't want to be the messenger. She had seen and heard so much down through the years. She couldn't be the one to break Karl's heart yet again.

So she told one of the bosses. That boss was Don McDonald.

By now, McDonald had quietly worked his way up from cleaning toilets at the original "crammed-in" Todd location to being branch manager of the 78,000-square-foot Hawthorne facility.

He had looked at the future—*a* future—and had made it happen.

"You need to be the one to tell Karl," Carol told him, "because I'm not going to!"

Don did tell Karl; Karl was still like a father to him. But Karl was *really* the father of Chris, and once again, Chris was in trouble.

Just another eclipse of the McMillen sun.

In the shadow, Don could return to his nice office, as Chris sparred with the law and Karl began the usual damage control.

It didn't take long for the details of that mess to be known. Since the city of Hawthorne had grown fond of Todd's contributions to the community and since this particular incident with Chris had happened *there,* all was "worked out" and the car-bumping mistake went no further.

But this latest sidewalk scenario was very, very different. Chris's bicycle-cocaine catch didn't happen in the friendly fields of Hawthorne; and drugs were a hell of a lot more serious than a fender-bender.

Everything was more serious now.

Mark was dead. What could be more serious than that?

Life for Chris, perhaps—*life behind bars.*

THE TIME BETWEEN DECEMBER 9, 1994, and Chris's eventual courtroom showdown on March 26, 1996, was a panic-sweat sprint to avoid the results of this damning twenty-dollar swing at a third strike.

For Chris McMillen (with son, Ty), Christmas of 1994 was the start of an all-or-nothing race, where losing meant a lifetime behind bars.

Some of this sprint was well within the legal lane lines. But the first lengths were far off the path.

To begin with, Karl writes a check and bails Chris out of jail—fifty grand.

MARCH 28, 1995

Sprung from his cage and poised for what might be his last court battle for freedom, Chris is cited by the El Camino College Police Department for violating California Penal Code 647(F): drunk in public.

This latest misdemeanor frays even more ends in an already unraveling mess. Chris simply cannot go to jail for the rest of his life on this third strike!

He jumps the fifty-grand bail and heads for south-of-the-border sanctuary in Mexico.

And Karl helps.

When your child is headed for life in prison, you do whatever you have to do...

Karl knew of a hotel down there where Chris could hole up—one of the first hotels in the Cabo San Lucas area, just north of the resort town.

Karl had a friend in the construction business who supplied air-conditioning units to this hotel and others. They had a working relationship. They grew close, learning how to work the system—they knew which *funcionario* was on duty and when, so the big-ticket air conditioners could make it down there with the fewest monetary obligations and duty dilemmas as possible.

But Chris opted to borrow Karl's tent trailer, hitch it to his truck, and set up camp on the beach.

Just like the Baja trips...

Karl also put about four thousand bucks in Chris's pocket, for amenities.

Two weeks later, Karl, Thelma, and Chris's newest girlfriend (Shannon's mother is long gone after these seven years of turmoil), fly down. They all need another plan. Karl assesses and analyzes the area, much as he had back in Morgan City. Except this time the situation is more desperate.

It isn't so much a real estate assessment now; it's: *Where can someone on the lam comfortably hide?*

Karl and Thelma find a nice apartment; they pay the required first, last, and security deposit. The plan in place, they fly back to the U.S.

Chris and his girlfriend spend their first night in the apartment.

Chris is now trapped in another kind of cell.

The nervous rush of being a fugitive isn't as pure as the nerve-bending rush of dropping down a giant wave. All that's looming up behind you on that swell is a mountain of water; it's a whole other worry to be looking over your shoulder in Mexico, waiting for a hammering knock to come on that apartment door.

AUGUST 2, 1995

The couple stays in the apartment for one night. And that's that.

They decide that a Bonnie-and-Clyde law-dodging lifestyle isn't going to work.

We need to face this head on.

They head back north to help in Karl's efforts to change the call on that third strike.

But right before they reach the U.S. border, a new idea jumps into the plan: ¡Matrimonio!

AUGUST 4, 1995

Two days after the rápido Tijuana wedding, the newlyweds fly to Las Vegas where they marry again on *this* side of the border. Just to make sure.

More obligations and complexity…

Time is key and it's slipping. They all need to get some of Karl's next plan into action. Whatever can push a legal decision in the right direction—a direction that might possibly fend off this unforgiving third strike—absolutely needs to be done.

Immediately.

It isn't quite Columbia or Duke, but Chris resumes his coursework at El Camino Junior College where he actually does well, achieving high grades. He jumps into Harbor Occupational Center and earns his Certified Structural Steel Process Welding License.

He enters a drug recovery program at a facility in North Hollywood.

Maybe this is working…

After the North Hollywood program ends, Chris checks into the Betty Ford Clinic in the resort area of Rancho Mirage, California, near Palm Springs.

Fourteen days later he walks out.

This wasn't part of *any* plan.

Your decision to enter treatment at the Betty
Ford Center was not an easy one and was the
direct result of your problems associated with
alcohol/drug dependency. Your decision to leave
treatment prior to successful completion is a
matter that impacts you and your family...The
nature of addiction is that, in spite of promises
to ourselves and others, without outside help,
problems with drugs or alcohol usually reoccur.

The Betty Ford Center

Chris, don't give up.

No!

Not now.

Twenty-five to life...

Chris spends the rest of the endless summer of 1995 at Progress
House, a twelve-step rehab center in Northern California.

EARLY 1996

*THE PEOPLE OF THE STATE OF CALIFORNIA, Plaintiff
and Respondent, vs. CHRIS ALLEN [sic] MC MILLEN.*

It took money, attorneys, and persuasion.

Chris didn't get along well at all with the first attorney Karl
brought in. That attorney was a three-hundred-dollar-an-hour guy.

Chris brings in his own defense lawyer, at a bargain price of one-
fifty an hour. But lawyer number two needs the help of *another* lawyer.

All three send their bills to Karl.

The two-attorney team studies Chris's case and searches for
precedents. No parallel can be found, but they conclude within
the complexity that it might be possible to get Chris's *second* felony
stricken. That would make this new offense not his third, but his new
second strike.

They study cases, and then they study them again.

Their legal strategy was unheard of at the time. But many attorneys' invoices later, it worked.

Chris's second strike was gone, leaving his bicycle bust as his new Strike Two.

But regardless of the penal numerics, that twenty of coke came with a high cost.

On March 26, 1996, Chris was sentenced to six years in state prison. It wasn't the "39/42 to life" that it could have been, but it was still too much.

April 1, 1996

Dear Honorable Judge Donald F. Pitts,

I am the father of Chris McMillen...It is because I have such strong feelings about my son and the sentence he received that I write this letter to you.

My wife Thelma and I very much love our son. Of course we are aware of his past problems with the law and with drug addiction. We have, however, seen since the arrest that gave rise to the present case significant positive changes in Chris's behavior and attitudes towards life... his being charged with a third strike felony and his general understanding that he could spend the rest of his life incarcerated led him to the realization that he had to change his ways and attitudes.

My son was married last year to a young woman...She regularly attended meetings with Chris and is an active speaker against drug addiction. Chris and my daughter-in-law are expecting a child in August.

Clearly, for the first time in his adult life, my son had begun to address his personal struggle with drugs and had taken steps to lead a constructive life...I do not condone or excuse Chris's actions. Our son's problems with the law have been a source of great pain and sorrow for myself and my wife. One of the ways we have dealt with our remorse has been to work hard and to share our success with others. Recently we provided a bequest of $1.5 million to the School of Business Administration at the University of Southern California to honor a former professor, Dr. Kenneth Trefftzs.

This letter by no means is meant as a criticism of your court, the District Attorney's office, or the able counsel who represented my son. Instead, it is a plea that the judicial system take into account the nature of my son's latest non-violent offense and the efforts he made to change...We urge everyone involved to consider a fair and appropriate reduction of the six-year sentence previously ordered and pray for an alternative sentence involving formal probation. Thelma and I desperately don't want our son's life and that of his family destroyed at this important juncture of his life.

Respectfully yours,

Karl McMillen

KARL'S MENTIONING OF THE CHAIR he purchased for Dr. Treffstz was not self-serving hype to prove his clout and position to the judge. Whether the judge discerned it or not, it was actually another example of Karl's optimism amid chaos. It was also the beginnings of his benevolence and philanthropy—also within the fractures of chaos.

The $1.5 million to USC for Dr. Treffstz' chair was also not a showy gift or bestowal. It was a lot of money, sure; but more importantly, it was a monument to what hard work can do. It was a monument to those rare humans whose personalities are woven into words and traits like perseverance, focus, drive, and honesty.

Karl loves to say that "It took a plumber to buy Dr. Treffstz his chair at USC!"

Karl was a proud "plumber" when he purchased a faculty chair at USC for his lifelong mentor.

And he's right.

But to refer to Karl McMillen as just "a plumber" might be as unfair as *not* calling him just "a plumber." He is both: the ultimate hands-on working class hero, while at the same time a man whose eyes and heart are always open to what life has to offer.

Now, this *plumber* was snaking the system. The third strike was gone and he was bent on cutting away at the six-year sentence. Addicts need rehab, not prison, right?

Once again, Karl McMillen was trying to save his son—and maybe even himself while he was at it.

CHAPTER 19

The High-Bottom Drunk

MAY 1996

Chris sits in prison, serving the majority of his sentence. The third-strike fastball has been dodged, but despite Karl's pleading, the six-year sentence for the .16 grams of coke—one year for each .026 grams of the dope—will stand.

Meanwhile, Todd Pipe & Supply has kept its streak alive, hitting 'em out of the park in terms of sales. New branches have opened in West Los Angeles and San Diego. In Nevada, the Las Vegas unit is getting ready for *its* grand opening.

But the grind of all of this—the good and the bad—is not having a zero effect.

Karl and Thelma are drinking.

A lot.

Thelma would often pass out early from drinking. Karl would put her to bed and she would wake up ready to go again a few hours later.

Exactly one month after Karl sent the hope-filled "alternative sentence" letter to the court, Karl received a letter of his own—from Terry Devitt. Devitt, by now of course, was a major player in this long tragedy. The best supporting actor in a drama that had so many acts and scene changes.

His scene changes had him moving to Hawaii. Apparently, with all the research and study he had done over there, the islands had grown on him.

And he was in a shaky mourning over the suicide death of his twin brother—a suicide associated with the twin's own plunge into the razor-rocked shore of drug use.

Devitt's recovery from grief was shaky because events in the lives of twins often mirror one another—even if sometimes those mirrors are cracked.

But Devitt was more concerned with Karl than with himself or his twin when he typed up this note in the spring of '96:

```
                                        May 1, 1996

Dear Karl:

    I wish I wasn't writing this letter but my
respect and affection for you compels me to
do so.
    In the past couple of weeks, I've received
three phone calls from the mainland, including
one from Thel, all expressing grave and sincere
concerns for your health, your very life. I've
heard the same things that were said about me...
"He's killing himself"..."Isn't it a shame to see
him like this?"..."He's lost his self-respect"...
"Why won't he get or take help?" Karl: YOU said
those things about me and you were right!!!! And
I wouldn't be here today if I hadn't stopped
drinking. I would have died a falling-down
drunk without pride or dignity. I'm so grateful
that didn't happen. I've done some pretty good
```

things in this life and I deserve a better death than that!!!

And so do you!! I've known you for twenty-five years and I've always had the greatest respect for you as a parent, a businessman, and a wonderful friend. Karl, I beg you—get detoxed and get treatment. Get your life back!!! You are needed. You've grandchildren to watch grow up. Chris could finally be getting it together—don't you want to see that?

Karl, please take all the love and respect and gratitude that people have for you and use it to reach into yourself to do what you must do.

I have been blessed to have you in my life for twenty-five years—I'm not ready to say good-bye. Please get well. I love you very much.

Terry

Devitt's claim was true: Drinking was hurting Karl personally and it had the potential to dam up Todd Pipe's surge.

And Terry had corroboration for what he was saying. Other friends and coworkers agreed behind the scenes.

They loved Karl, but they also recognized that amidst the emotional free-for-all that had consumed Karl's and Thelma's savior energies with Mark and Chris, Karl now needed to turn some of the healing focus on himself.

Maybe, just maybe…

AS MANY VOICES FROM THE STREET cry out about alcoholism as about drugs. More, maybe. After all, alcohol is legal.

And certainly more *accepted*.

The Disease Can Take You

It possesses you. It becomes the most important thing to you. It is above anybody or anything else. You'll lie, cheat, steal, or whatever it takes to get that drug—and alcohol is as much a drug as the rest of them.

The reason most people drink is because they're restless, irritable, and discontent as the Big Book of AA says. They take alcohol and drugs because that's what relieves that sense of restlessness.

But ninety percent of alcoholics never recover from this disease. It's a terrible, terrible thing. Despite any amount of love and caring from family and friends, the disease can take you.

You have a drinking career that you may stop. But the disease inside of you progresses as if you had just kept going.

Back in Baja, Karl had asked himself if he and Thelma drank because the boys took drugs, or if the boys took drugs because he and Thelma drank.

It's still a question with no answer.

The adult drinking and partying began with the hip ambience of the beach and the social atmosphere of the businesses—right about the time that the weed grew into heroin and both took their high toll on the brains, bodies, and beings of Mark and Chris.

Usually it happens that way. You know, just social fun. Then it all takes a nasty twist. And there are always the triggers—like that first drink. You can ask yourself if you can control and enjoy; if you can control your alcohol usage. That's fine. But the real sign of an alcoholic is that when they take their first drink, they can't put it down—especially half-full. With the alcoholic, once he takes that first drink, the physical craving for alcohol takes over, and he has no defense against it. The physical part of it—the physical cravings—

take over like an allergy. You need another one and another one and another one—obsession and compulsion.

Actually, Karl didn't drink *every* day. But there *were* times he would wait for the liquor store to open.

When you know the hours of the liquor store, that's not a good sign.

But so many do.

Drinking was such a part of the social scene of the WWII generation and the generation after that. Every social setting was centered around drinking. Super-stiff Crown Royal and vermouth Manhattans went down like water, along with all this other heavyweight stuff. It was just part of it. You turned on the TV, and you not only had Dean Martin and Frank entertaining us with drinks in their hands, but the audience had 'em, too! Jackie Gleason would come on stage, take a big hit, and tell his fans, "How sweet it is!" It was a fundamental part of the times.

But now, unfortunately, it's even crazier; because there's not even a pretense of sophistication or fun or ignorant innocence. Alcohol binge abuse among freshmen college students ranks number two in causing the most violent offenses on college campuses. High statistics on rape, pregnancy, STD transmission, and DUIs are all alcohol-fueled among the young.

Eventually it takes what it takes to get you to hit bottom—to want to get sober. Everyone's bottom is different: your wife leaving you, getting fired from your job, whatever. Some need to lose every-thing before they wise up. Others—called "high-bottom drunks"—don't have to sink nearly that low.

Of course, there's a saying that the only difference between a high-bottom drunk and low-bottom drunk is that one "pukes" and the other "throws up."

We all have the same disease. Just varying levels of suffering we're willing to tolerate to feed it.

And the disease is so, so powerful.

"...while some alcoholic subtypes may function better than others, in all cases, alcohol dependence must be viewed as a severe disease with a significant adverse impact on health and well-being."

—Howard Moss, MD,
Associate Director for Clinical and Translational Research,
National Institute on Alcohol Abuse and Alcoholism
(NIAAA)

A severe disease...

There's one addict who passed out in the doorway with a bottle of vodka while his kids played in the living room like nothing was happening. They were numb.

The guy's sponsor came by and the first thing he did was address the kids: "You know your dad would do something different—if he only could," he told them.

Some just can't kick it.
"If he only could..."
But others can.

KARL MCMILLEN'S FRIENDS and business colleagues—and his wife—knew exactly how to intervene with Karl.

It would be all about numbers.

Thelma found her opportunity at a company event in Palm Springs. She talked with one of the key execs at Todd, a man Karl was close to: branch manager Dan Patrick.

"Karl is killing himself with his drinking," she told Dan. "Can you please talk to him? Tell him he's hurting himself and the business?"

Dan agreed; and he met with Karl by the hotel pool that same evening.

"Karl, you're going to die from the alcohol!" Dan was straight up. "And you're embarrassing Todd Pipe. You miss dinners with vendors, and at times it's even worse than that!"

Dan Patrick knew what he was talking about—he was a recovering alcoholic himself.

He got it.

So did Karl—now.

Jesus, I'm hurting the business with this drinking? I can't...I can't do that!

Bingo!

Karl agreed to quit drinking.

Just like that.

The next day Karl asked Dan to be his sponsor at AA. Dan explained that he couldn't do that, but said he would introduce Karl to *his* sponsor, Jack. Dan, Karl, and Jack went to lunch and then to a meeting.

Meetings always start with numbers, a tangible tidbit Karl could chew on. But this was a sum gain he hadn't been added into quite yet.

"Who has five years?"

Hands go up.

"Who has four years?"

More hands.

"...three?

"...two?"

"...one?"

"A month? A week?"

At the very end, Karl proudly raised his hand. "I've got two days!"

Eventually, Karl increased those numbers. He's received sobriety chips year after year, with no lapse.

Karl also attended Al-Anon—*once.* With Thelma.

> *Al-Anon will chew up enablers. When your kid or your loved one comes to you all messed up and you give them money, you don't want to go back to Al-Anon and have to report that!*

True enough. In fact, all of the voices and the wisdom from the street are based in truth.

Uncomfortable? Sure.

Helpful? Certainly.

Insightful? Absolutely.

And Karl probably could have used a few more sessions. But for now, and for once, he was focused on healing himself. He was bailing out himself and his business rather than his sons.

You'll Always Find Reasons to Drink

> *There's going to be triggers that are going to make you want to drink. Tough times are going to come up. You're going to see old friends.*
>
> *There are all kinds of reasons you come up with to go back to the old lifestyle: Life is hard. Life is tough. But I know I can easily go over and live that other way.*
>
> *You have to work very hard to go through the twelve steps to try to get rid of all that.*
>
> *But it is so, so worth it!*

It was sure worth it to Karl. A solution here was easy to analyze. Karl could simply not hurt his business.

That was *his* bottom.

Karl's to-the-point reaction could be the key antidote to transforming the lives of addicts in every gutter and in every boardroom around the world, if it could only be "medicinalized" and prescribed.

Why is it so hard to understand that it's not a good trade-off when getting high on *any* substance outweighs success and prosperity and love and an easy enjoyment of life?

It seems so basic and logical. But then again so does "Just say no."

And so many conflicting levels lie below and above logic when it comes down to the devil in drugs.

Not for Karl, though.

Karl's recovery went beyond cold-turkey; *that* booze-bird was frozen solid. It was too important.

Hawthorne.

Garden Grove.

Sepulveda.

El Monte.

West Los Angeles.

San Diego.

Las Vegas.

Business was booming…

Chapter 20

All That Is Left

Summer 1996

Chris's third child, another daughter, is born.

Her father is in prison, on his way to serving eighty percent of his sentence.

Inmate number E-87808, Chris Alan McMillen, is in Delta Conservation Camp #8, in Suisun City, near California's wine country, above San Francisco.

As incarceration facilities go, it wasn't exactly Sing Sing or Pelican Bay.

> Delta Conservation Camp CC#8...is located on 22 acres in the rural area of Solano County...The inmates are classified as Level I and Level II (minimum security risk)...Inmates who participate in the camp program must be physically fit, cannot have more than 7 years remaining on their sentence, nor convicted of any capital crimes, sex crimes or domestic violence. After meeting these requirements, each inmate must meet CAL FIRE's

requirement of 67 hours of training; the same training that an entry-level firefighter receives... The main mission of the camp is to provide inmate fire crews for fire suppression in the Sonoma, Lake, Napa, and the Solano County areas.

During their stay at the camp, inmates must undergo continuous training...Inmates are taught useful skills that are transferable to employment in the community upon release or parole. While housed at the facility, inmates are able to obtain their GED and continue their education.

—CALIFORNIA DEPARTMENT OF
CORRECTIONS AND REHABILITATION,
DELTA CONSERVATION CAMP,
2009-2010 Solano Grand Jury Report

And maybe even continue their lives in a productive way.

Training.

Useful skills.

Education.

But, as always, there were *issues.*

Must be physically fit...

Inmates must undergo continuous training...

The initial damage that occurred when Chris leapt two stories down was a broken fibula and tibia.

The first operations included the insertion of a metal plate. That became infected and was removed. A Hoffman device, described as a "temporary prosthetic fitting," was inserted, along with a bone and skin graft.

The Hoffman device became infected, so it was removed.

Next came another bone and skin graft. That lasted awhile, but its results, too, were failing.

Even the Delta Conservation Camp, with all of its "minimum security" amenities and scenery, was a painful hell for Chris.

THREE HUNDRED NINETY-EIGHT MILES SOUTH, in the amenities and scenery of Manhattan Beach, another hell was burning.

Thelma was sick, and getting sicker.

She was a smoker; so many of her generation were.

The ads and the persuasion and peer pressure of the fifties and sixties were brutal!

More Doctors Smoke Camels than Any Other Cigarette!
As Your Dentist, I Would Recommend Viceroys!
There's Never a Rough Puff in a Lucky!

Stars of the day all had cigarette endorsement deals—Bob Hope, Perry Como, Ronald Reagan, Kirk Douglas, Lucille Ball. Even sports stars like Hank Aaron, Ted Williams, and Stan Musial were telling everyone to light up.

And everyone did.

Karl was one of the "everyone" as well. Until back around the time he got sober, when his doctor detected a circulatory problem he was having. The doc expanded on his findings: "I can give you this prescription for your circulation, but if you throw those cigarettes away, you're going to solve the problem."

Again, numbers: The prescription costs *this* much and the cigarettes are costing *this* much. Together, they're costing *how much?!*

Karl threw his last pack out the window and he was done, leaving another very chilly turkey.

First the booze, now the butts. If only everyone had Karl's resolve.

If only that "everyone" had included Thelma.

She wasn't done. She remained hooked on the nicotine and developed cancer in her throat.

Now it's time for her operations and treatments to begin.

Karl loses track of just how many Thelma endures. But he never loses track of his optimism.

Thelma will beat this.
Chris's leg will heal.
Chris will turn his life around.

Thelma's medical processes go on and on. More and more sections of her throat are removed. She and Karl anticipate the cancer treatment effect of hair loss, so they order a custom wig.

A thousand dollars deposit.

Thelma doesn't lose her hair, but she and Karl want the wig finished anyway. Just in case.

Keep working on it...

But the cancer keeps working, too—spreading and lingering.

Thelma's sister arrives to help. She can care for Thelma while Karl is at work.

JANUARY 27, 1999

Karl and Thelma turn in for the night. Thelma gets up and goes to the bathroom at about midnight, where she begins coughing up blood.

She makes her way back to the bedroom.

JANUARY 28, 3:00 A.M.

Karl wakes up and finds Thelma on the floor, clinging to the bed. She is gone.

KARL'S OLDEST SON IS DEAD.
His second son is in prison.
His wife has succumbed to cancer.
It would be enough to break most people.
Most.

But Karl keeps going, doing what he does best. It's time once again for action; but this time it's hard. Excruciating. He needs help and finds it with the son that never was, Don McDonald.

McDonald's phone rings well before dawn—*those* are the calls that bring emotional ice down the spine and a quick awakening.

Karl tells him that Thelma has just been taken away.

Don is there. He helps make the rest of the calls. And he unlocks the complex process with prison authorities to allow Thelma's youngest son to come home for her funeral. Chris is not "between jail stays" like he was during Mark's memorial.

Don works with the system, makes the correct contacts, and fills out the proper forms. Thanks to his efforts, Temporary Community Leave (TCL) is granted. But Karl will have to pay all the travel expenses for Chris and a law enforcement escort.

No problem.

Checks are written.

FEBRUARY 6, 1999, 7:45 A.M.

Chris and his own personal guard board a jet in Sacramento bound for LAX.

Touchdown, then directly to the church where they are part of a standing-room-only crowd of all those who shared in sixty-nine cherished years with Thelma Beatrice McMillen. Fronted by Karl and Chris—and Chris's armed marshal—they all listen to the eulogies and the love.

They listen to the final soundtrack that the family put together for Thelma; from the carefree joy of *On the Road Again* to the statement of *My Way*.

But then comes the Righteous Brothers' *Ebb Tide*, its lyrics inspired by the film *From Here to Eternity*, with its famous scene of Burt Lancaster and Deborah Kerr locked in an embrace on the sand as the waves wash over them.

Thelma Beatrice McMillen, 1929–1999

Ebb Tide was not only a part of Thelma's final soundtrack; it was a melodic mirror held up to the McMillen family's life, from the beach-based beginning to now to a series of ends. Nothing was more fitting than this ocean allegory…the ebb and flow of the tide…the highs and lows of life…the "love"…whether in the "rain," the "dark," or in the warmth of the "sun."

And, *"like the tide at its ebb,"* the "peace" now felt by Mark and Thelma.

By 7:45 that evening, Chris and his escort are back in Delta Camp.

IN THE LATE-WINTER DARKNESS of that February evening, a grieving Karl and a shattered and imprisoned Chris—separated by nearly five hundred miles and by layers of steel bars and razor wire—are all that is left of the brightest young family on the beach.

What now?

What now?

Don't give up.

No!

Never. Karl keeps going, stays in action, focusing on what can still be saved.

At this point, make a final decision…

Chris did make at least one decision. Perhaps his mother's death and the way he had to attend her funeral made him consider responsibilities and the ramifications of actions.

On March 24th, Chris contacts Karl's attorney, Gary Michel.

Chris's son, Ty, and Ty's girlfriend had come to visit Chris. He'd learned from them that Sally's friend who has been caring for Ty since Sally's death—and remains on the dole for the four grand a month—is selling her house in Hawaii.

Ty is now eighteen, maturing, and getting ready to rent an apartment with his girlfriend. Both have jobs and steady income.

It's time to cut back to just three grand a month for Ty.

It's time for some responsibility and an assessment of priorities all the way around.

The first priority for Karl after Thelma's passing is Chris's leg.

With legal help from another of Karl's attorneys, Chris is moved from Delta Camp to the California Correctional Center at Susanville, where new processes begin on his leg. On June 18, 1999, he receives an "open window" cast and stitches.

More infection, more failure.

More pain pills…

The cast is removed.

Three weeks later, Chris sees a nurse.

She does nothing. No real examination, no antibiotics for the infection. Nothing.

And this time no pain pills, either.

Karl and his attorneys go back to work. Their first thoughts are to get Chris moved to the Vacaville, California, prison which has a larger medical department. But nothing can top private care. Offer them a deal:

July 13, 1999

CALIFORNIA CORRECTIONAL CENTER
DR. M.S. BARDO
P.O. Box 790
Susanville, CA 96127-0790
RE: CHRIS ALAN McMILLEN (No. E87808)

Dear Dr. Bardo:

...Karl McMillen is the President of a major corporation. As an alternative to treatments at Vacaville, he is prepared to pay for all treatments and any required security staffing for Chris to receive immediate treatment at a qualified private medical facility...

Sincerely,

Michael T. Ungar

The request is ignored.

AUGUST 1, 1999

Chris is transferred south to Chino where he receives a split-thickness skin graft.

It doesn't work.

Then, more surgery.

Chris spends six months in the prison hospital at the California Institute for Men at Chino.

The system has gotten Chris out of Susanville, but beyond that, it hasn't been overly anxious to accept Karl's offer of independent outside help. No one has gone out of their way to fly in surgeons from Johns Hopkins or to get Chris a private room at the UCLA Medical Center.

Throughout this longest of Chris's prison stretches, Karl and Ty become regular visitors.

Karl is allowed to sit in Chris's lockdown hospital ward with him. It's a tiny slice of hell, far from the spatial sweetness of Manhattan Beach.

He sees his son penned-up and hurting, with a leg so damaged he would be shot out of his misery if he were a stumbling animal. The small "pens" of his cell and now this ward are reducing him to nearly that level of species-status.

Chris's wife is also a regular during those cattle-call visiting hours and she sees behavior in Chris that Karl does not. She knows Chris and can't be fooled. Chris is getting drugs through the easy underground of the prison. He is again "self-medicating."

And she can't deal with that.

She files for "separate maintenance." Her attorney negotiates with Chris's attorney. The demands are that Chris seek help upon his release before she will even consider letting him back.

Meanwhile, Karl is still supporting her and her daughter with a monthly allotment. Of course, by doing this—and by supplying Chris with his own counsel—Karl is essentially paying both lawyers to do battle with one another!

For Karl, this latest woe-woven web is yet another eye-rolling, confusing drain on everything and everybody. Another frustrated shrug of *Why?*

For Chris, this is all yet more of that torture-in-restraint.

October 3, 1999

To be honest, Dad, I don't know what I'm going to do when I get out. As you could probably tell, I'm in a bad way right now. I'm depressed, frustrated, angry, and a little scared!... When you've been locked up in a cell for months, put in this type of situation, your mind plays games with you if you let it. I have to remember to take this stuff one day at a time... I can't let it break my spirit. I have too much to live for when I get out; too many good years ahead of me.

I know it's got to be difficult to see your son in this position. If Ty was in this position, it would be heartbreaking for me, too. I just want to assure you, Dad, I'm an ol' saddletramp and I will get thru this. I'm as tough as they come when I want to be.

CHRISTMAS 2000

Chris spends the holidays at CIM Chino, agonizing over his leg and what is becoming an angry and ugly parting with his wife.

Another Merry Christmas and a Happy New Year...

But this new year will produce at least one positive: Chris is scheduled for a mid-year release. By February, Chris is looking ahead—and looking back. Back to those days in Baja:

Dad... When I get out, hell, I might even take ya down to Punta San Francisquito and do a little dorado fishing, dirt roads from Bahia de Los Angeles to Punta San Francisquito; you know the trip... You remember when you and mom got ol' yeller stuck... that was one hell of a trip! I'm thinkin' you ought to write a book...

While it's yet another less-than-joyous Christmas for Karl and his remaining family, potential positives can be seen on the horizon.

JULY 14, 2000

Chris is released.

From Susanville.

He had been transferred back there for the remainder of his sentence to just possibly get some final medical care for his deteriorating leg.

He does.

And it seems to take—*this time.*

But he is now left with a pronounced limp; and the limp is causing problems with his hip.

Chris is forty-three years old and the father of three children.

He has served four years, three months, and eighteen consecutive days; eighty percent of his six-year sentence. Four years, three months, and eighteen days for possessing a few bucks' worth of low-grade rock cocaine, and all for the initial probable cause infraction of not having a light on his bicycle.

CHAPTER 21

No Heir to the Throne

THIS RELEASE FROM PRISON was a far cry from all the rest.

No plane ticket was offered. No one was there to pick him up. And no one remembers why. Recalling the reason for the lack of fanfare this time is another of those dim, grim occurrences lost among the twists, turns, detours, and secrets of drug abuse.

Maybe it was just that drone of numbness—on everybody's part.

Maybe it was because this had happened so many times before.

This time Chris climbs aboard a Greyhound bus. He gets on at the Susanville stop; newly released inmates are a common passenger-base at this particular pick-up point.

He heads home. Home to Southern California. Home to his father. And maybe, just maybe, to that fishing trip to Baja he dreamed of back in his cell.

He dreams of it now, looking out at the farmland of Northern and Central California blurring by, the hum-rumble of the bus his only conversation.

It is a long conversation.

A multi-stop Greyhound route is called a "milk run" in the transportation business. Passengers have plenty of opportunities to get out, stretch their legs, and regroup.

At about the halfway mark in the lumbering six-hundred-mile trip, the bus stops in Modesto. Chris's stretching and regrouping includes buying beer and whiskey.

The results of that little stop make a long trip much longer.

Not until four days after his long-awaited release does a disheveled and hungover Chris finally knock on his father's door.

From 1972 until 2000, a span of twenty-eight years, Chris has spent eighteen of them in lockups of one form or another.

Welcome home…

CHRIS WASN'T ALONE in experiencing the heavy, revolving door of prison. Neither was Karl.

This time, Richie Davidson's voice from the street echoes through both freedom and lockup, showing the confusion of the addict in both.

Your Mind Changes

I would come home to my mom, fresh out of jail, and I know she'd be scared, full of fear.

This one time I'd been in county jail for a year. I told myself I was through with this life I'd been leading. Never again!

But two weeks before I got out, I had this thought in my head. The thought was that, you know, when I get home, I'm going to get a little wine and go down to the beach and smoke a joint.

I deserve that.

I've been in here a year.

Sure.

A relapse always happens way before it happens.

Once a thought like that comes into an addict's mind—just a hint of an idea that they can have or do "just a little" and be okay (which is completely impossible)—it becomes an obsession. It stays in your head and metastasizes. You start to believe the story that you're telling yourself.

You became more and more disconnected from the truth and from your power. You have to stay connected and focused on being present in reality.

For me, that thought was my relapse—the beginning of the end.

And when I got out, it was exactly what I did. I was on the beach, I was drunk, I was loaded, and within two weeks I was right back in the lifestyle.

I knew what I'd done to my mom, I knew it was wrong, and I wanted to do right; but I didn't have a chance—and that was the part I didn't know.

Your mind changes without your permission.

I have friends who have had twenty years sober—now they have two days.

For an addict, there's absolutely no correlating drug use with consequences.

Even after all that I'd been through, having just been released from jail, I really didn't know that the beach and the joint and the wine would do that.

An addict can't differentiate.

After about the twentieth time I called my mother from jail, she finally told me to f— off. She stopped being my buddy. I was so mad until I got it through my head that I couldn't keep torturing her like this!

That got my attention.

THE LAS VEGAS BRANCH of Todd Pipe & Supply was up and pumping out product. The ninth and final arm of the company, the Escondido, California, facility, was nearing completion.

Even though Chris had a long way to go in his recovery, he was home. The prison visiting hours could be taken off the schedules.

It was time.

It was time for Terry Devitt's prophesy about Karl's "inspiring others" to come down from the mountain in a sublime-divine way. Mark's life-insurance money had certainly made Hawaii a better place. And Todd's expansion had helped water to flow neatly and drip-free throughout the West. But now it was time for a deeply personal push.

Karl McMillen was going to turn the deaths of his wife and son, along with his own lifetime of hard work and potato-packing, gold-panning grit, into a center-stage display of genuine goodness.

The war waged on, and the enemy of drugs and nicotine and alcohol would not win.

Karl and Mark's passionate charge was now joined by the spirit of Thelma.

APRIL 10, 2001

Another spirit that powered and inspired so many of Karl's charges joins Mark and Thelma. Karl's beloved mentor and advisor over the past four decades, Dr. Ken Trefftzs, dies in San Diego.

Dr. Trefftzs suffered from Alzheimer's. Toward the end of his life, he told Karl in his professor-like advisory way, "Karl, I won't be able to help you anymore. My mind is going…"

But what his mind did for Karl and his businesses, and for the subsequent help that the McMillen enterprises would provide, will never be gone.

GOOD TURNS

Donor Gives to Honor Wife and Save Lives

Businessman is moved by his success and his setbacks
to pledge $5.3 million to a medical center
for a program to fight substance abuse.

Karl B. McMillen has savored some of life's sweetest gifts: a long and happy marriage, a Midas touch in business, and the robust health, at age 74, to keep on expanding the firm...

McMillen also has endured some of life's toughest challenges: the death of his firstborn son from a drug overdose, the loss to cancer of his wife of 48 years, and his own battle with alcohol abuse.

Now the Manhattan Beach man, who made his fortune in plumbing contracting and supply, has dug deep into his pockets in a carefully planned gesture that ties together the blessings and the pain. McMillen has pledged $5.3 million to Torrance Memorial Medical Center to develop a comprehensive program to combat drug and alcohol addiction.

The Thelma McMillen Center, named in memory of the businessman's wife, is scheduled to open next August. The outpatient facility, to be housed in a newly purchased building next to the hospital, will be large enough to serve more than 400 patients a year. That will at least double the capacity of the medical center's chemical dependency program, now limited to adults.

McMillen's donation, which Torrance Memorial officials said is the largest private gift in the hospital's 77-year history and one of the largest ever to any community hospital, will enable development of a program for adolescents and will help pay for treatment for uninsured patients. The center will have dedicated rooms for counseling, treatment, and meetings, plus a library and exercise space.

"There is so much need for these programs," McMillen said during a recent interview in his tidy office at the Hawthorne headquarters of Todd Pipe & Supply, the firm he co-founded in 1966 after selling his interest in a previous firm and "retiring"...

Through his donation, McMillen believes he has found a far more effective way to join the war on addiction..."Through the Thelma McMillen Center, we can save lives...I feel fortunate that I am at a point in my life where I am able to give back something"...

—*Los Angeles Times*, November 17, 2002
Jean Merl, Staff Writer

"Thelma's Place," as it has become known, delivered a punch that will get an enemy running. The impact was more like a sledgehammer when it came to the center's focus on young abusers.

A large part of [founding Thelma's Place] *involved the creation of a program to help adolescents troubled by drug and alcohol abuse—a dream fulfilled by the creation of the Thelma McMillen Teen Outpatient Program.*

According to Moe Gelbart, Ph.D., executive director of [the Center], *"With every teen that this program helps, we continue to realize the vision of our benefactor, Karl McMillen, whose generosity made it all possible."*

—From the History of the Thelma McMillen Center
for Chemical Dependency Treatment

"The First Step in the Right Direction" is an appropriate motto used by Thelma's Place. The first step inside tells a potential patient that this isn't a hospital or close-walled rehab. Its atmosphere is more of a private office or college; a place of respect and learning. With its mentoring staff, library, reading room, weight and exercise facility, and conference centers, Thelma's Place feels comforting and it feels positive.

Thelma's Place has a warm atmosphere of respect and learning.

It is certainly both.

The emphasis on bringing family members and loved ones into a patient's support network rounds out a total package of compassion and cure.

In his speech at the dedication of Thelma's Place, Karl delivers a somberly paternal perspective:

> *"I know that drug and alcohol abuse touches many lives...*
> *I know from personal experience the devastation addiction can bring...*
> *If there had been a teen program like the one we are launching at the*
> *Thelma McMillen Center, I believe my son would be alive today."*

Thelma's Place was now open for business.

2004

The funding of the $1.5-million–dollar chair Karl pledged for Dr. Ken Trefftzs is fulfilled completely.

Generosity is becoming a full-time job. And that full-time job is benefitting so many lives in the name of Mark and Thelma.

It was time...

By '04, Karl had been working hard and successfully for sixty-five-plus years.

It was time to retire—*again*. Karl's first "retirement" back in the 1960s didn't really count; it didn't offer the opportunities, nor the complexities and obligations, that this one did.

This one would require a plan.

A big plan.

And an extensive examination of data.

Underlying everything was that direction-draining question of succession. And underlying *that* was the blood-letting truth that Mark was gone and Chris was in no position to even stand in that kind of line.

> *Every human being is born an heir to an inheritance*
> *to which he can succeed only in a process of learning.*
>
> —Michael Joseph Oakeshott

Karl studied the options. He wanted to retire and dedicate more time to his philanthropy and to enjoying life; but he would never do it at the expense of his Todd Pipe family.

They would have to be taken care of.

Todd's employees appreciated the practicality and caring of all of this—but, oh, how they would miss Karl McMillen!

On so many levels and for so many reasons.

The notes, cards, letters, tributes, and thank-yous that came to Karl from his employees as he stepped away from Todd were anything but corporate protocol and formalities. They were love:

"Thank you for being a blessing to me and my family. Your thoughtfulness has been unsurpassed by anyone I've ever worked for..."

"Karl, thank you for your generosity! We will never forget all that you have done for us."

"Thanks for the Mexican Riviera cruise, thanks for the Caribbean cruise, and many other nice vacations. Without your generosity they would not have been possible."

"Thank you for all that you have done for me personally. You have always gone over and above a normal employer. You made me feel like family."

The sale of Todd was not done lightly or easily. After all the lengthy investigations, considerations, and negotiations, Karl sold Todd Pipe & Supply to Hughes Supply, a mega North American, forty-state-and-two-Canadian-province-wide construction wholesaler that was expanding into the West. Karl was assured that Hughes would maintain the personal-touch *"hard work, honesty, integrity, and a respect for both customers and employees"* that he had utilized as he built Todd.

This family would be taken care of...

But just a year later, the entire Hughes Supply operation—including Todd Pipe & Supply—was purchased by Home Depot for $3.2 billion.

The personal employee loans, getaway resort trailers and condos, and countless "family" perks were now completely lost in the high-stakes shuffle.

Not lost in the turnovers, however, were the standout skills of Todd's employees—another result of Karl's Golden Touch. Those triumphs were never overlooked or missed by Todd's competitors—especially the quality of Todd's management staff.

Managers had been promoted from within. Like Don McDonald, they grew up at Todd Pipe & Supply; they received educations at Todd Pipe & Supply and through Todd Pipe & Supply. They had attended practical seminars, classes, and college courses. Their experience, talent, and knowledge were as valuable as Karl's 24-carat caress.

It was a front-office fire sale. Any of Todd's management team who eschewed Home Depot were snatched up like chum in the water by predator-rivals.

THE RADICAL CHANGES that Karl was seeing at Todd Pipe haunted him—you don't sell a thoroughbred race horse to have him turned into a plow-puller.

Karl was disturbed and distressed at the latest sale news; but how Todd operated was no longer his call. Right now, he was retired.

CHAPTER 22

Marriage, McMillen-Style

As a TWENTY-SEVEN-YEAR EMPLOYEE in the offices of Todd Pipe, Carol Campbell had seen a lot.

She knew the business. And she knew Karl McMillen.

She knew Thelma and she knew the boys and she knew what had happened to them all. She had witnessed so much from a professionally distanced yet personally caring vantage point.

Carol was the one who had seen Chris in yet another confrontation with cops while on her lunch hour. And she was the one who couldn't bear to deliver more pain to a man like Karl.

Professionally distanced, personally caring…

In 2004, after the sale of Todd, Karl called up Carol. He explained to her that since he wasn't her boss anymore, he'd like to take her out to dinner.

Sounds logical…

They began to know each other better. And they began to travel together—well, travel not in the sense that one might expect from a retired multi-millionaire. But in the back-to-Baja back-roads way

Karl had and has always liked to travel: in a pop-up camper with no bathroom.

"But," he promised Carol when the discussions began, "we will always stay in five-star hotels at our destinations. *When* they're available…"

SEPTEMBER 2004

The couple's first trip cinched the tone of their adventures together. Carol had three suitcases, a hanging clothes bag, a carry-on bag of cosmetics—enough clean luxury for six months. Karl had one little bag and his pickup truck.

It was more than enough.

Carol kept a journal of the trek. You can almost hear the spirits of Jack London and John Muir echoing in her words!

> On our way to the north rim of the Grand Canyon. As we travel to Tuweep Point it becomes more and more obvious that you need a four-wheel-drive vehicle to make it. The further we go, the more I begin wondering if I made the right decision of wanting to experience "an off-road dirt trip"!
>
> But Karl is having a wonderful time proving that his Toyota Tundra can blaze trails and conquer the world. I'm wondering how anyone ever even found this road!
>
> Now we're behind our schedule and it's dark. There's no choice but to push on to Tuweep—there's nowhere to pull off and nowhere to camp and it's too dark to see anyway!
>
> We catch a rabbit in the headlights and he keeps on running for a quarter mile before he gets out of the rut.
>
> Maybe he's the smart one!
>
> Then come the bats flying out of the darkness!
>
> Then the owls!

Rabbits, bats, and owls: Oh my! But this is Karl's yellow brick road. It's the release that balances his business wizardry. It's who he is. From sliding brakeless down the Indio grade with Chuck to bouncing over Baja ruts and rocks with Mark, this race and run with feral nature is Karl McMillen.

We can see nothing but what is directly in front of the headlights. The road is like a lunar crater and we finally bounce into Tuweep Point. But there are only a couple of places a vehicle can comfortably stop and camp— and both are taken! (It's hard to believe that other people have found their way out here!)

Karl pulls the truck up to four small rocks; he parks and sets up the camper for the night. Chili, fried potatoes, and onions are part of the "setup."

We go to bed and open the window so I can see the stars...

In the morning, I leap out of the camper to see where we are. No guard rails! No barriers! No nothing to stop you from walking off the edge of the Grand Canyon!

"How glorious a greeting the sun gives the mountains!"

—John Muir

Later in this "off-road dirt trip" we head for a magical place called "Hole in the Rock" in Utah. It has to be special with a name like that! On the way, we have lunch in the town of Escalante. A local tells us that the area's last rainfall trapped everyone who was where we are going!

Yes... this is magical!

Karl says we'll be fine—we have plenty of food and water!

Trapped?!

We're on another of those roads that really aren't roads. (Definitions in the wilderness differ vastly from where people actually live!)

And believe it or not, there's someone behind us on this "road"—two guys in a truck. Karl pulls over and lets them by. He figures they'll make good scouts—he can see where the biggest bumps are by watching them bounce all over the road!

I ask Karl if this is the "bad" part of the trail that the people in town told us about.

"Nope…not yet…this is nothing!"

We get to a part of the road where two vehicles are parked—including the truck that went in front of us. The people are getting out; they're going to hike the rest of the way up. They aren't going to risk their vehicles trying to navigate the huge asteroid-sized rock directly ahead!

Karl doesn't share in their apprehension.

We pass them and Karl hangs out the window: "So far, so good!" He smiles!

> "The Wild still lingered in him
> and the wolf in him merely slept."
>
> —Jack London, *White Fang*

I have a simple question at this point: "Karl! You are not going to drive up this rock, are you?!"

He is.

"Carol, you need to trust me," he says. "Just hang on and I'll show you."

I figure General Custer gave the same speech to his men—right before they saw Crazy Horse!

Well, we made it! And we saw the famous "Hole in the Rock." I learned that in 1880, pioneers formed a community nearby and called it Bluff.

I also learned that "bluff" is something Karl McMillen never does. What he says he's going to do, he accomplishes!

"Just hang on…"

On the road with Karl. So far, so good...

CAROL HAD KNOWN KARL since 1978, but primarily as just "the boss." She was never really aware of his pioneer personality or that he could talk and interact beyond numbers.

Now she was getting close to the guy who had grown up panning gold, working in the fields, plumbing housing tracts, and preferring denim and flannel to pressed pants and ties.

She could also see that Karl was comfortable in almost any setting; as long as he was connected to that "lifeline of savvy" his father had thrown him and "studying the Tobes of the world and analyzing characters and character." And as long as he could share it with someone he loved.

From 2004 to 2007, Karl and Carol alternated between the pickup truck, planes, and cruise ships. (Yes, Carol finally got her five-star vacation adventure, too!)

Monthlong road and off-road trips from Alaska to Florida melded with Mexican cruises and treks through China and South America.

For the first time in over thirty years, a little of that second goal in Terry Devitt's 1976 report was finally being realized for Karl.

Goal B: Removing from your lives the constant strain and tension that has now been present for more than half a decade.

That "half a decade" had expanded into an excruciating three decades–plus, but Karl—and now Carol—were finally living with at least a little less strain and tension.

JULY 11, 2007

Karl and Carol are married in Ely, Nevada; not far from "the hill."

Carol had always referred to their other trips as "Adventures, McMillen-Style." This adventure was "*Marriage*, McMillen-Style."

The plan was to be married in Ely's circa-1900s courthouse, "an old-fashioned white three-story building, sitting on a green grassy hill…simple and tranquil."

And they'd be married by a judge, with only Karl's cousin Bill (who just happened to be in the area) as a witness.

Simple and tranquil…

This was a dash different in grandeur from, say, Prince William and Catherine's Royal Wedding, the Kardashian bash, or the years of fantasy-speculation about how Brad and Angelina would eventually tie their tangled knot.

"Marriage, McMillen-Style" began with a couple of days at a local inn before the big day, allowing time for an expedition into the maw of Karl's old dusty stomping grounds. Karl showed Carol the bright lights and high times of big apples like Strawberry Creek, Major Junction, and Ruth.

But they had some slight hitches.

First, a recent hip replacement had Karl teetering around with a cane. It would take him some time to recover, but the surgery had gone well. No complications or surprises. Torrance Memorial had even given him a private room with fresh fruit and vegetables each day.

(Not long after, Karl would further extend his generosity to the hospital by making them, through a highly complex series of accounting and tax rules of bequeathment, the beneficiary of a three-million-dollar life-insurance policy. Carol figured it was a good thing the policy wasn't in effect yet when they opened him up to fix that hip!)

The other slight concern was that the night before leaving, Carol had fallen in Karl's garage and broken her foot.

Now, some may have thought this a bad omen, a jinxed way to start off a marriage—like when actress Hilary Duff lost a tooth hours before her wedding! But, hey, Hilary worked it out so that she could smile and eat, and Karl and Carol worked it out so they could walk.

These minor injury-setbacks didn't hinder the romantic atmosphere of the trip at all.

No siree.

The happy couple may have been hobbling (Karl with his cane and Carol with a big black orthopedic boot housing her entire right foot), but in the spirit of Jim Henry, Karl and Carol hiked and marched the area around the hill while Karl conducted a firsthand tour of his childhood.

They even dedicated a big nugget of time hunting for the famous "Hercules Powder box toilet" again. The one that Mac had rigged up for young "Karlie" seventy years before. It had been twenty years since Karl and his buddy Omar had embarked on the same mission and had found the lost toilet in all of its rustic utilitarian splendor. This would be like a second climb to the top of Everest, but on this triumphant return, Karl was accompanied by his soon-to-be blushing bride! A pre-honeymoon hike to the field of dreams!

Their search-and-observation operation rivaled salvaging the wreck of the *Edmund Fitzgerald*. But unlike that great ship's bell, this time the Karl-commode could not be found.

But it had been well worth the try.

A couple of days later, it was time to add a new excursion to that autobiographical tour.

Karl McMillen and Carol Campbell arrived at the Ely City Hall for their wedding.

Still teetering; still limping.

But smiling.

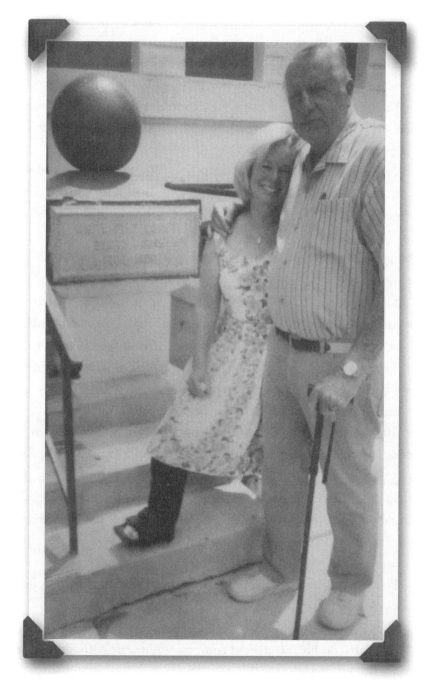

Karl and Carol on their wedding day—teetering and limping, but smiling.

Luckily, the judge's office didn't have much of an aisle for them to walk down. But the listing lovebirds *were* faced with a long flight of stairs in order to get down to the judge's chambers.

And no elevator.

That would be no excuse for backing out of this, Bill and Carol told Karl. They even offered to lower him by a rope if necessary.

It wasn't.

Karl may have limped and winced as he made his way slowly down those stairs, but he made it—humming some touching and sentimental lyrics courtesy of Johnny Cash (*"I fell into a burning ring of fire…I went down, down, down and the flames went higher"*…the "Wedding March" it wasn't!).

I do…

Next was the honeymoon. Now, to again compare landmark nuptials—after Britain's Royal Wedding, the new Duke and Duchess of Cambridge honeymooned at a private resort in the Indian Ocean's Seychelles Islands at a cost of $72,000 a night. The Kardashian party basked on the Amalfi Coast in Italy.

Karl and Carol opted to be a little less extravagant.

After *their* wedding, Karl, Carol, and Cousin Bill piled into the pickup truck (Carol in the tiny back seat) and headed for a local junkyard.

Some vintage treasures of Americana and Western motoring history were rusting away in there that Karl just *had* to share with his cousin.

And Carol.

Then it was on to a spaghetti dinner at a local café and a good night's sleep.

They'd need it.

Up early and hit the ground running (or at least with focused and purpose-filled limps!).

Roll up Route 93.

Stop at a pawn shop in Wendover looking for old guns.

Up through Salt Lake, Bonneville, and into a camp at Bear Lake on the Utah/Idaho border.

Perfect…

Karl was always willing to keep his promise to Carol about staying at five-star hotels. None, however, seemed to be along the trail on that first day of the McMillens' new life as a married couple.

But it didn't matter.

Not here; not now.

It didn't matter if they were bouncing along a dirt road in Utah or walking along the Great Wall of China; climbing aboard a cruise ship bound for the Mexican Riviera or climbing up and over a low-gear rock in the wilds of Alaska. They had each other and the enjoyment of the world around them.

Karl and Carol did finally enjoy a fun family wedding celebration! But more importantly, they enjoy each other and living life to the fullest.

Karl McMillen had persevered and fought hard to make his way to the top of the business world; he never quit. Neither would he ever quit on life, or his family.

Even when it felt like those tragedies might sometimes be outweighing the triumphs.

It didn't matter…

Triumphs and tragedies are a part of any normal life, of course. But there are degrees. And like everything else with Karl, *his* triumphs and tragedies never failed to be extraordinary.

Triumphs and tragedies provide perhaps the most telling bellwethers of how someone fares with being human.

Triumphs and tragedies…

Ultimately, the truest successes in life are measured by how you handle both.

CHAPTER 23

Hana Hou!
One More Time Around!

BACK IN 2000, when Chris staggered up to Karl's door after finding his way from the Greyhound stop, he was forty-three years old.

Then forty-four.

Forty-five.

Forty-six.

It's 2004, and change *has* occurred. The drunken bus ride appears to have been Chris's last bottle-bout. Like an addict who loads up on meds right before checking into rehab, it's common to have one final binge before committing to sobriety.

"Final" doesn't necessarily mean forever. But for now, Christmases and summers are producing the right amount of family and personal warmth.

Maybe...

Chris is trying to make his marriage work.

Karl gives his son's family the $1.4-million home in Manhattan Beach; he moves back up to a "house on the hill" in Palos Verdes.

When Chris is clean, he is never happier. He goes to his youngest daughter's softball games. He coaches, works on the playing field, and helps the kids out. Everyone loves him.

Clean and sober, Chris is never happier than when coaching and spending time with his kids.

But now an old issue is reshuffled, coming back for yet another deal.

Along with the drug and health horrors, Chris's "enjoyment" of gambling has long ago developed into a problem.

You don't have a gambling problem as long as you're winning…

Chris wasn't winning.

With this last marriage, Karl gave Chris several life-insurance policies that he and Thelma had taken out on him, each for about 10K. So now, Chris takes out loans on the policies, and that's that.

More insane amounts of money flushed and shot.

Between the drugs and the gambling and the related medical and legal bills, this treasury of trouble becomes a magnifying glass— joining with Karl's benevolence to allow others to see closely what all of this leads to.

Chris attends meetings; his wife accompanies him. Supports him.

When he speaks to other addicts at various stages of use progression they "fall off their chairs" with the impact of what Chris says and expresses. The force of unmatched charisma applied to "I've done it all" revelations is impossible to ignore.

An assignment from one of the meetings materializes as an especially powerful lens. Chris was required to recall and write down instances when his drug use reversed the meaning of fun. Where the "kick" of drugs turned into just the opposite and destroyed something that could have been pleasant or constructive.

This up-close self-examination by Chris causes more head-shaking and more deep peers into that glass. And more of those questions—*Why would I want to live like this?*

One time my friends and I were going to a Rolling Stones concert in Hollywood. We were drinking pretty heavily and had to park about a half-mile away from the stadium. A few blocks before we got to the stadium, I was arrested for being drunk in public—I missed the concert.

I had a great job in Louisiana working for a company called Oceaneering. I was working as a 3rd class diver and had an opportunity to become a 1st class diver, and then a supervisor. As a result of drinking and taking pills on the job, I was fired.

I always wanted to go to work in my father's business, be a good son, and follow in his footsteps. Due to my alcoholism and drug addiction, the opportunity has passed me by.

And it gets worse and more internalized:

Assignment #3

My emotional nature seems really scattered. I can't seem to get any balance…a lot of the time I'm depressed or just miserable or in a funk.

I'm not working, and fear crops up when I apply for a job because of my past. I feel useless—less than, really. I'm not good enough, stupid and slothful.

Chris shared what he'd done and been through, creating an in-depth diary of what it's actually like to live like this—the disappointments, the missed opportunities, the shame.

This view is clear and it is frightening.

Add in Chris's time spent in prison, his short stint on the lam, his shattered leg, his broken marriages and relationships, his estranged children, and his legal, financial, and personal problems, and what you have isn't a simple little "scaring straight" story. No. The look explodes into I-can't-even-scream shock. No one wants to live like this.

No one.

Chris wanted to magnify that.

And he did. Just by being who he was, and by Karl being who *he* was. Chris had been blessed with maximum-swell potential; he had everything he needed to have the most amazing life ever. The world had always been at his fingertips.

It *still* was. But he still couldn't grasp it. Instead, he remained under the hold of that unretreating enemy.

But Chris *was* able to turn his life into lessons. Those listening knew he spoke from a place of hard-won wisdom; in-the-alley addicts aren't bluffed easily.

And Chris had a giving heart and a forgiving heart. He'd pick people up and take them to meetings; he'd spend hours and hours helping them. He'd let people stay with him and take them to dinner and breakfast. He knew they were all sharing the same walking shoes.

Even when Chris was using, he was helping other people. He'd get loaded one day and be out giving help the next day.

If you needed help, Chris was there.

Forty-seven years old.

Forty-eight.

Other than the limp, Chris is looking like himself, physically. He's even back in the ocean and on the board.

And this restoration and resurgence offered the time, place, and energy for a task that had been in emotional suspension for years.

It was time to face that shark of reflections and memories once more.

Mom...

The boys' best friend.

The best friend who once said: "Remember the good times. That is what I do, and I often laugh at the bad times."

Chris paddled out alone to scatter his mother's ashes, along the same Hermosa shore where he had rejoined Mark with the Pacific.

That monster was still biting and thrashing, but it didn't matter. Once more he did what he had to do—what he wanted to do.

No kau a kau, makua hine...

> *"Out of the water, I am nothing."*
>
> —Duke Kahanamoku, the Father of Surfing

Chris paddles back in.

But he needs more.

"I saw the early years, the good years with Mark and Chris and
our friends like Richie and Charlie Q.
All these guys, we grew up together surfing Hermosa.
When we'd paddle out together,
people would be amazed watching us all rip!
I never saw Chris pass a wave that he thought he could ride;
he'd just whip around and go!"

—Another of Chris's lifelong friends

Chris prepares for a trip back to Kauai, to catch an old taste of the endless summer.

Cousin Jeff is over there at the same time on his honeymoon—a harmonic equinox convergence.

Hana hou! One more time into the *moana* with Jeff.

Jeff remembers it well:

> *I was a day ahead of Chris in hitting the water. I was surfing this place on the south shore called Brennecke Beach. It's a little reef, and there was this local out there trying to control the point. He kept on taking all the good waves.*
>
> *This one wave came in and it was the biggest set of the day. I looked at this guy and said, "I'm taking this wave!"*
>
> *He goes, "No-how, this is my wave!"*
>
> *I say, "No, man, this is my wave!"*
>
> *I take off in front of him.*
>
> *I'm paddling.*
>
> *He yells, "Comin' right, hale, comin' right!"*
>
> *I don't even listen to him. I just take off. I cut him off and I ride the wave.*
>
> *My wife is on the beach watching me, waving to me. I've caught the biggest wave of the day and I'm surfing it in.*

I kick out and paddle back out and the guy's sitting there waiting for me on the outside. I paddle up to him and I say, "Hey, I apologize for that."

He goes, "You beat it! You beat it now!"

I go, "No, I'm not beating it, but I do I apologize. I won't do it again."

"You beat it!" he repeats. "You beat it now or we have a beef."

"I'm not beating it," I tell him again. "Let me tell you the deal: I'm forty-five years old, I'm on my honeymoon, and I don't beat it for nobody."

And he goes, "You no beat it?"

"No man, I ain't beating it. You can deal with this right now or accept my apology. I won't do it again."

He's thinking.

He goes, "Where you from?"

"I'm from La Jolla," I tell him.

"Oh, La Jolla," he says.

So we sort of bond, right.

But as I paddle in to my wife, these other local guys are standing out there on the shore. There's about five or six of them and we have to walk by them to get to our car.

I tell her that if they come at us, run as fast as you can. But they don't say or do anything.

Chris comes in that night, and we plan to surf the next day. Chris asks me where we're going.

"Well, there's Shipwrecks," I tell him. "And then there's this cool point called Brennecke's. But we can't go out there because I got in a beef with the locals this morning and I don't feel I can go back out there again."

He goes, "Dude, we're going out there first thing in the morning!"

"I never saw Chris pass a wave that he thought he could ride."

So Chris gets up bright and early and wakes me up—you know, now he's waking ME up to go surfing like I did to him and Mark back when we were kids in Hermosa.

We get out on Brennecke's, he takes off his shirt, and he's just ripped. He's got his tattoos and he's looking like Arnold Schwarzenegger. He paddles out and I paddle right behind him. We go out to the point and they're out there.

He controls the left; I control the right.

He says, "Don't worry about it, Jeff. We're going to take this place over. No one's going to mess with you today!"

And I felt like, "I got King Kong on my side, man! No one's going to stop us today."

That's the way it was with Chris; he came there to take care of me. He was like a big brother watching out for me. And there's nothing like that, especially when you're surfing in the water; because it's usually a one-on-one thing, but having your big brother out there, these locals knew, "Hey, you mess with him, you have to mess with me."

And that's exactly what Mark did for Chris, too.

It was that harmonic convergence.
Mahalo, kaikua'ana.

BUT, LIKE THE SURFERS in Jan and Dean's classic beach tune "Ride the Wild Surf," it looked like Chris had finally taken "that one last ride."

Not long after Chris returned from Hawaii, the problems caused by his bad leg and limp worsened, and he had to have his hip replaced.

Chris was sad and in pain. He told Jeff that he wished it hadn't gone down the way it did in his life.

He was grateful for his children, but he was sad with the way it went down for them, too.

Of all people, Jeff understood.

All he ever wanted to do was to be like Chris. In every way…

Jeff accomplished just that. He never found his way into heroin, but cocaine became his distorted mirror-image of Chris:

For me and for so many, it all started off as emotional addiction, but if you do it long enough it becomes physical.

Once you cross that line, you're like a caged animal. Whatever you have to get, whatever you need to survive, you'll do anything to get it. And that's how I lived.

The only thing that mattered to me was getting what I needed to get through each day.

And I was dying.

Literally.

But Jeff got—and accepted—help. He "lives in recovery" and he helps others who are trying to do the same. He is the alumni president of the McDonald Center in La Jolla, part of the Scripps Clinic and Research Center; and he's involved in drug and alcohol treatment centers all over Southern California, including the Thelma McMillen Center.

From Chris's times in the Betty Ford Clinic and other rehabs to his times passed out on a floor, Jeff was there—counseling, mopping up, or just supplying love.

He knew. He *knows*. He's been there:

The Wreckage of Your Past

You carry the emotional baggage for years. The emotional baggage runs with you forever, really. If you party and get high for twenty years and all of a sudden you're cleaned up for a couple years, you've still got twenty years of what you lived through encased in your brain. And with that, you have all this shame and guilt and remorse and fear that goes along with those years of addiction. It's a mess!

So now, you've got two years of sober memories over here, and it doesn't hold any weight to those twenty. So you've got to do a lot of work to get forgiveness and make amends and clean up the wreckage of your past and learn how to live; to find a design for living that will work with and for you. Some kind of faith and some kind of higher power that can help guide you through tough times.

Chris was trying. He was ever trying to find that "design for living." But by now his emotional baggage was far overweight, and the cost to transport it was becoming prohibitive.

You're thinking, "I know I can rob, steal, and cheat over there and do okay in my old life." You start to think that this honest life is the tough life.

And for many addicts, it is.

But still, Chris would attend the addiction meetings with Jeff. They would cry together and they would learn and they would teach.

The tears increased.

But, as always, *if you needed help, Chris was there...*

When Jeff had to have heart surgery, arriving at the hospital at three a.m., Chris was already there. He was the only one in the parking lot; sitting patiently in the dark with a cup of coffee.

Waiting for Jeff. Waiting to give support.

Karl arrived soon after.

This was a family.

Chris did the same for Richie:

> *My mom was an alcoholic; my sister had addiction problems. I've definitely lived through a series of times that were not too good. But during it, Chris proved again that he was the most giving, caring guy.*
>
> *He touched my life.*
>
> *I came out of the hospital at one point and I couldn't even walk because of what the drugs had done. I was like a patient in* One Flew Over the Cuckoo's Nest. *I was crazed, seeing stuff come out of my body. I felt like a different human being—just completely gone.*
>
> *But Chris picked me up—literally. Physically. And he nursed me back to health like I was little kid. "Let's take a walk on the beach," he'd say. And then he'd invite me for Thanksgiving because my family had disowned me.*
>
> *Chris was my sponsor and Chris was on track. We would discuss stuff in a real good way. He made me happy when he was so happy at his daughter's softball games; and seeing how much he loved his kids...*
>
> *He wrapped his arms around me like a brother and he loved me until I could love myself.*

Chris turns forty-nine.

Fifty.

Never give up…

A half-century of years behind him, Chris looked back and reflected, as he had so often before. This time that reflection shone with his thoughts about the father-child relationship. The thoughts were intense. With what he and his father had been through and what he had been through with his own children, they had to be:

My perspective of the father-child relationship is that I believe a father always has unconditional love for his children. He might not like what they do all the time, but the love is always there.

Fathers always forgive their children and want what is best for them.

A father is someone you respect, like an old oak tree—solid, firm, strong, and unwavering throughout the storm of life.

The father is someone you can always depend on. It is a constant; always there.

With Karl as his father, Chris was completely right.

2006

Chris enters an apprenticeship program with Local Union 250 of the Steam-Refrigeration-Air Conditioning-Pipefitters & Apprentices of the United Association of the United States and Canada. On his first day on the job, he is welding at an awkward angle; his hip goes out.

That's that.

And it wasn't the last time for the hip to slip. While working in the attic of Karl's home, it went out on him again, requiring paramedics to lower him down.

Chris's welding jobs were now limited to Karl's charitable projects; Chris would do work on some of the facilities like the House of

Hope. But he would never take any form of payment or any credit for the work.

He just wanted to help.

He loved giving.

2007

Fifty-one years of age and still with these damned issues; feelings and cravings that hang in there like a noose swinging in the wind right outside. Always a reminder of another type of potential.

You've got to do a lot of work to get forgiveness and make amends and clean up the records of your past and learn how to live…

Chris's wife has finally had enough of the struggle.

They divorce amid a settlement that involves the house in Manhattan.

This time, the trust writes a check.

To Chris, losing his wife was the worst part of all of this, a choking cinch-knot in that noose.

Chris loved her, and she loved him. But no one loved all those issues.

DECEMBER 10, 2007

The McMillen Family Foundation files Articles of Incorporation. The resolve forged by what this family has suffered for so many years is finally formalized for positive battle. The potential for good to come out of all this is now limitless.

The year 2008 begins with the Foundation releasing a determined war cry of a mission statement:

The McMillen Family built a very successful wholesale plumbing supply business consisting of nine highly-respected facilities located in California and Nevada. That success was the result of hard work, honesty, integrity, and a respect for both customers and employees.

Those same values will guide the McMillen Family Foundation in providing support to nonprofit groups and agencies dedicated to improving the lives of those in need.

The mission of the McMillen Family Foundation is to provide assistance to eligible groups in Southern California that are dedicated to helping men and women who have been impacted, directly or indirectly, by alcohol and/or drugs. We will give priority in funding to those nonprofits that share our values and have produced tangible and measurable results.

The Foundation was set and ready for combat.

Give.

Help.

Fight the battle!

Those *"eligible groups in Southern California that are dedicated to helping men and women who have been impacted, directly or indirectly, by alcohol and/or drugs"* began with Pathways to Independence and House of Hope, both of which provide safe, nurturing environments for abused and/or substance-dependent women.

The sister of Chris's wife had been helped through House of Hope. The head of Pathways, Dave Bishop, was a customer of Todd Pipe in Orange County and shared an AA/Al-Anon closeness with Todd's Dan Patrick. Those personal relationships provided a befitting bridge to the foundation's first beneficiaries.

And it was just the start. So many people need help.

Unfortunately, Chris McMillen was still one of them.

CHAPTER 24

"Stay Clean and Your Life Will Be Set. Choose Drugs, You Are on Your Own."

JULY 2, 2008

Nearly a year to the day after Karl's marriage to Carol, Chris suffers severe throat pain.

He sees a doctor and is referred for a CT scan at Torrance Memorial, home of "Thelma's Place."

As Chris walks through the doors aside the Thelma McMillen Center, he obviously thinks of his mother. *Reflects.* How can he not?

And how can he not stand for a moment and look at the full and formal name: The Thelma McMillen Center for Chemical Dependency Treatment. This is *his* mother and this is *his* disease.

This is *him.*

This entire facility of hope and help is about *him* and people *like him.*

Drug addicts.

It's a lot to handle.

Tears.

Embarrassment.

Please, Mom, don't be ashamed…

IT'S APPARENT RIGHT FROM THE START that something serious is wrong with Chris. His CT scan is overseen by the head cancer doctor at the facility. After reviewing the results, Chris is referred to Dr. Uttam Sinha at USC's Keck School of Medicine. Sinha is recognized as the best of the best.

Chris has throat cancer, like his mother. And like his mother, he has been smoking for years—another serious addiction to add to the list.

By October of '08, Chris has had surgery and heavy doses of chemotherapy.

Everyone—from Chris's three children to his sponsor, Merle, to every other friend and family member—is at Chris's side during these hospital stays.

The cancer was caught quickly and stopped, but Chris was left with a hole in his throat due to a procedural tracheotomy.

Yet what didn't stop was Chris's smoking.

He just *couldn't*.

He'd plug the hole while he smoked and cough it down.

Throat cancer is often described as the most excruciating. The diagnosis was devastating to Chris in every way; even in its remission. More medications were awakening cravings.

More using—*heavy heroin using*—followed.

Chris was giving up on life; and no longer giving up drugs.

Less than four months later, in February of 2009, it was time for a final, *final decision*.

Intervention.

> Things are moving in a positive fashion...Still, I know there are difficult times ahead. Behavior doesn't change overnight or even in months. But we have taken good steps and I think things look as good as they have in some time.

—Terry Devitt,
Final Report and Recommendations, June 1976

FEBRUARY 4, 2009

Thirty-three years since things were looking "as good as they have in some time."

And the behavior that "doesn't change overnight or even in months" sometimes becomes a monstrous way of life. A monster that simply couldn't be allowed to grow any more.

Enough was more than enough.

Intervention was a specialty at Scripps Memorial Hospital's McDonald Center for Drug and Alcohol Treatment on the edge of the Pacific in La Jolla, due north of San Diego. McDonald's chief interventionist, John Seaman, understood addicts, addiction, and intervention:

> "Intervention is the best way I know to help break through the delusional thinking of the addict or alcoholic and help him or her gain insight into the problem and become willing to accept help," Seaman says. "The delusional thinking is 'protected' by a rigid defense system, which, of course, leads to denial."
>
> What's delusional thinking? "The addict fails to make the connection between the consequences he experiences and the substance he's using," Seaman says. "You need to understand the cunning, baffling aspects of this illness. A person loses control, and the drug takes over."
>
> The goal of an intervention is to get the alcoholic or drug addict to agree to enter a treatment program immediately, as soon as the intervention is completed. Seaman, who has conducted more than 1,300 interventions, says this goal is met about 75 percent of the time. He says a fair percentage of the remainder will eventually seek help.

—From "When One Drink Is Too Many,"
San Diego Magazine, 2005

Intervention is what saved the life of Cousin Jeff. It was a major turning point that he remembers so well:

The Power of Intervention

A full ten years before I got sober, I knew I had a problem. But I was always taught to beat my problems on my own.

I couldn't.

I tried for all those ten years to stop.

My family knew I was going to die because of this. They finally did an intervention on me, and right then I had a moment of clarity. I had a spiritual experience where I was able to stop the lies and admit the truth to my family. That I was a drug addict and I needed help and wanted help.

Before that I was full of shame and guilt. I knew I wanted to quit, but I couldn't bring myself to admit the truth to anybody. Especially my family. I couldn't tell anybody how bad it was for me.

I received exactly what I needed with that intervention. Everyone in my family was there. They begged me not to die like Mark died— please don't die like Mark died!

And at that point I looked at the sky and said, "God help me, I don't want to die like this. Please don't let me die!" And something happened to me in that moment. Chills went through my whole body and the desperation and willingness came to me and I became willing to accept help, and that whole process began.

I wasn't cured instantly, but I was willing to go.

I made a decision to give twelve-step programs a chance and put my whole self into them and see what might happen.

When I went to treatment, I was there long enough to get some clarity, hear miracles of recovery, hear the message, and get some hope that maybe I could do it too, and I could have a life.

Since then, I've had that life; the best years of my life. I've been doing it one day at a time.

Ultimately, it's about permanent sobriety.

Now it's Chris's turn.

An army of Karl, Carol, Jeff, and Ty, along with longtime family friends Merle Countryman and Richie Davidson, intervene in Chris's failing life and health.

And they seem to make it through, behind enemy lines.

Chris is thin and frail, making the hole in his neck even more pronounced. He agrees to go.

This army of love brings him to the McDonald Center. The facility is a heavyweight in the field; so is its cost. Karl writes a check.

With intervention so close to Jeff's mind, heart, and soul, he is relieved that Chris is in treatment. But when he finds out that the center is letting Chris smoke, Jeff is not happy.

Are you blind?!

This man has throat cancer!

We must address the smoking—the smoking wakes the pain, the pain wakes up the drug addiction!

Heal the whole body, heal the whole mind, heal the whole spirit—let's get him on a healthy track of life all the way around!

Jeff is told that they will deal with "one thing at a time."

It's February. Maybe, just maybe, by spring and summer *this year*, Chris could be back and enjoying the beach.

February 14, 2009

Chris walks away from the McDonald Center.

Cousin Jeff knows why:

Chris knew he had some drugs at home and he was really hurting…he hadn't surrendered, even yet. At this stage in his drug-life, he'd still do anything, including walking out of rehab, to get what he needed to make himself feel better, feel comfortable.

Chris "walks" but he needs help. He gets in touch with a girlfriend in the San Diego area. She works with him and they engineer a $225 taxi ride back to his $1.4-million Manhattan Beach house.

Four days later, Karl and Carol receive a call. After nearly four decades, the phone ringing at the McMillen home is still met with a shaking anticipation.

For good reason.

Chris has apparently overdosed. He is rushed to the hospital and his life is spared.

Back to the McDonald Center, the battle with Karl and Carol gets verbally bloody. This prisoner of the drug wars is not going back into confinement. At least not there.

Okay, fine. But the next final, final decision is going to be in the form of a final, final contract.

The final deal.

FEBRUARY 23, 2009

First, pre-contract, Chris is removed from any financial aid or association with Karl's trust.

Done.

Ty and Richie check Chris into the Betty Ford Clinic in Rancho Mirage—the same rehab center he walked out of back in the mid-1990s.

This time, maybe, just maybe, things will be different.

This time the contract is legally binding.

Chris is presented with the agreement—very formally prepared by Karl's lawyers:

March 19, 2009

Dear Chris:

As a trustee of your trust, I want to assure you that we will work with you in your treatment program. But I also want to state as clearly as possible that under no circumstances will we use the trusts to enable your habits. To achieve both of these objectives, you have agreed to the following (which we will reevaluate every six months with input from you and from your treatment professionals):

You will comply with the current and future recommendations of the Betty Ford Center. At the present time, this involves your enrollment and participation in, and your successful completion of, BFC's Residential Day Treatment program.

You will participate in a random drug testing program to confirm your sobriety. The precise terms of this program will be developed by your BFC treatment professionals.

You will remain productively engaged in the board activities of the McMillen Family Foundation and the Thelma McMillen Center.

To confirm your agreement to the foregoing course of conduct, please sign and date where indicated below.

Agreed to and accepted as of this _19_ day of March, 2009.

Chris A. McMillen

Chris A. McMillen

Chris is in Betty Ford. Karl is there too, along with Carol, Ty, and Jeff, for the events of Family Week. The events aren't fun and games. It isn't a hats-and-horns carnival of social jumps; not with lives on a thread of the line.

This isn't entertainment; it's education.

While the patients absorb and learn, so do those around them. And it's never too late.

After thirty-seven years, Karl begins to understand the meaning of enabling. He is taught the addict-axiom that "If an addict talks with his hands—or even if only his lips are moving—you can pretty much bet it's all B.S."

For the next few days, Karl lies awake in that deep heart of the night trying to fathom this new understanding…

For the next few days, until another of those calls comes through.

Three days after the Ford Clinic Family Week, an emaciated and weak Chris has trouble breathing. He is rushed to the adjacent Eisenhower Medical Center, rated as one of the top one hundred hospitals in the United States.

Karl arranges for an eight-hundred-dollar ambulance ride to take Chris from Rancho Mirage back into Los Angeles where he can get further treatment back at USC's Keck Medical Center.

The doctors find that Chris has stayed cancer-free, but fluids are building up in his throat and cutting off the air supply due to a lack of self-therapy.

Chris still smokes.

The doctors further tell Chris that the reason he is not healing or gaining weight is due to his drug abuse.

My God…

This horrific last stage of addiction has gone on for so, so long. Constructive damage control has become a panicked holding-on while the parachute of survival spins and collapses. Heartbeats and the unceasing mental pounding of desperately seeking the *Whys?*

are flatlining. The "rehab, promises, tears, repentance" and the ever-nearing firestorm of death are now loud, smashing ticks of the clock.

How long?

How long?

Chris, my only son,

I am writing this letter to you because talking just does not come out right and I can't seem to say all I need to say.

Son, I know how hard these last ten months have been on you and I am so very proud that you were strong enough to stick with the treatments and beat the cancer. It is time for you to fight the next battle, and that is your powerful drug addiction. You are cancer-free. The doctor has told us the pain level is now to a tolerable level and there is absolutely no reason for drugs to go into your body.

You seem to be in total denial as to how heavy your drug use is. That is the ONLY reason you did not gain your weight back or the strength. Chris, you were wasted most of the time and did not take care of yourself. That is why you did not bounce back and probably why your throat is swollen with fluids now. You don't even know how bad you were using heroin or how often you were drugged up.

Chris, you came very close to dying that night before we took you back to the McDonald Center. You think your kids are not there for you. Well, let me tell you, they would have been if you had not been so loaded on so much drugs, and you were so mean to Ty. They could not handle watching you nodding out and wasted most of the time.

I know you will blame me for being controlling, but if you think about that, you

will know that I had to be because you would
never take control of your life and break away
from me taking care of you.

I have been there for you your whole life. I
have bailed you out of every situation you ever
put yourself in. I have financially supported
you, your children, and your future generations.
After going to the Family Week, I have painfully
discovered that everything I tried to do to
help you was hurting you instead. I am suffering
more than you know, knowing that my enabling
stopped my sons from facing the punishments for
the mistakes you both made and probably would
have stopped you from taking your situation for
granted. Son, I am not sure if you will ever
understand, but I have no choice but to cut you
out of everything from the trust and from my
living will.

You will be left with nothing.

I worked my whole life to make sure that my
family was taken care of and now I know it was
a mistake. If you choose to go home instead of
following the contract, then I have no choice.
I REFUSE TO GIVE YOU THE MONEY TO KILL YOURSELF
WITH. If this is the road you choose to take, you
will have to kill yourself without my help.

If you choose to follow the contract, your
life will be put back to being trusted with
money. You have no idea how much you could help
other people from your experiences in life. You
would make a GREAT drug counselor and could stop
others from following the wrong path. It only
takes staying clean and sober and taking a class
in counseling and you could have a rewarding and
productive life and have the financial backing
you are seeking from me.

```
I can't put it any clearer, Chris.
Stay clean and your life will be set.
Choose drugs, you are on your own.
I love you more than you will ever know.
```

Dad

April 1, 2009

Thirteen years to the day since Karl wrote the letter to the judge, attempting to get Chris's longest prison sentence reduced, more persuasion is needed to try once again to free Chris—from the *real* enemy.

Chris is discharged from USC. He is met again by the strike force of Karl, Merle, and Richie to escort him back to Betty Ford.

More battle.

More anger and shouting.

Karl and Merle and Richie huddle up to discuss a plan B; then they look around—no Chris. They drive around in circles for an hour looking for him.

But he's gone.

Chris has grabbed a cab—*again*—this time headed for his ex-wife's house. He can't talk so he has to write notes to the cab driver. He's determined!

Back to Betty Ford?

No way.

Everyone needed a breather. Everyone needed a time-out.

What next?

Maybe a family gathering. Not a "Family Week" seminar, but a bound-by-blood family get-together.

Karl and Carol had moved to the cliff side of the beautiful Palos Verdes Peninsula, a short sea breeze down from the Mediterranean inspired California-nirvana resort of Terranea. From the backyard you can almost reach out and touch Catalina Island.

Whale- and dolphin-watching is a part of the daily scenery and ambience.

It really is heaven.

And heaven can help everyone and anyone—certainly.

In 2008 and 2009, Karl and Carol's corner of heaven donated a total of $1,007,000 to worthy charities, through the McMillen Family Foundation.

APRIL 26, 2009

Heaven has a family reunion.

The family gathers for a barbecue at the estate. All three of Chris's children are there. More friends. More family. More support. More angels of mercy.

And Chris spends most of this special time in heaven nodding out.

APRIL 27, 2009

The smashing ticks of the clock are getting faster and more deafening.

The day after the barbecue, Chris nods out again. But this time the situation for a drug swoon is not so opportune.

Chris is in the driver's seat of the latest pickup truck Karl has given him. He fades away and side-swipes a parked car. Thankfully no one is hurt.

A breath test administered by cops on the scene shows no alcohol intoxication, but no blood test is given. A search of the truck uncovers no drugs. Chris is taken to his ex-wife's house; she brings him to Karl's.

Official police pronouncement or not, Chris is clearly loaded. He is put to bed.

APRIL 28, 2009

Chris has a therapy appointment at USC. Carol will take him. His drugged-out state from the day before has not fully worn off, so Carol calls Ty to help her.

It is not a pleasant ride to the Keck Center—more nodding out.

They arrive and get Chris inside. More cold facts from the doctors: continued smoking will bring back the cancer, and the drug use prevents further treatments for his neck and throat.

The truth.

Matter-of-fact.

They all head home to Karl and Carol's, and Chris is once again put in bed. Keep it dark. Keep out the sunlight and the ocean breeze. Sleep. Sleep it off. There will be no enjoyment of heaven on this day, either.

APRIL 29, 2009

Chris hasn't left the bed. Karl and Carol keep checking on him. He finally gets up to go to the bathroom. Carol fixes him some soup, trying to coax him into eating and building up some strength. He never makes it to the soup. As he walks down the hall toward the kitchen, Chris passes out, falling flat on his face.

He is cut and bleeding badly.

Karl and Carol rush him to the emergency room where he gets six stitches in his head. He is placed in the hospital for observation.

And he is given pain pills.

Chris indicates that he is fine with staying there awhile.

MAY 4, 2009

Chris is released from the hospital and put back in bed at Karl and Carol's.

MAY 6, 2009

The clock is louder and faster…

At 5:00 a.m., Carol's cell phone rings. Chris is calling from downstairs. He has fallen and can't move. Karl and Carol rush downstairs and find Chris on the floor with his hip badly displaced.

Call 911.

The paramedics get him to the hospital. The doctors discover that they don't need to give him pain meds as they try to fix his hip—Chris is completely loaded on heroin. He isn't feeling much.

The doctor's attempts to put the hip back into its socket are unsuccessful; and all the while, Chris is lost in his self-medicated nodding out.

Chris's blood pressure is extremely low because of the drugs, so a withdrawal program is begun. He needs an operation and it isn't going to happen with him in this state.

MAY 10, 2009

Top orthopedic surgeon Dr. Don P. Sanders is brought in to perform the operation.

While the medical team is reassembling Chris's hip, Karl's intervention team is also reassembled—and expanded.

The final decision.

Again.

Intervention.

Again.

This will be *the* intervention, and it will occur just as Chris is released from the hospital. Chris will be going to Casa Palmera behavioral health treatment facility in Del Mar. Like Scripps, the place is good (described by the Thelma McMillen Center's Moe Gelbart as the "toughest of the tough"). And, with that class of clamp-down quality, it's not cheap. It's twice what Betty Ford was.

Karl writes another check.

Eleven names were already on the team's list; more are added. A plan is drawn up, and it is more precise this time—like a military maneuver. Maybe *that* will translate into the entire process being more binding on Chris.

This time.

. And as always, this war is being funded by Karl. He adheres to his tactical general's philosophy: *If you control the money, you can control the plan. Even if it doesn't work.*

But this plan *had* to work.

MAY 15, 2009

The key is that Chris is completely unaware of what is about to happen. The director of nurses and Dr. Sanders have been alerted to all of this. They know what is going on.

Chris will be in a wheelchair, ostensibly on his way to have X-rays taken.

Shannon and Ty will escort Chris back to his room to change his clothes and check out of the hospital.

We will begin at 8:15.

By 10:15, we will be done and Chris will be on his way to Casa Palmera.

The plan is orderly, it is regimented…and it works!

Chris is overwhelmed, outnumbered twenty to one. And he surrenders.

More or less…

Karl gives him a speech: "Here's what you're absolutely going to do…"

But then Chris asks how long he must stay at Palmera.

"Goddammit, Chris!" his friend Kevin shouts. A recovered addict himself, Kevin has helped Chris in the past and his patience is waning. "Don't you get it?! Don't you understand that we're trying to save your life here?! Let the people at the program decide how long you have to be there!"

Karl also brings up the legal agreement Chris signed back in March before going to Betty Ford; and that is a cold reminder to Chris to that his funds are still cut off.

Chris asks when his monthly trust will be reinstated.

Now it's time for Karl's frustration to rise. He tells Chris that he has completely missed the point of all this. He tries to explain to Chris that the theme of the intervention was to bring his lifetime of friends and family together in an effort, reiterating what Kevin has said, to *save your life!*

Chris's funds will be reinstated when he "regains his senses, thinks logically, and is absolutely drug-free. If it takes three months, six months, or more."

And that's that.

BUT AT CASA PALMERA, the detox can't immediately begin. Chris—the one-time King of the Beach—is so physically fragile that at least some degree of wellness must be restored before the program can be started.

Chris is transferred by ambulance to the nearby Scripps Medical Center. More treatment on his throat is needed; a tube is inserted to help him breathe.

It takes eighteen days for a nursing-back-to-health and a detoxing of the drugs in his system.

Another summer begins, Chris's fifty-second. Another summer with the sun and sand and Pacific swells so close. But another summer that Chris will not enjoy.

And as the weather heats up, Karl's introspection about the sink-hole of addiction also intensifies. What he discovered about himself during that Family Week at Betty Ford burns through him over and over:

Dear Son,

I have come to realize, after almost thirty-nine years of having been the enabler, it's not working. I have been a slow learner. Sometimes loving someone (my son) gets in the way of doing what is best for him.

Everything that is being provided for you is in an effort to save your life. I have seen your recent behavior as follows: You left the McDonald rehab center in a cab, drugs in your boots and underwear, nodding out in public, falling in the hallway, falling in the bedroom dislocating your hip, three car accidents in one month caused by drugs, a near-death overdose at the Manhattan Beach house...then to the USC hospital, resulting in you walking away and getting a cab...while the Betty Ford facility was waiting for you to return...and now there is Casa Palmera.

Chris, in the recent past, any open discussion we have had by your bedside, on the phone, etc., has been like a debate. I am doing what I feel is necessary to save your life. Your denial has been so powerful that you have not understood that you need help now. Period...You will first get to a drug-free position so that you are able to begin to understand and accept the help that Casa Palmera is giving you. To do this, it is imperative that you be cooperative and stop trying to do things your way. It's time for a change in your attitude. It is time to surrender...

One final note to you, son—if you choose drugs over recovery, I will with great sadness honor your choice and let you go with love.

All my love, *Dad*

P.S. Please make me proud of you.

Also on May 15, 2009, forty-one hundred miles away, Terry Devitt dies quietly in Wailuku, Hawaii.

Terry's words, thoughts, love, and reports had been such a part of the McMillens' lifelong ordeal.

But as the years passed, Terry had become more and more distant, not just geographically but emotionally. And more reclusive. The long-ago suicide of his twin brother never left him; nor did a deepening depression.

As Chris was being wheeled into Scripps, the westerly breeze off the Pacific carried one last wave of love and insight for the McMillen family from Terry Devitt, the echoes of a letter he had written to Karl twenty-one years before:

> Please read and understand this more than any report or recommendation I've ever made. I very much want and need [you and Thelma] to be a part of my life for a long time. That won't happen until we accept that, try as we might, life sometimes deals us a bad hand. And then, as Mark and my brother would be quick to point out, we shuffle the cards and move on.
>
> I love you both, have from the gate, worry about you and most of all, miss you.

—Terry Devitt,
Final Report and Recommendations, June 1976

JUNE 3, 2009
Chris is back at Casa Palmera where he remains for three months.

SEPTEMBER 3, 2009
Chris completes Casa Palmera's program and is released. He begins their outpatient schedule of Thursday follow-up visits.

Chris makes two of them.

SEPTEMBER 17, 2009

Chris is back on drugs. Ty takes him back to Casa Palmera.

SEPTEMBER 21, 2009

Chris walks out of Casa Palmera.

For weeks everyone wrestles with decisions.

OCTOBER 31, 2009

Chris Alan McMillen turns fifty-three years old.

At this point, make a final decision…

Karl and Carol make that final decision. One more intervention. This one will be from the inside. Casa Palmera refers four "freelance" caregivers to stay with Chris in teams of two as part of a live-in intervention. They, too, will be supported by Karl.

More checks are written.

NOVEMBER 11, 2009

Karl begins *this* plan by taking Chris's truck. As the truck leaves, two of the four mobile drug counselors move in.

This is it.

NOVEMBER 15, 2009

After four days, it seems that the internal battle is being won. Karl and Carol meet with one of the facility members for an early report. Chris is accepting the live-ins. He is eating well, his prescriptions from the doctors are being monitored, and he has already attended meetings.

Maybe, just maybe…

Karl does some mathematical analysis—some elementary arithmetic, really.

Numbers.

He sends a quick note to Chris:

```
The McMillen family life expectancy:
My grandfather, 84.
My grandmother, 80.
My mother, 96.
My father, 72 (but he was killed crossing the
street).

The point is, Chris, that you are 53 and
cancer-free. You could live for another 30-plus
years.

It's time to quit drugs! Please remember that
I quit smoking and drinking 14 years ago. And you
can get back to the gym and to surfing.

You have so much time in which you could help
so many people...All of your past life experiences
could be used as a background for a new life of
helping others to avoid so many years of pain,
loss, and suffering.

I believe God is not done with you here on
Earth. He needs you to do what you do best:
help others with their addiction...you would be a
wonderful counselor if you choose to be.

By being a mirror in which others can see
themselves and their loved ones, your life and
what you have been through will impact countless
people...you could be helping so many with your
life story.
```

CHAPTER 25

Unyoking Another Type of Thoroughbred

CHRISTMAS 2009

Thirty-four years ago, Karl and Thelma visited their sons in jail. Then they went back home to their beautiful Hermosa Beach castle on the sand with its million-dollar view; but its resort-like warmth had cooled. The festive party house had become a logistical headquarters for the shower of what-comes-next hammers being dropped by Mark's and Chris's addictions.

Thirty-four years of hollow holidays and wasted summers—lost moments that held every potential-promise. Thirty-four years of bright sun and life-shine that were tarnished more and more with each passing season.

Mark is gone.

Thelma is gone.

But Chris…

Christmas for Chris this year may finally be merrier and brighter. His house is being shared by interveners, yes; but it's an invasion driven by love and support. Chris spends a calm holiday with his family at the home of Fred Morrow, Jeff's brother.

Things *are* turning around.

And what may have been the most effective personal therapy for Karl throughout all of this turmoil is that he never lost his passion for his work. Haunting thoughts about what had happened to his beloved Todd Pipe & Supply after the sale to corporate giants became a renewing boost in that passion.

He wanted to unyoke his thoroughbred and get back into the race!

In 2009 and into 2010, Karl had his chance. The positive life-turnarounds finally happening for Chris were paralleling Karl's energized sprint back into business.

One of the main reasons Karl had sold Todd in the first place was that question of succession. He cared. He cared about his employees. He cared about their future.

The terrible truth was that Mark and Chris were never able to assume prominence in a McMillen & Sons picture.

The sale to Hughes seemed to be a fail-safe way to cinch down a future for Todd's loyal employees and allow Karl to rest easy. But the quick resale to Home Depot/HD Supply Company had unsealed the deal.

Couple Karl's concern for his former employees with his now ever-expanding philanthropic desires, and you have roaring and resurfacing thoughts about that succession. *All of this needs to continue—and it needs to continue in the right way. The McMillen Family Foundation must be dedicated to helping people forever.*

A new Todd Pipe would take care of everything.

IT WAS TIME FOR ANOTHER of those harmonic convergences. In late 2009, the non-compete agreement Karl had signed with Hughes (and via the subsequent sale, Home Depot) expired. Building leases also included in the initial sale were expiring. It was then that Karl happened to run into Dan Patrick at a charity event for Pathways to

Independence. Dan, of course, was Todd Pipe's former Sales VP and the friend who'd gotten Karl off the booze. Patrick had stayed on after Hughes' purchase of Todd as their Western Sales VP. But after the company's acquisition by HD Supply, he'd left to take a similar position with Mueller Industries.

The two got to talking, and the question came up: Wouldn't it be fun to open up a new Todd? Karl tells Dan he must be nuts; what with the economy and all.

But Karl's mind launches into its calculations: *I had ten years as a plumbing contractor; plus from '68 to 2004 I put in thirty-six more as a wholesaler. That's almost fifty years of experience.*

With Dan, together we know all the principals in this industry; we know the contractors and have their respect; we have a history of having a happy family of key people as our employees. We have great access to bank funds. We still own our old key locations—with the lease periods about to expire.

Hmmm…

And then Karl thought back to what Dr. Trefftzs had once said about it being time to get Karl "off the street."

Well, maybe it was that time once again.

Karl told Dan that his idea was a good one! But the key point for Karl was the ownership plan they devised.

The new Todd would have five partners with an age factor that provided built-in succession. All five would be from the old Todd: the group had all worked together, got along well together, and had fun being together. Tom Morrow, Jason Kemp, and Aaron Olsen joined Karl and Dan as the owners of the new Todd Pipe.

Morrow had been with Todd since the original Garden Grove location days; Kemp began as a truck driver in 2000; and Olsen worked his way up from the receiving department where he started in '97. That's the way Karl McMillen operates.

That's the Golden Touch.

And it works.

Succession…

Kemp and Olsen are still in their thirties; Tom in his forties; Dan is enjoying the mature mindset of his fifties; and Karl is, well, eighty-something. The succession problem is solved.

As the elders eventually depart, the plan is that they'll sell their shares to the younger partners.

And Karl has set up *his* shares so that after his demise his one-fifth interest in the company will pass on to the McMillen Family Foundation. The Foundation will have a steady stream of income into the future—and that's a great source of pride for *all* the partners.

The pride hits maximum level in that a legal-maximum of twenty percent of all of Todd's profits, now and forever, are donated to the McMillen Foundation and its work. It's the most a corporation may donate within the tax structure, and Todd wants to go all the way.

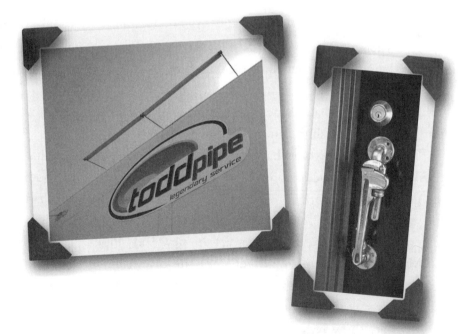

The sky's the limit for the new Todd Pipe. It opened its doors in 2010, geared up to donate a full twenty percent of its profits to the McMillen Family Foundation, now and forever.

By means of comparison, American companies gave a median of 1.2 percent of their 2008 profits away to charity in 2009, according to *The Chronicle of Philanthropy* website.

The first tangible result of Dan Patrick's idea was Todd Pipe, LLC, which opened a facility in Anaheim in February 2010, followed by another in San Diego in January of 2011, and a third at Todd's old headquarters in Hawthorne in March of '11.

Karl is happy, the partners are happy, employees are happy, and the Todd Pipe customers are happy (they had always remembered and longed for the "legendary service").

Todd's competitors—well, like any healthy competition, they may not be overjoyed, but one thing is for sure: they're not going to knock Todd too much for how it operates. You don't want to be the guy bashing a company that dedicates itself to helping so many people!

As the new Todd began to *re*establish itself, writer Jim Olsztynski, who had written about Todd being selected as the industry's Wholesaler of the Year back in 2002, revisited the company that represents so much more than just commercial success:

The Rebirth of Todd Pipe

Besides the partners, many other former Todd veterans have joined the company in key positions. More would return if they could, except the reconstituted company with 75 employees at this stage is much smaller than the hundreds employed at the original version..."everyone wants to come back and work for Karl."

"We're proud of Karl," Jason Kemp voiced. "He's done a lot of favors for employees and customers over the years, and set an example for us. When he's in the building you overhear people saying, 'Hey, Karl's around!' He's a legend in the supply business."

...The market is a lot different than it was when they left the business...What hasn't changed is the company's culture. It's centered around an unmatched commitment to customer service, which has led the reconstituted Todd Pipe to incorporate into its logo the slogan, "Legendary Service."

...McMillen and all the other partners arose from blue collar roots, and they never forgot where they came from. All of the partners and most if not all of the firm's other managers started their careers in the warehouse or as truck drivers. They dress like their customers and speak the same lingo. I asked if Todd Pipe employs outside salesmen and the reply was, yes, except they're called truck drivers!...

"Our success is built on relationships with customers and vendors. People shop where they feel comfortable"...Morrow weighed in with an episode that happened a few days before my visit. A contractor

had a problem with a tub and wanted $200 for his
labor in fixing it. "I made a decision on the spot
to give it to him," he related. "I'm going to try
to get it back from the vendor, but whether or not
I succeed, the customer is taken care of. Is a
customer worth $200?"

Said Patrick: "Something Karl has always said
is do the right thing, no matter what it costs."

Turning serious, he added: "The reason we're
back in business is Karl's passion for drug rehab.
It's like a dream come true knowing that 20% of
our profits are going to help recovering addicts.
Being around Karl is something to aspire to."

...I asked McMillen to contribute any final
thoughts. He paused to reflect, then said: "I look
back on my life as having three phases. The first
was to study hard and learn. Then came working
hard and making a lot of money. Now it's time to
give back."

—*Supply House Times,* August 11, 2011
Jim Olsztynski

The giving back—to his employees, to his customers, and to the
charities he supports—is simply what this man does.

The resurrection of Todd Pipe brought back an iconic company
to serve the plumbing industry, certainly. But it also returned to
corporate America a model business; a firm that should be looked at,
studied, and emulated.

For a massive operation, the warehouses are spotless and organized.
Employee camaraderie is easygoing and warm. And more warmth is
generated by the every-morning blueberry muffins that greet Todd's
customers (along with the filling flavor of "Taco Tuesdays"). Clients
are treated like kings, and the staff of each facility like royalty.

Golden...

The Todd "Recipe for Success" was another tasty item placed back on this business's menu as part of the company's official history:

- *Over-service the customer (If you make a mistake, own up to it and fix it).*

- *Strategically locate branches with unmatched inventories and fill rates.*

- *Build employee morale—building a team atmosphere leads to one common goal.*

A Customer

"A customer is the most important visitor on our premises. He is not dependent on us — we are dependent on him. He is not an outsider in our business — he is a part of it. We are not doing him a favor by serving him....he is doing us a favor by giving us the opportunity to do so.

"Over-servicing" the customer may best be seen in yet another result of Karl's years in the biz. Karl recognized way back at Alert Plumbing and in his work in Alaska that the main variable in a job was the labor factor: if you can control the labor factor, you can make money. This was reaffirmed much later by wholesaler association studies of wasted labor. Class A jobs (commercial buildings), in particular, suffered a labor waste of up to 35 percent. Along with obstacles like the material bull pens being too far away, plans being revised, air-conditioning lines in the way of other infrastructure, and other measurable errors, "service" elements like back-ordered material and late deliveries also contributed to the waste.

So, as a supplier, Todd Pipe aspires to a 100 percent fill rate (currently maintaining an astounding 98 percent) and to be on time.

That helps Todd's customers to reduce their 35 percent waste factor. And *that* helps Todd to grow and to keep those muffins warm!

EVEN WHEN KARL has to assume the role of big-business owner, he keeps that ring of the common man. Like the time he had to swing into a public-relations round of golf with an important customer.

It went about as well as expected, considering the axiom "Plumbers don't golf!"

And the other old axiom about first impressions...

On the very first hole, the customer's very first shot hits a tree and bounces back to about thirty yards *behind* the tee. Karl shrugs and politely asks all the groups behind them if they'd like to play through. He could see the paint-pen writing on the wall: it was going to be a long day!

Back to basics...

The common man...

What Karl does works.

Who he is works.

"Do the right thing, no matter what it costs..."

The "right thing" was Karl picking up exactly where he left off as he reacquired and reinstituted the Legendary Service of Todd Pipe. Again, with that telling bellwether of how one faces down both triumphs *and* tragedies. Do you use the triumphs to make life better for others as well as yourself? Do you look at tragedies as lessons, taking what is learned and, once again, making life better for others?

The answers to these questions matter.

The answers mean so much in business, and they mean so much in life.

CHAPTER 26

Numbers Do Not Change Lives

EARLY 2010

As Karl first sets about rebuilding Todd Pipe, he is excited in thinking that Chris, too, can now finally be a part of this glittering "time to give back."

The interventions have brought so many "teams" together at different times. The support system has apparently worked.

Along with the revelations and epiphanies that Karl is accepting about his enabling of Chris, his thoughts about how Chris's story can help others are being steeled and reinforced.

As in Jeff's loving testimonies, Karl is told over and over about Chris's abilities to teach and guide. From the jails and the prisons to the rehabs to the where-am-I stupors, Chris has always been able to offer some kind of help to someone.

Finally, a future looks clear—a *positive* future.

By being a mirror in which others can see themselves and their loved ones, your life and what you have been through will impact countless people...

JANUARY 2010

The mood shifts.

Concerns arise about what appears to be Chris's return to drugs. How is he getting them through the wall of his housemate interveners?

He isn't.

Chris's cancer is back.

Aggressive.

Strong.

And it has metastasized into Chris's brain. That is what is making him "nod out" now. The smoking and drugs don't allow for the production of healthy cells. Your body can't recover.

The positive future is certainly going to include the reflection of Chris's life—Karl knows *that* will never die—but the weakened flesh of Chris is another story.

FEBRUARY 1, 2010

Karl, Carol, and Ty gather with Chris and Pastor Steve Mays in the office at South Bay Calvary Chapel.

The *final*, final decision occurs in that room on that day.

The final steps are taken.

The last steps in a fifty-three-year odyssey of broadsided emotion and hard wisdom.

It was surely a final memory ride for Chris. A final drop down the steep face of a towering North Shore swell as the sun was setting and the light dimming.

That room, on that day, would become Chris's *pu'uhonua*—his final "place of refuge."

That fifty-three-year odyssey was like the Hawaiian legend of King Kamehameha:

*He rode gladly on the crest of the surf waves. He delighted to drive
his canoe alone out into the storm. He fought with the monsters of the
deep, as well as with men. He captured the great shark that abounds
in the bay, and he would clutch in the fearful grip of his hands the
deadly eel or snake of these seas, the terror of fishes and men.*

—"Kaala and Kaaialii: A Legend of Lanai"

Chris's rides on the crests of surf were epic. His lone languish in the
storm was his deep-heart-of-the-night mad prison-cell meditations.
The monsters and men he fought were many and unfathomable.

But the most deadly terror he had to fight with was himself. On
that day, in that room, like Kamehameha, Chris indeed captured that
great shark. His battle victory and his fearful grip would be the story
of his life and struggle; helping others to find their own *pu'uhonua*
before it is too late.

It's fitting that the Hawaiian word *aloha* is used to both greet
someone as they come into your life *and* to bid them farewell.

MARCH 6, 2010

Karl McMillen bids *aloha* to his youngest *keikikane* in a memorial
service held at the Thelma McMillen Center.

A standing-room-only crowd of three hundred people fill the
largest meeting room at "Thelma's Place." Maile vines—"the lei of
royalty"—are brought in from Hawaii. Their "open-ended, horseshoe
fashion" is placed around the necks of Chris's immediate circle of
family and friends, "exemplifying the bestowing of honor and respect,
and also the spirit of aloha."

It is time to join together—*ho'oku'i.*

Pastor Dan Bradford of King's Harbor Church in Torrance is at
the memorial.

Pastor Bradford had taken Chris, along with other members of his church, to New Orleans to aid in reconstruction work after Hurricane Katrina in 2005.

"Chris was not a talker," Dan explained. "He was a doer. He was not flashy. He cared about using his experiences to help others…He was not the kind of guy who was going to tell you how to live, but he would say, 'My experience is…'

"He wasn't preaching; instead he was using that experience to teach you how to choose well in your own life."

As always, if you needed help, Chris was there…

Chris's son, Ty, filled the room with what exactly his father was all about—apart from the experiences. Ty unlocked the door and let the blue Pacific flow in.

"He was a big-wave charger…always with the soul style…so hard to get…so hard to come by…but Dad always had it. Always just dropping into a big wave, just laying it out, right on the nice flat bottom, and taking that bottom turn and just hookin' it right up into the barrel. That's what he loved doing…

"'Suit up and show up' were his famous words, and that's what he lived by…that's what he did…

"We all knew his ups and downs, but he always found a way to make the ups drown out any downs…"

The eulogies continued.

Jeff.

Richie.

Shannon.

Chris's ex-wife.

Merle Countryman.

Testimony after testimony; outpourings of love and gratitude and sadness for Chris.

But it was Pastor Steve Mays who helped Karl to say a father's final good-bye as he described in heart-crushing detail just what happened in that church office, on that day:

Son,

We are looking at this great picture of you on the beach with that big, big smile of yours. All your friends are here and your family who love you so much are here…I am learning more and more about you from your friends; how easy it is for you to love people—to reach out and touch them because you can feel their pain and sorrow. I wish I could express myself the way you did. My gift seems to be in my head talking about numbers—lots and lots of numbers. This is where I live. No one in their right mind will ever challenge me with numbers. But numbers do not change lives, nor do they bring peace and real happiness.

Numbers can make you and others rich, but they cannot build a family. They can provide shelter, but they cannot heal a broken heart. They can provide security, but they cannot take away someone's pain deep down inside.

I see so much of your mother in you. She was able to express her love so freely and to give with no strings attached. I love you so much—I realize only now how I wish I could have expressed it in a different way.

I know, as your dad, I did the best I could. I was so sure we would win this battle together. Then we would be able to help so many others with the same problems you faced in your life daily. I was willing to do anything, take you anywhere, pay for everything; but I never really knew how sick you were. I am just now hearing from so many of your friends how you reached out and helped so many who were hurting like you. I am so proud of you, my son.

Where do I start? What can I say? I guess I am a slow learner. My God, it's only taken me eighty-one years to learn how to say I love you, to put my arms around you, to cry in front of you, and to say I am sorry also. The great news is I am still learning at eighty-one.

Chris, what you did that day in Pastor Steve's office at the church is worth more than all the money I have ever made in my life. In one sentence, you chose to set me free forever. I will never forget that moment as long as I live.

Pastor Steve said, "Chris, is there something you would like to say to your dad?"

You lifted your head up, looked right into my eyes, and said, "Dad, I love you."

Then you said, "Dad, I am so sorry for all the pain I have caused you. Please forgive me."

My son, all the years of pain were over. All of my shame was removed. The tears began to flow; I couldn't hold them back. And I found myself getting out of my chair to hold you and tell you the same: "Chris, forgive me for all the things I put you through."

At that moment, I realized for the first time how strong you really were. To suffer so much, and yet be so loving. No wonder everyone loves you and misses you so much.

But then Pastor Steve looked me right in the eye and said, "Karl, will you let your son die?"

And I said yes.

He turned to Carol.

"Carol, will you let Chris go right now?"

Carol said yes.

He looked to Ty.

"Ty, will you let your dad go and will you be okay?"

Ty said yes.

Then the Pastor said, "Chris, is this what you want? To be set free from this sick, feeble body?"

And with that crazy, big smile of his, Chris said, "Yes, Pastor Steve, I am ready to go."

"Chris," said Pastor Steve, *"as your Pastor, you are free to go. You have our blessings."*

My God, at that very moment, Chris's growing tumor burst through an artery and blood began pouring out of his mouth.

Pastor Steve called 911.

In all that blood, there were still those big blue eyes and that goofy big smile saying, "See you guys soon...Love you all..."

The crazy kid did it again to us; he snuck out the back door. But this time, no one would ever catch him.

As I rode in the ambulance, I knew my boy had found real happiness and peace—the stuff that money cannot buy.

I love you, Son...

Epilogue

Mark and Thelma had both been returned to the sea years before—by the hands of Chris.

Now it was Chris's time to go back. Now it was everyone's time to feel a shark-rush of memories and reflections.

Jeff called together the paddle-out:

"After the service…we're all going down to the beach at 21st Street and The Strand, and we're going to circle up. We're going to hold each other and we're going to stomp our feet. We're going to throw our hands up in the sky. We're going to yell at the clouds. We're going to talk to Chris; we're going to get some kind of closure. We're going to go around and say how much we loved Chris and how much we miss him. Then we're going to have a paddle-out and have one last surf session with Chris.

"Ty's got a little part of Chris he's going to take out there, and we're going to catch a couple more waves for Chris one more time…"

In terms of a caring circle, this fifty-strong grouping of friends and family was not unlike the ones who had tried so hard to herd

Chris into help during the interventions. But this circle was decidedly different in spirit.

As they all paddled west, away from shore, their thoughts connected with the water. So much was now becoming one. They knew that every wave has its crest and trough. That so many hopes and dreams have the same rise-and-fall flow as those waves. And they knew that when the hard winds of reality and just-too-much-damage go on and on and on, those waves of hope become blown out and impossible to ride. All you can do in the harsh face of that is stand silently on the shore and watch; thinking about the perfect ride that could have been.

Many on that paddle-out must have been thinking just that: how Chris could have had that perfect ride. That perfect wave. The perfect eternal set that he could have worked forever.

It was March in the Pacific and it was cold, but no one cared. As Ty scattered Chris's ashes into the water, the others freed a thousand Hawaiian orchid tips into the sea. It all melded with the tears of those on the paddle-out and with the life force of the ocean.

So much was now becoming one…

Ty and his two sisters would preserve some of their father's ashes to be brought back to Hawaii—to be scattered where Ty's mother, Sally, had been given back to the peace of the waves and the blue warmth.

No kau a kau, makua kane…

CELEBRATING THE LIFE OF

CHRIS MCMILLEN

OCTOBER 31ST 1956 – FEBRUARY 1ST 2010

*"I dropped a tear in the ocean.
The day you find it, is the day I will stop missing you."*

By being a mirror in which others can see themselves and their loved ones, your life and what you have been through will impact countless people…you could be helping so many with your life story.

—Karl McMillen,
November 15, 2009

LESS THAN THREE MONTHS before Chris's death, Karl wrote these prophetic words to his youngest son. These words were undeniable… Chris's life—and death—is the ultimate cautionary tale for drug addicts and would-be drug addicts.

But it is an examination of Karl's life that provides even deeper lessons. About both triumphs and tragedies.

"Karl, I've watched you in your life. The tragedy and the loss in your life and the man you've become is unbelievable; you are a force of nature. Through all of this, you've taken your hard-earned money and your time and you've invested in something that is like a rolling snowball; it goes out and touches other people's lives and it touches more people's lives and it just goes on and on. I thank you so much for being who you are. You should hold your head high!"

—Richie Davidson,
at Chris's Memorial Service

Throughout all of his tragedies, Karl truly was and is "a force of nature." How did he become that type of man? How did he scale those high walls and survive those devastating sheers?

He Always Did It Right

by Chuck Monnich

Chuck Monnich has been Karl's best friend since childhood. From the mining days on the hill to their

Karl (left) and Chuck got an education together on "the hill."

college days in New Mexico, from the drug-escaping Baja trips to Karl's struggle with alcohol, Chuck was there. And Chuck was there when the hearts of the McMillen family were being torn out, one by one.

Chuck shared all of Karl's life. As boys, they explored the still-new and very wild West together. As men, Chuck has been handshake- and hug-close as the triumphs and tragedies of his best friend's world have played out like the pair's adrenaline-pumping, no-brakes shot down the Chiriaco Summit Grade so many years ago. From the tops to the bottoms, Chuck has been there.

The trips up into Northern Nevada with Karl's dad, Mac, were the real "first days of school" for Karl and me as far as our practical education in life goes. Sometimes we'd be gone a month; sometimes Mac would load us both up on a Friday after school and have us back in time for class on Monday. And all that was done in an old truck that would go maybe forty-five miles per hour over roads that weren't equipped for even *that* kind of speed! Mac was the ultimate adventurer. Even Karl's mother, Frances, would go with us from time to time.

Karl had pure pioneer blood running through his veins from the very beginning.

We'd pan for gold every day, and we met all those characters—Jim Henry with that anvil he used for brakes on his truck; and of course Tobe Barnes. We'd eat at Tobe's—the best sourdough biscuits in the world, pinto beans, cabbage, salt pork. We had many a good dinner on his big cast-iron stove.

There was also once a guy named Boone Tilford up on the hill; he was one of the original prospectors there. He'd been dead for years, but his log cabin was one of the only solid structures around. Long after the hill heyday was over, I was up there, taking the caulking out from between the logs, and the newspapers mixed into the caulk had dates in the 1880s.

Then there was that time when we lost the brakes in Mac's truck; and *we* didn't even have an anvil to throw out! Mac and that other guy we strapped down in the back had been drinking homemade wine up on the hill all day. No wonder they didn't wake up!

Years later, after the growing up we did on the hill, Tobe moved down to Searchlight; a small 1890s Nevada mining town in the Colorado River Basin. At that time, they'd let water out of Boulder Dam maybe once every three days. That would cause the river to go way down and the trout would get caught in the holes on the sandbars. You could catch them with your hands.

I'd go visit Tobe once in a while in Searchlight, and occasionally he'd send me trout—by mail! Until one time when his care package swam right into a holiday weekend. When the now not-so-fresh fish were finally delivered, the postman told me, "I don't know what's in this package, kid, but it's been sitting in the post office for three days and it smelled up the whole place!"

Our time on the hill as kids was definitely a foreshadowing of what Karl would be as a man. It would be eight in the morning and Karl would be completely done with tasks like washing Mac's truck. I, on the other hand, would still be asleep!

Karl was always a go-getter!

In 1939, I went to Butte, Montana, for a big McMillen family Christmas. Butte in those days was somethin' else, with all of the activity and commerce that was happening around the mammoth Anaconda Copper Mine; Butte even became known as the "Richest Hill on Earth." Mac knew the foreman of the mine and they showed us around. They dropped us almost a quarter mile down in a car on a cable that was stretching out like a rubber band! They had a regular city down there in those days.

Then Karl and I grew up—sort of.

We would go back to Montana—to the city of Divide, in the southwestern corner of the state—to go elk hunting. And we'd drink. While we played poker, we'd kill a big bottle of scotch between the two of us. Maybe that was another foreshadowing, because the problems with drinking—and drugs—sure came.

When the drugs hit Mark, the Baja trips became more of an exercise in escape; getting Mark away from the friends and the temptations at home. I liked Mark as a kid real well, and he was the one who usually came with us on those Baja jaunts. But *both* he and Chris had trouble from such a young age. They were such bright and talented brothers. They could have been good students if they wanted to be. They could have followed Karl in his business, too.

But they just weren't able to do it.

Just like Thelma couldn't stop the smoking. She was such a good person, but maybe it was that overt goodness—that friendliness—that hurt the boys. A lot of people have said it: she really was like a best friend to them.

And she drank. And Karl drank. One time they were at my house and we'd all had too much. Karl was planning to go home, so I pulled all the spark plug wires off his pickup so he couldn't drive. He slept in a chair all night.

The idea of finally explaining to Karl about how his drinking was hurting Todd Pipe was the perfect revelation for him. Karl wasn't going to mess up that company, because—throughout everything—Karl McMillen, Jr., was and is a super businessman.

And he always did it right—being so good to his employees, always helping everyone out. And now he helps more people than any of us can even grasp. He is still doing it right. The idea that he has brought back Todd Pipe at this stage in his life is incredible.

Maybe there was a little more foreshadowing on those days up on the hill. Maybe that's where that kid panning for coarse nuggets out there in that dusty wilderness stumbled onto the magic that brought him his Golden Touch—the Golden Touch that has helped him to achieve his triumphs and weather his tragedies. And to turn those tragedies into so many positives for so many people.

KARL'S SISTER RUTH recognized her brother's Golden Touch back in 1954 at his graduation. His best buddy, Chuck, saw it even earlier—a reflection in the small bits of gold and life-learnings they worked so hard for as kids.

Everyone who has ever worked with Karl McMillen has felt it, seen it, and been touched by it themselves.

A quick, overall look at Karl's "Golden Touch" provides an extra-educational review. A running time-lapse spin through the life of Karl B. McMillen, Jr., projects the perfect template for triumph in business—especially for those who still believe that good guys can't make it to the top. And for those who *don't* believe that back-to-basics decency and respect in the workplace can chew the heads off of more complex and overthought business models.

Karl's Golden Touch

From the beginning, Karl McMillen, Jr., listened to and emulated his father. "Outwork them all!" became not a barked order but a clear credo and a fundamental way of life.

Then it was on to proficiency in a staple and stable trade—plumbing—realizing, however, that some mental mettle would be a good complement to the gray gloves and blue collars. That's where the degree in finance from USC came in handy.

Keeping eyes, ears, and opportunities open helped bring Dr. Kenneth Trefftzs into Karl's network of friends and business associates. Keeping those eyes, ears, and opportunities open allowed Karl to accept Trefftzs' advice and guidance. It's a good policy to recognize that there is always someone out there who can teach you something!

Karl's brother-in-law often branded Karl as "reckless"—making daring, double-XL business maneuvers. But Dr. Trefftzs saw things differently. He perennially referred to Karl as "the most conservative businessman I have ever known"—always working with all cash, up front. The two divergent perspectives of Karl's drive and means—to some very impressive ends!—could both be accurate.

Then came the direct dedication to business—Karl's putting of "Outwork them all!" into practical play through his ten years as a plumbing contractor, his years in real estate investment, and then in his joining Ralph Todd in a business that had obvious potential.

So far, so golden.

Knowing when—and how—to expand came next.

But by age seventy-six, Karl had to face that he had no successor for his business. Dr. Trefftzs was gone. His eldest son and wife were gone. His youngest son was simply not capable. It was time to reassess: Todd was sold. But building leases were retained as part of a diversified portfolio of investments.

The future was always out there; looming.

But for now, the charities were set up. The Thelma McMillen Center was established. This part of the Golden Touch got even more polished.

Five years passed and that finite future arrived. Those expiring deals were called in and a new Todd Pipe was built with the same ethics and people-power as before. The McMillen Family Foundation and the way it makes the world a better place was set up forever through Todd and its newly-assembled "succession."

With the rebirth of Todd Pipe, Karl McMillen has been able to raise the results of his triumphs even higher. With this line of succession in place, he has now produced a limitless source of giving that will benefit countless people he will never know or meet; but people who will share directly and indirectly in the tragedies that so terribly touched those whom Karl loved most.

That is solid gold.

That is success.

"Very few men could do what you did, Karl. It's not about the money—you would have done it without the money; but God blessed you with money. I deal with thousands, tens of thousands of people, and not many fathers would deny themselves by giving so much…this is the beginning of something great. Amen…"

—Pastor Steve Mays,
at Chris's Memorial Service

THE LIVES AND SUFFERINGS of Mark, Thelma, and Chris McMillen will never be in vain. What they and their family endured, Karl and Carol never want anyone else to experience.

As of the end of 2012, Karl and Carol McMillen and the McMillen Family Foundation have given in excess of $12 million to Southern California charities that are *"dedicated to helping men and women who have been impacted, directly or indirectly, by alcohol and/or drugs"* and who *"share our values and have produced tangible and measurable results."*

The McMillens' hearts, their on-fire benevolence, and their resources are making that wish and hope a reality for so many people. People whose lives have been lifted by these organizations:

Pathways to Independence.

Villa Center.

House of Hope.

Beacon House.

First Step House.

Lynn House.

Friendly House.

Shawl House.

Ashland Home

Al-Anon.

Turrill Transitional.

Mary & Joseph Retreat Center.

The Thelma McMillen Center.

A sign commemorating each donation is appropriately framed in copper piping.

The Legacy of the Thelma McMillen Center

In one hand you've got death, drugs, misery, and destruction. In the other hand, you've got a happy, wonderful life.

But it's impossible for someone who's addicted to make that choice.

It's not clear to them.

The drugs are what they know—the easy way; the clear way seems impossible for them. And that's why the Thelma McMillen Center exists. That's why they're doing their work, trying to make a difference in these kids and people before they get to this confused point.

And if they do get to that bad point, then the staff tries to give them a way out and a way up.

The people there understand.

They understand that with the addict, the physical craving can be taken away, but the mental obsession stays strong. You wake up and think of it.

This is common; very common. And no one on the outside really knows what you're going through!

Addicts talk about a man, like forty years old. His son was nineteen and addicted to heroin, and he wouldn't stop.

His dad goes to him and says, "Shoot me up!"

The son says, "What?!"

"I want to be addicted, too," the father tells the son. "And I want to beat this together—with you. You're not going to go through this alone!"

That is love; that is love when you're willing to give your life up like that.

—A final voice from the street,
a former patient of the Thelma McMillen Center

So many counselors, doctors, and good, caring people right off the street give so much, and so much of themselves, to help sufferers of addiction.

That is what the McMillens have done. But on a massive scale. They have used their hard-won resources from Karl's Golden Touch to, in turn, touch the lives of addicts everywhere. The McMillen Family Foundation is working to ensure that no addict has to suffer alone.

That is love.

Afterword:

What's a Parent to Do?

At Chris's memorial service, Pastor Steve Mays read out Karl's thoughts:

As your dad I did the best I could…

No one would deny that Karl McMillen went to exhaustive extremes to try to save his sons. But the always-haunting *What could I have done differently?* lingers.

And there's no perfect answer.

Some parents are enablers; others will tear their kids' rooms apart looking for drugs. Neither may work.

And different people have differing ideas.

> *I don't know what Karl and Thelma could have done differently. Moving? Maybe. Taking the boys on more trips? Doubtful. How do you run from drugs if they're on every corner, everywhere, for someone who really wants to go out and get them?*
>
> *But I have learned that a parent has to control whom their kids are friends with. It's hard—the kids have to go to school—but you have to try. I never allow other kids into my house that I don't*

know—until I know they are not involved in drugs. And I've taught my kids never, ever to be around kids who do drugs because they will steal everything you have.

I saw Mark and Chris do that to Karl and Thelma, over and over again.

—Don McDonald

I think we need to be present in our children's lives. To understand what is really going on with them. We don't want to interfere with them growing up as people, but we need ask questions: Are my kids on the right path? What are the boundaries I need to set up? And, Is what I am doing really the best for my child?

Maybe we even need to take a parenting class.

And like Karl, we can never give up hope.

But sadly, one other answer I have for "What's a Parent to Do?" is this: We have to help addicts to meet their own collapse.

You can tell someone not to smoke pot, you can tell them how much they're hurting themselves, killing themselves, but I know from experience that an addict can't access that until he or she has hit bottom.

It's the only way.

—Richie Davidson

Karl's thoughts about "numbers"—business—as related by Pastor Steve, may provide the most intense insight into all of this: *Numbers can make you and others rich, but they cannot build a family.*

That's a hell of a statement. It's huge.

It shows just how big and powerful addiction is. It will transcend the largest of "numbers."

It will transcend the greatest amounts of money.

And love.

And potential.

June 3, 2012

Dear Karl,

After reading your story, I had some deep feelings about the pain a parent goes through at the loss of a child. When that loss is due the use of drugs or alcohol, the feelings of remorse and responsibility are stronger than all others. When I lost my twenty-eight-year-old son, I had those feelings.

It was a while before I realized that no matter what I did, I could not help. Some things are beyond a parent's help.

Your story goes over and over a loving family's efforts to provide help for their drug-addicted children. The very best recovery facilities in the nation were used but with no success. This is a priceless example that only the addict's desire for help and willingness to surrender can provide recovery.

This story needs to be told.

Sometimes we have to give up our personal needs and desires to serve a greater good. You have served this good by revealing your family's struggles in an effort to help many others.

And your donating of resources to recovery facilities will without exception save the lives of alcoholics and drug addicts who are ready for and in need of help, for years to come.

Thank you. I love and admire you.

Jack Clower

The McMillen Family Foundation

The McMillen Family Foundation is proud and honored to support the following charities.

Ashland Home
P.O. Box 3676
Laguna Hills, CA 92654
(949)460-0375
www.ashland-home.org

Beacon House
1003 S. Beacon Street
San Pedro, CA 90731
(310)514-4940
contact@thebeaconhouse.org
www.thebeaconhouse.org

First Step House of Orange County (Charle Street & McMillen House)
P.O. Box 1904
Costa Mesa, CA 92628
(949)642-2941
info@charlestreet.org
www.charlestreet.org

Friendly House
347 South Normandie Avenue
Los Angeles, CA 90020
(213)389-8810
www.friendlyhousela.org

Garden Grove Alano Club
9845 Belfast Drive
Garden Grove, CA 92844
(714)534-2244

House of Hope
235 W. 9th Street
San Pedro, CA 90731
(310)521-9209
www.houseofhopesp.org

Lynn House
Costa Mesa, CA 92627
(714)438-0110
www.thelynnhouse.org

Mary & Joseph Retreat Center
5300 Crest Road
Rancho Palos Verdes, CA 90275
(310)377-4867
www.maryjoseph.org

Pathways to Independence
P.O. Box 43
Los Alamitos, CA 90720
(562)493-9048
www.pathwaystoindependence.org

SHAWL
936 S. Centre Street
San Pedro, CA 90731
(310)521-9310
www.shawlwomenshouse.org

South Bay Alano Club
702 11th Place
Hermosa Beach, CA 90254
(310)374-2131
info@southbayalanoclub.org
www.southbayalanoclub.org

Southwest Alano Club
2130 Birch Avenue
Hawthorne, CA 90250
(310)973-9898

Thelma McMillen Center
3333 Skypark Drive, Suite 200
Torrance, CA 90505
(310)784-4879
www.torrancememorial.org

Turrill Transitional
1396 North Waterman Avenue,
Suite 100
San Bernardino, CA 92404
(909)888-7173
ttap.operations@t-t-ap.org
turrilltransitionalassistanceprogram.org

Villa Center, Inc.
910 North French Street
Santa Ana, CA 92701
(714)541-2732
villacente@aol.com

www.mcmillenfamilyfoundation.org

www.toddpipe.com

In loving memory of

Chuck Monnich
December 20, 1925 – October 31, 2012

Jack Clower
August 20, 1928 – November 30, 2012